# LIFE IS FULL *of* SWEET SPOTS

With best wishes
and hopes that
your life is more than
full of sweet spots!

— Mary O'Connor

# LIFE IS FULL *of* SWEET SPOTS

## An Exploration of Joy

MARY O'CONNOR

abbott press®

A DIVISION OF WRITER'S DIGEST

# LIFE IS FULL OF SWEET SPOTS
## An Exploration of Joy

Abbott Press books may be ordered through booksellers or by contacting:
Abbott Press
1663 Liberty Drive
Bloomington, IN 47403
www.abbottpress.com
Phone: 1-866-697-5310

Grateful acknowledgement is made to the following for permission
to reprint previously published material:

W.W. Norton & Company: Excerpts from The Wild Braid  by Stanley Kunitz with Genine Lentine,
(New York: W.W. Norton & Company, ©2005). Reprinted by permission of the publisher.

Algonquin Books of Chapel Hill: Excerpt from Last Child in the Woods by Richard Louv ©
2005, 2008. Reprinted by permission of Algonquin Books of Chapel Hill. All rights reserved.

Bollingen Foundation: Excerpts from Paul Valéry, The Collected Works of Paul Valery, Vol. 13,
Aesthetics, translated by Ralph Manheim (© 1964 by Bollinger Foundation).
Reprinted by permission of the publisher.

Random House: Excerpts from Gift from the Sea by Anne Morrow Lindbergh, (New York:
Random House, Inc, Vintage Books Edition, 1965). Reprinted by permission of the publisher.

Cover photo by Jupiterimages.
Cover design by Words by Jen, Jennifer A. Payne

ISBN: 978-1-4582-0803-3 (sc)
ISBN: 978-1-4582-0802-6 (hc)
ISBN: 978-1-4582-0801-9 (e)

Library of Congress Control Number: 2013901218

Printed in the United States of America

Abbott Press rev. date: 3/6/2013

*For all who walk the earth and want more*

*that together we may look to the sky and see its rays of hope,*

*breathe the air of the sea, of the garden, of home, and inhale its goodness,*

*touch the earth and put its flowers in our pockets,*

*turn our eyes and ears and souls to the sights and sounds of morning waking,*

*and be energized with open minds and joyful hearts.*

# Contents

Acknowledgements . . . . . . . . . . . . . . . . . xi

Introduction . . . . . . . . . . . . . . . . . . xiii

PART 1 - DRAWING ON NATURE

The Earth . . . . . . . . . . . . . . . . . . 3

The Sea . . . . . . . . . . . . . . . . . . . 31

The Sky . . . . . . . . . . . . . . . . . . . 53

PART 2 - TAPPING INTO OUR BODIES

The Vista of Sight . . . . . . . . . . . . . . . 71

The Pulse of Sound . . . . . . . . . . . . . . . 95

The Essence of Touch, Taste & Smell . . . . . . . . 117

PART 3 - STRETCHING OUR MINDS AND SOULS

Frontiers of Wonder . . . . . . . . . . . . . . 141

The Heart of Giving . . . . . . . . . . . . . . 163

The Spirituality of Life . . . . . . . . . . . . . 185

Afterwords - Finistère . . . . . . . . . . . . . . 209

More to Explore . . . . . . . . . . . . . . . . 213

In Their Words . . . . . . . . . . . . . . . . 249

About the Images . . . . . . . . . . . . . . . 251

Notes . . . . . . . . . . . . . . . . . . . . 257

# Acknowledgements

To all the men and women, artists, gardeners, mothers and fathers, lovers of music, of the wild, of the stars, who agreed to tell their stories of finding joy: my warmest thanks, not only for the firsthand experience you bring to this book, but for your personal outreach of friendship and introductions to your favorite spots of joy.

To Jennifer Payne, friend of many hats, words, encouragements, red ink, hugs and cheers: my incalculable gratitude, not only for sharing your love for words and images, but for using your design and editing skills to coax the best out of me and all that appears on these pages.

To Jan Logozzo, longtime friend who recognized from the beginning the call for this book and doggedly pushed for its fruition: many years' worth of thanks, both for your support and encouragement and for your sharp and questioning proofreader's eye.

To Margot Larson, writing colleague and brainstorming comrade: *merci beaucoup* for the many hours shared in the sunshine on my deck in planning and discussion, recharging any flagging determination with the energy of illumination and creativity combined.

To Karen and Gary Rancourt, always there with an idea, a contact, an introduction, a perspective: heartfelt thanks for your interest that reinforces the capacity of friendship.

To the women of the York Correctional facility who wrote in their poetry classes of a hunger for peace and joy that can't be quenched: my deep appreciation for revealing the presence of light that shines in even the darkest of places.

To the myriad of friends, family and acquaintances, contacts in-town and online, all too numerous to name, who offered expressions of interest, encouragement and suggestions of content: my sincere thanks for your thoughts and ideas, all of which have proven to be an invaluable part of this journey.

# Introduction

There is an old Native American belief that the world is a circle and that all natural things in that circle are connected. Animals, plants, rocks, mountains, the earth, the sea and the sky—each, in one way or fashion, teaches something to another.

Writing a "circle poem" is a basic creative exercise I often use when teaching poetry writing to inmates at a nearby correctional institution for women. Draw a circle, I tell them. Populate it with words representing elements of life. Next, randomly connect the words in pairs, describing how one may relate to the other. Typically, the women look blankly at their circle of interconnected words, ponder, then begin to write. They write of a tiger lily just as beautiful as a first time mother. They tell of the rock that holds the house of the family together, the bright stars that they see while sitting on top of the hills.

Sometimes I take the women for a walk in the woods. The woods are made of colored magazine photos spread throughout the classroom, photos of bugs and squirrels, of ponds clogged with fallen leaves, trees fighting to let their crowded branches see the sky. I tell them to be quiet and simply listen to the pictures in their minds.

It is an exercise that helps build powers of observation and of creativity. It also brings an understanding of connection—between themselves and the pieces of the world around them. It opens their eyes to seeing things in new and surprising ways, to observing that even when living in a world seemingly stripped of beauty and pleasure, there is a way to find fresh air. The women thank me for helping them open closed windows, and ask if next time they can write about love.

There is a parallel in what these women are doing and what this book is about. The parallel is in the process of exploration that is at the core of this book. It is in learning how and where to find happiness and joy in so many things that surround us, in drawing our own circles and connecting what we see: all the sweet spots of life.

## Places to Know and Love

Sweet spots by definition are places that invigorate, lift our spirit, stimulate, enliven—special spots that delight and bring us pleasure. Sweet spots of all sorts and descriptions have been talked about since the days of Adam and Eve and the apple tree, from the time of the ancient Romans who built a culture based on pleasure and passion, and on into the years of the Renaissance and beyond as both mind and body exhibited a gusto for life.

William Safire, the late *New York Times* political columnist and oracle of language, brought sweet spots into the present in 2007. Observing that sweet spots represent a pleasant or favorable place, an area surrounded by or lying between less favorable conditions, he identified some of the more common of such places. The thickest part of a baseball bat is one, *Treasure Island* another.

A true sweet spot, in the eyes of Safire, is a place that is beyond lovely, more exhilarating than the happy medium. It is a place that allows one to hit the longest high drive possible. But the world is large and its sweet spots of joy are many. They lie, as Safire said, in the neighborhood of less desirable, more mediocre, options.

So what exactly do we mean when we talk about the sweet spots of life? What makes them sweet, where are they and how do we tap into them? We'll set out to answer these questions here.

## How to Use This Book

The geography of joy is, by its very nature, a case of boundless discovery. It is an exploration of the world's horizons, a look at where we are most likely to find joy, and a start in the course of gathering ideas on how to make such places our own. We'll want to remember that word, *start*, as the exploration of joy is an unending process.

The words in the following pages are exactly that: starting points. They introduce us to some of the many elements and species that distinguish the earth, the sea and the sky, and help us realize how their beauty, harmony and powers make us inwardly hum. Then, moving deeper into the life-force of the natural world, we'll explore the gifts of our body and its natural senses, of our minds and our souls, and observe how they contribute to such miracles as feeling and hearing, to the calming power of spiritual strength.

We'll be guided along the way with both anecdotal and research-based narrative, words that bring us back in history to the days when kings bathed their bodies in precious oils, or take us to the present with studies that prescribe just 20 minutes of daily walking in the woods to energize our bodies and our souls. We'll keep an eye out, too, for helpful lists that pop up throughout the book, suggestions of favorite places to see the stars or to fill our pockets with shells.

Accompanying us on our journey are a mix of people from across the United States, Canada and Australia—artists, gardeners, mothers and fathers, lovers of music and of the scent of saffron, those who have traveled beyond the edges of a particular sweet spot. Not surprisingly, the things of which they speak are ordinary as well as remarkable—things like digging in the dirt in the backyard and finding delight in the digging, or taking lessons from the butterfly and discovering joy in its magic.

Told in an individual's own words, each Case in Point is a personal story of how and where he or she personally found relief, fulfillment or simple contentment in life. Each is given as a real life illustration of the dynamics of joy—how its discovery is an everyday affair. Then, in a nod to the everyday-ism of the discovery of joy, notable quotes from characters as dissimilar as Winnie the Pooh and Albert Einstein appear from page to page for thoughtful reflection.

The French novelist George Bernanos once said that the secret of happiness is to find joy in another's joy. The stories told in the following pages go a long way towards paying off those words, though they still leave a long way for each of us to go on our own. Each story, each reflection, each little detail, is simply an opening. They are intended only to suggest ideas and provide encouragement in our continuing process of discovery. It is up to each of us to make of them what we will. I found myself mulling them over, reflecting on them, tucking them away for further thought and deliberation. In the hopes that you, too, will enjoy chewing over what you read and hear before coming up with your own personal take-aways, many of mine are offered as "Food for Thought" at the end of each chapter.

As with the women who found a breath of fresh air when writing their circle poems, we will want to think about what we see and hear throughout the book, to learn from its stories and prescriptions of such things as walks in the woods and journeys to places unknown and set about making them our own. To help us do so, the book concludes with a section of More to Explore—a directory of Internet links to relevant resources, destinations and activities. Including websites and listings of museums, galleries, and cultural venues, More to Explore is a virtual smorgasbord of interactive tools for finding and exploring sweet spots.

That, after all, is what *Life is Full of Sweet Spots* is all about. It is a guide, a companion piece, an entertaining, as well as inspirational, way to find and explore those special spots that may delight and bring us joy in our journey through life. So let us begin.

# Drawing on Nature

# CHAPTER ONE

# The Earth

❉

*The old people came literally to love the soil and they sat or reclined
on the ground with a feeling of being close to a mothering power...
The soil was soothing, strengthening, cleansing and healing.*
—Ota Kte, Native American author

Walden Pond is a seemingly unremarkable kettle-hole of a pond tucked away in 2,680 acres of forest in Concord, Massachusetts. Made famous by author and naturalist, Henry David Thoreau, its pristine and tranquil shores and waters own a place on the map as a National Historic Landmark. It is also a starting spot for our own understanding of the Earth as a rich and powerful source of joy—a place that is good to touch and walk on.

Thoreau was drawn to the pond and its surrounding woods as a place where he might confront only the essential facts of life while learning what it had to teach. He got permission from his friend and mentor, Ralph Waldo Emerson, to use a piece of land that Emerson owned, and on that bit of land built himself a cabin, moving in on the Fourth of July, 1845. He chose a spot on the side of a hill, offering a front yard in which strawberries, blackberries and "life-everlasting, johnswort and goldenrod" grew. It was there in this 10' x 15' shingled and plastered house with its brick fireplace, garret and closet, a window on each side, two trap doors and a door at each end, that Thoreau lived for two and a half years.

The tiny cabin was a quiet place where he could live simply and comfortably, albeit without the so-called comforts of life, while observing and writing about the wildlife and the earth around him. In the end, his journal notations became the fodder of his classic *Walden* and the substance of a philosophy of living that is referred to even today.

Thoreau saw nature as a force that will steer us right—if we just let it. He tells us this in his essay, "Walking," a favorite read for anyone who has ever succumbed to the magnetism of nature. If we are to nurture our health and spirits, we will take his advice and spend four hours a day at least, usually more than that, "sauntering through the woods and over the hills and fields, absolutely free from all worldly engagements."

*I go to Nature to be soothed and healed, and to have my senses put in tune once more.*
*—John Burroughs, American naturalist*

### Take Twenty Minutes a Day

Appreciate the splendor of nature. This, after all, is what Thoreau would have us do. Look up and around, look to the west, to the wild, to the hills and to the fields. There is so much to discover—so much more of the earth and the heavens than we have allowed ourselves to see—so many sweet spots.

The good news is that we don't need to spend two years living in a cottage by Walden Pond as Thoreau did, or even four hours sauntering daily through the woods, in order to appreciate all the earth offers. If we look at the research findings of University of Michigan Professors Rachel and Stephen Kaplan, we would be delighted to know that twenty minutes is all that it takes to benefit from an increased vitality. As they theorize in their studies, natural settings have a positive influence on both mental and physical health. It all comes down, they say, to brain function and to what they describe as "soft fascination"—a state in which the brain is left free to wander and to soak up pleasing images. With a scenario such as this, respite and revitalization can be found in something as simple as a stroll along the beach or a walk in the woods.

Nature, as University of Rochester professor of psychology Richard Ryan suggests, is an underutilized resource; it is something within which we flourish. "We have a natural connection with living things. ... It is also fuel for the soul." Given the extent to which we live and work in built environments, he concludes, it is critical that we find ways to make it more a part of our lives.

As it turns out, while research such as that of the Kaplans and Ryan lays the scientific groundwork for describing what happens when humans come into contact with nature's finery, sometimes it is unvarnished stories of the personal encounters of others that capture our attention in ways that drive the truth home and make us think. Consider this anecdote told by *Last Child in the Woods* author Richard Louv about his early tree-climbing days:

> It was frightening and wonderful to surrender to the wind's power. My senses were filled with the sensations of falling, rising, swinging; all around me the leaves snapped like fingers and wind came in sighs and gruff whispers. The wind carried smells, too, and the tree itself surely released its scents faster in the gusts. Finally, there was only the wind that moved through everything.
>
> Now, my tree-climbing days long behind me, I often think about the lasting value of those early, deliciously idle days. I have come to appreciate the long view afforded by those treetops. The woods were my Ritalin. Nature calmed me, focused me, and yet excited my senses.

### Make Life Your Garden

Looking closer to home than the woods, we find that plants and flowers fit nicely into the role of building a sense of well-being. Often, while we're not even watching, they manage to weave their way into our unconscious minds as a source of both spiritual and physical renewal.

There is an old Japanese saying that some people like to make a garden of life and to walk only in its paths. U.S. Poet Laureate and Pulitzer Prize winner Stanley Kunitz came close to making this the case when he declared in his ninety eighth year that all he wanted to do was to write poems and be in the garden. Reflecting on a century of doing just that, he wrote of his tendency to brush against the flowers while walking in the seaside garden of his Provincetown home, anticipating the fragrant eloquence of their response.

His love of the garden went beyond its ultimate gift of bloom, beyond the rose, just ready to unfold, and reveled in the broader comfort of a kind of relationship that could be "transacted wholly without language." The spruce represented the rising of the sun; even the snakes brought satisfaction as they became so accustomed to his stroking that they seemed to quiver in a kind of ecstasy.

I feel I'm not only sharing the planet, but also sharing my life, as one does with a domestic animal. Certainly this is one of the great joys of living in this garden.

—Stanley Kunitz, U. S. Poet Laureate

# Case in Point

## Reawaken through Flowers

BARBARA PARSONS
Kent, Connecticut
*Mother, grandmother, home health-care provider, gardener,
writer. Best way to experience joy: Stop and smell the flowers.*

Flowers, in the words of American botanist Luther Burbank, "always make people better, happier, and more helpful; they are sunshine, food and medicine for the soul." For Barbara Parsons, former inmate turned gardener, flowers brought just that: sunshine and food for her soul.

> "There are arbors throughout the property…cutting flowers swaying in the breeze, delphiniums in shades of blue and lavender, poppies, lilies in all their splendor, coneflowers, buddleia, spirea, and fields of sunflowers, a favorite of my grandchildren. The sight is breathtaking and pulls your soul in close to the peacefulness we all crave."

Barbara wrote these words to picture a world for which she greatly yearned while serving time for manslaughter due to emotional duress. The image and her prose, "Dream Cottage," was fiction. The state of mind it described was not.

For someone who had enjoyed gardening since childhood days when she worked with her grandfather in his vegetable garden, the loss during imprisonment of such simple tasks as planting, even weeding, was devastating. Initially written as somewhat of an idyllic dream piece, her words reflected the deep love of nature instilled in her as a child by her mother.

While incarcerated, Barbara took advantage of as many rehabilitative activities as she could. She earned an associate's degree, tutored other prisoners, joined the institution's hospice program and trained service dogs to help others. But it was her love of nature and the facility's writing program that helped her find her voice and reopen her heart and her soul. It was a love that helped her survive, one that "helps me endure the harsh, unnatural world of this maximum-security prison."

Access to the natural world was highly limited, and so it was her work on the prison grounds as a gardener, a much sought-after and favorite assignment of the inmates, that gave her the sun, the therapy, even the spiritualism, of nature for which she longed. She weeded and planted, nurturing tiny marigolds and zinnias in paper cups covered with plastic wrap until transplanted, often using plastic spoons as make-do gardening utensils.

Following Barbara's release and return to the community, she turned to the restorative therapy of gardening, this time through a paying job in a nearby garden center and nursery. In one sense, the new world in which she worked mirrored the "Dream Cottage" gardens she had invented in her mind while confined to the cinderblock world of prison. It was, as she saw it, a welcome lifeline as she adjusted to the world outside the prison walls.

Delphiniums, poppies, lilies in all their splendor, coneflowers, spirea, and fields of sunflowers may not have actually been present in her life, but their calming influence and peacefulness were. Even today, working among the "happy faces" of the sunflower, Barbara continues to look for and to draw on their restorative peace that she continually craves. Sunflowers remain her favorite flower.

**In Barbara's words...**

*I craved being out in the sun. Once, one of our teachers brought in a sprig of lilacs, one of my favorites. I saw them and I started crying and said, "Oh, my goodness, can I smell them?" It was just so overwhelming to see them there on her desk in the prison. It's the simple things that bring you joy and comfort.*

*There are so many things that have happened in my life, especially in the past 15-20 years. Sometimes I feel that happiness is an illusion, that if we become too happy, then something happens to betray us, to set us straight.*

*You know, we're not here to be happy about everything. I think that every time I'm really happy, there's a crisis, a tragedy where something happens. I lost my son, [killed in an accident while Barbara was in prison]. My children don't laugh anymore, I don't laugh anymore. Since he died, since my crime, I feel like it's a betrayal to my past if I'm happy.*

*So I'm very satisfied to be content. It took me a long time to find peace and contentment, and I'm satisfied with that. I listened to the singer Josh Groban the other morning on "Good Morning, America." I cried. It's his voice, it's just so beautiful. It's the little things that we don't stop to pay attention to that really affect us, that touch us.*

*Do I really find joy in gardening, in all these things? What I'm seeing here is that peace and contentment are an emotional state. And I can get peace and contentment from working in the garden, playing with my dog, my grandchildren.*

*I love it when they call me grandma, there's just something about that little voice. They're so excited and everything is new. There's joy in that, and it's very simple. My dog just loves a bouncing ball, and when I play with him, you would think he's the happiest creature on the face of the earth.*

*Why do I like the sunflower? It's the little brown face, surrounded with sun rays—it just seems to be a happy face. They stand so tall and aggressive. There's something about them that makes you happy.*

*So it's the little things that we do in life that really matter. Gardening. The flowers. They bring me a peace and contentment; they allow me to find joy.*

## Create a Theme Garden

The beauty of backyard gardens thrives on attention and creativity, on hours of picturing and planting, weeding and pruning. But it's not until we step back and admire and appreciate both the inherent and resulting fruits of our labor that we fully appreciate the feelings of peace and serenity they bring. It is a sensation of joy that creators and followers of such popular garden themes as Japanese and English, butterfly and hummingbird, midsummer night, secret and faerie gardens alike, invariably affirm.

## Japanese Gardens

Stones, water and plants, all arranged to give the visitor a sense of peace, harmony, and tranquility, are often seen as the core of an Oriental-themed garden. Additional elements, such as moss, koi, tea houses, gravel gardens, reflective ponds, lanterns, bamboo, stepping stones and aesthetically pruned trees, may complete the picture. But it is such intimate traits as subtleness, natural beauty, moderation, and human scale that the judges of *Sukiya Living, Journal of Japanese Gardening,* tend to look for and favor when they rank North America's top 25 Japanese Gardens.

# Case in Point

## Build an Art Project to Walk Into and Through

### LINDA BRAZILL and MARK GOLBACH
Madison, Wisconsin

*Linda: Journalist and gardener. Mark: Retired security
officer, photographer and gardener. Best way to experience
joy: Soak up the magical moments of creativity.*

Linda Brazill and Mark Golbach can attest to the peace, harmony and
tranquility they have found in their own Asian-style garden. Working
together over a period of 12 or more years, they transformed a once
ordinary—and limited—space into a place of meditation and joy. It
was an endeavor that followed a crooked path of detours, of exploration
and of hard work as they excavated a pond, constructed a bridge and
tea house, and carefully placed plants, stones, gates and roughly 900'
of paths for strolling on their 100' x 200' house lot. It was also a process
marked by creativity and the joy of sharing.

**In Linda's and Mark's words...**

*We actually see the garden as very much a creative process where you're
dealing with the same issues as if doing a painting or a sculpture. It's kind
of a multi-dimensional art project; color, texture, form and scale, as well
as light, affect it. Then there is the effect of time, not only the different
times of day, but the seasonal changes over longer time.*

*Sometimes we think the garden is better in the winter than during
the growing season, almost because we don't have to do anything with it.
We can sit back and enjoy it. There are magical moments in the winter
when there is a full moon and snow on the ground and we just look
forward to those rays. Rather than trying to recreate them with lights,
we made the decision not to use artificial lighting and we just wait for
those moments.*

*The tea house particularly was slow in coming, but now it's actually
enclosed and you can get a real sense of what it will be like when the stucco*

*finishes are on. Then I always wanted what's commonly referred to as a meditation garden or gravel garden. Of course you can't have everything in a space this size. But the moon garden was sort of my version of that. There's a small area off the deck where there's also gravel and even though they are relatively small, they do have that calming effect.*

*Among the Japanese aspects of the garden that we tried to incorporate was the idea of a stroll garden. So in our 200' deep lot, we have about 900' of paths. There are spots where you can go left or right or behind something or in front of it, a wonderful place for just walking around. But we also designed it to be viewed from the back of the house, where we have two large banks of windows. All the changes that we made with the landscape were made with the idea that it would be viewed from the house, so it's kind of a theatrical place in that regard.*

*The strolling aspect of the garden is one that we both share. Usually the conversation goes something like:*

*Oh, there's something that needs to be done.*

*Don't think about it, just enjoy!*

## English Gardens

If we want to make anything grow, then we must understand it—and likely have green fingers. So admonishes Russell Page, British landscape designer and author of the classic *The Education of a Gardener*. Green fingers, he writes, are a mystery only to the unpracticed. The fact is that seeds and plants and trees must each obey the laws of its nature, and good gardens "cannot be made by somebody who has not developed the capacity to know and to love growing things." For Page, green fingers are "the extensions of a verdant heart."

It is, perhaps, this capacity to know and to love growing things that so successfully feeds Britain's national affection for a pursuit that is constantly changing—thanks to both the country's changeable weather and a climate conducive to plants from around the globe. English gardens, Page observes, seem to be always in a state of flux. "The fugitive pleasures which gardening affords seem to be enhanced...by a subtle and deliberate disorder that softens the emphasis of a straight line and never allows the garden to appear static or achieved."

# Case in Point

## See Life from a Garden Viewing Platform

GEORGE SCHOELLKOPF
Washington, Connecticut
*Art historian, antiques dealer, president, Hollister House Garden.*
*Best way to experience joy: Share garden's beauty with others.*

George Schoellkopf, creator of the Hollister House Garden in the hills of Litchfield, Connecticut, has both a vision and a passion. Both are built around the creation of what he describes as an old fashioned garden in the manner of famous English gardens, formal in structure but informal and rather wild in its style of planting.

Ironically, this ardent gardener had little experience in cultivating nature's beauty beyond his childhood days of trying to create a garden in the harsh Texas climate, and later, by using containers in Manhattan. He attributes the idea of the Hollister House Garden to a trip he took to England, when he fell in love with some wonderful, but rather elaborate, gardens. One in particular, the Sissinghurst Castle Garden near Kent, created around the surviving parts of an Elizabethan mansion, particularly caught his fancy.

**In George's Words...**

*I wanted to make a garden in that style, in that tradition, and I came back and all the books said you can't do that in America. But you can learn how to do it. I had a vision in mind. I kept making experiments, lots of experiments with plants to see what would work, what wouldn't, how to make it better.*

*The wonderful thing about the English style that I fell in love with is that you start with structure and the walls and the hedges and paths so they become a framework. This allows the plants to be a little more free in the way they grow, which I like. It's part of my aesthetic. I like the naturalness of the way plants grow, but I like a real structural plan in which that happens.*

*I always choose the plants; it's part of the great fun. I often say I want my plants to look as if they're enjoying—even better, that they are enjoying themselves. Sometimes we create an illusion that the plant doesn't really live there. Most of the plants are perennials. But the ones that I do replant, I try to make look as if they actually live there.*

*When I found the house, there was no garden. Nothing was here—it was a slope. It's not very comfortable to arrive and be on a slope, so I terraced it. When I started this thirty one years ago, the American styles of garden design were very different and very antithetical to this kind of style. That's a very American idea that we're not supposed to have form. In New England it's not so true. I've always treasured that about New England— its order and its little picket fences.*

*I think the old fashioned order and form of New England goes very well with nature, but it's separate from it. With Frank Lloyd Wright and others, the idea was to sort of meld and become part of nature. It's a very different way of viewing the world. I think there is nothing wrong with being perfectly honest and saying that a garden is made by man for mankind. Nature is then organized for mankind's enjoyment, experience. It gives you a viewing platform, so to speak, from which you can enjoy nature.*

*My favorite time is walking out in the garden, meditating or noticing and thinking, "Ah-h-h, isn't that wonderful!" I like views very much, so I'm always trying to place a bench where you look back at the house and you get the structure and you get the plants and you feel the difference, the layers of space. I very much enjoy just looking, especially in the morning. The morning is the best time, it's wonderful.*

## Butterfly Gardens

There's a reason butterflies are sometimes called flying flowers. With their delicate wings of color and their seemingly fanciful flights—dancing, as it were, from one site to another—they are both a source of enchantment and a gardener's best friend. As they flit from flower to flower, they inadvertently carry with them bits of pollen that stick to their long legs as they probe the blossoms for nectar, all the while helping to pollinate our gardens.

Planting a butterfly garden begins with learning what types of flowers attract these delightful creatures. Butterflies, of which there are some 12,000 known species in North America alone, generally are attracted by scent and color, especially bright yellows, reds, purples and pinks with strong sweet scents. They are partial to wild as well as pesticide-free blossoms; hanging baskets receive as much attention as flowering trees and shrubs.

For starters, it's helpful to know what kinds of butterflies frequent the area, and to understand a bit about their life cycles and their favored plants. The popular black-striped Tiger Swallowtail, for example, tends to visit nectar-rich flowers that grow four feet or more above the ground; the delicate Spring Azure, one of the first butterflies to emerge in the spring, may be found feeding on small white flowers. That's the beauty of butterfly gardening. Give them their choice of flowers and they will come.

# Case in Point

### Find Therapy in Beauty

SPRINGS ROMANO
Kahaluu, Hawaii
*Counselor and Founder, Women of Wisdom Institute. Best
way to experience joy: Use beauty to restore beauty.*

Springs (Christine) Romano knows the secret of planting one beautiful thing to preserve another. The planting is actually of crown flowers, host plant of the Hawaiian Monarch butterfly. The combination of the two—the crown flower and the butterfly—are at the heart of a restorative program known as the Pulelehua Project.

Pronounced pooh-lay-lay-who-ha, the word actually means a combination of blessing or prayer (pule) and the name of a most sacred flower (lehua). Believed to be the favorite flower of the last reigning monarch of Hawaii, Queen Liliuokalani, the lavender crown flower is used symbolically to represent the cherished value of all flowers.

Springs launched the Pulelehua Project in the late nineties in response to a devastating decline of the Hawaiian Monarch caused by a combination of invasive lizards, ants and wasp predators, as well as overuse of pesticides. At the same time, the essential crown flower was dying out, leaving the species with no place to lay its eggs and seriously cutting into the food supply for the baby caterpillars.

As volunteers began to plant their own butterfly gardens and the project took hold, Springs and her fellow counselor, Susan Denham, recognized its therapeutic value for women and girls undergoing their own life transitions and co-founded the non-profit Wisdom of Women's Institute. Today, hands-on participation in butterfly preservation initiatives is an integral part of the Institute's therapy programs, another perfect example of how planting one beautiful thing helps preserve another.

### In Springs' words...

*In some languages, the words soul and butterfly are the same. Although, on the surface, we use the word pulelehua to mean butterfly, it's actually* describing the spiritual purpose of the butterfly—to carry and share the unspoken blessings of flowers during its ritual of pollination. In Hawaii, we use butterflies for every kind of blessing ceremony, for weddings, memorials, birthdays, anniversaries, new beginnings.

The pulelehua has taught me that if we are persistent, the day will come when we can stop, rest and reflect and, when the time is right, emerge and let our spirits fly free into new beginnings. Just having the presence of such a delicate and beautiful creature fluttering about will shift the focus off personal problems for anyone.

It's really quite simple. Begin with planting Crown flowers. They just need a sunny place to grow with well-draining soil. No need to buy expensive potting soil…adding sand to almost anything will work. Make cuttings and share them with everyone. Keep caterpillars out of harm's way in safe cages. Get ohana [family], keiki [children] and friends involved.

A butterfly garden can do several things. Perhaps most important, it can add to your enjoyment of nature and that of your ohana and friends. You can use it to raise butterflies and help children learn about nature and how to restore our natural environment. Few outdoor activities are more rewarding and easily available than attracting butterflies to your well-loved garden.

We know of no better teacher to show us the art of starting over than the enchanted butterfly. The butterfly teaches that something can change its form and that what looked like an ending is really a new beginning. They create opportunities for all involved to understand that all things are connected and in so doing to heal and transform troubled relationships and unfulfilled dreams and purpose—to begin to feel alive, connected and free again.

There are those who are happy and fulfilled in their own lives, but just want to lend a hand in keeping one of the most delicate and beautiful creatures thriving on earth. There is something very magical and pure that happens when a person connects with nature through the actual experience of caretaking a caterpillar during all of its stages of becoming a butterfly—then letting it go, with a wish. How does one describe the joy of that?

*Happiness is a butterfly, which when pursued, is*

*always just beyond your grasp, but which, if you*

*will sit down quietly, many alight upon you.*

*—Nathaniel Hawthorne, American author*

### Follow Your Feet

The Japanese have a special way of enjoying nature's greenery. It's called *Shinrin-yoku*, which translates roughly as "taking in the forest atmosphere" or "forest bathing." The term was introduced by the Forest Agency of the Japanese government in 1982 and, thanks to subsequent research on the physiological effects of forest exposure, has come to be known as one of the most accessible ways to lower the body's stress levels.

Studies conducted in both actual forests and the laboratory measure the physiological effects of various elements of the forest environment on our natural senses, such as the smell of wood, the sight of its scenery, sound of running water and feel of the trees and leaves. Resulting data and observations of physiological functions point to a deep-seated connection between the natural world and the sense of comfort and relaxation humans feel with *Shinrin-yoku*—or when enjoying a "forest bath."

To take our own forest bath may be easily accomplished simply by following our feet in the great outdoors. Open our own back doors, or venture further and set foot on one of the many scenic and historic trails that crisscross America's lands. Whether it spans the thousands of miles of a geographic corridor, such as the Appalachian Trail, or links ancient fishermen's trails into a 175-mile long cultural and geological network along the shoreline of the island of Hawaii, there is bound to be a match for our interests. For starting points, visit the online sites of the National Park System (www.nps.gov/findapark) or the GORP National Park Guide (www.gorp.com/parks-guide).

# Case in Point

## Touch Something Wild

PHIL DOUGLASS

Hooper, Utah

*Regional Outreach Manager, Utah Department of Wildlife Resources.*
*Best way to experience joy: Pass the wonder on to others.*

Phil Douglass takes away a feeling of deep-down satisfaction every time he helps others to touch something wild, to make connections with the land. For him, it is a sense of both appreciation and awe, an unfailing sensation of gratitude that comes through his understanding and love of wildlife.

The ways in which Phil realizes it are many, ranging from classroom visits in cities beyond the fringes of the state's natural assets to the Utah Department of Wildlife Resource's Great Salt Lake Nature Center and its program for volunteer naturalists. One of his favorites is the Department's Hardware Ranch Wildlife Management Area in northern Utah, with its 14-15,000 acres used to feed the elk in the wintertime. Developed to provide good habitat and winter range for big game animals, it simultaneously offers individuals and families an opportunity to view elk in the wintertime, literally *en plein air.*

**In Phil's words…**

*I'm a person that has ties to the Earth, so wonder and gratitude and joy are not something that are hard for me to find. They're surrounding me in the world every day. Sometimes you have to look for them, but when you have ties to the Earth, you don't have to look very far. I spent much of my growing up years with the mud from the Great Salt Lake squishing between my toes as I was looking for frogs in the marshes. So those types of things were part of my upbringing.*

*A big part of the wonder and gratitude that I feel are not only in my own personal experiences, but in helping others have those experiences as well. We bring the children out and provide them with the experience of feeling that mud squishing through their toes that many of us had growing up, but that we now see kind of slipping away.*

*I will never forget this one class from the inner city in Salt Lake. One of our things is to provide them with these little nets to go out and sample some of the insects and even frogs in some of the areas that we have. And this one lad had picked up a frog. He's holding it, cupped in his hand, very gently, just trembling with excitement.*

*I asked him, "Is this the first frog that you've held?" He just looked at me with this huge smile and said, "Yes!!!" So it's to be involved with the likes of that, and to know that these experiences are very real—and hopefully lasting—that I want to see happen.*

*One of my favorite activities in my years of working with wildlife is bird banding. Banding often requires 24 hours of straight work, but it is such a rush that you just don't notice the lack of sleep or food.*

*Often, when I hold a snow goose in my hands and gently put a band on its leg, I can't help but feel arctic wilderness dropping off of its wingtips in droplets of water. And as I release them and watch them fly away, I know where they're headed. Anticipation is a big part of joy. But also, it's just fascinating. It's one of those things that comes back to having the sense of wonder, just to see how these animals complete such herculean travels as they do.*

*Every time I think of classroom visits, it reminds me of the responsibility that I have. After one presentation to a fourth grade class in Bountiful, which is just on the outskirts of North Salt Lake, a little girl came up to me and handed me a note that said, "I want to be like you." What she saw is someone who loved wildlife and wanted to save a place in it for her. And if she wants to experience the joy of wildlife in her life, and the joy of being in wild lands and having something wild touch her life, then that's exactly what I want to have accomplished.*

*There is a real hunger to have joy. It's human, it's innately human. We all search for happiness and joy. I've played the harmonica my whole life. It's a great little musical instrument for a person who spends time in the outdoors. In my profession, I spend a lot of time at campfires alone and yet I've never been lonely with the harmonica; it helps remind me of the people, places and things that I love.*

*About six years ago I put together a little DVD of how to play camp songs on the harmonica, weaving in scenes of the west and of wildlife. I greatly enjoyed making this available, to the point where I put together a charitable organization called the Rocky Mountain Education Trust. I think about children such as those that are in foster care and who move through the system with very little possession, and so have been giving them harmonicas that they can take with them wherever they go and can create their own happy music. I've named the harmonicas the Campfire Companion and they're part of a program called A Song in My Pocket, Hope in My Heart.*

*There is so much in the world today of what I call artificial entertainment, so much external stuff that comes to you. But the things that are the most meaningful to me are the things that come from within. Joy comes from within. And so I'm giving them these simple little harmonicas. It's a piece of you that you're just so hopeful will make a difference.*

### Dig in the Backyard

Mary Oliver is a favorite poet—of mine, and of all those who fall captive to her powers of observation and her words that turn peonies and poppies, snow crickets and marsh hawks, into an enchantment of reasons at which to marvel. Perhaps what I enjoy most is her willingness to crouch down to the height of eye-level, close enough to watch a mink tiptoe along the edge of the creek, to be covered with blossoms and sugary vines, to hear a voice in the weeds. She writes of all the questions that a spider's curious life makes her ask and then suggests that though their answers most likely appear in some book of knowledge, it is in the palace of discovery that they are found. Would that we, too, might stop and see, to discover with wide open eyes all that is around us.

# Case in Point

### Learn from the Woods, the Frogs, the Flowers

### KARRIE MCALLISTER
### Orville, Ohio

*Mom, writer, dirt lover. Best way to experience
joy: Show others the fun of nature.*

Self-described mom, writer and dirt lover, Karrie McAllister not only realizes joy for herself in nature, she finds ways to make sure that her children learn how and where they, too, might find it. Recalling her own childhood with its weekends at her grandparents' farm in rural southern Ohio, as well as the simple pleasures of her family's home garden, Karrie believes such experiences basically shaped her life.

Today, she builds on those memories, using backyard dirt, sunflowers and simple sticks as just a few of her tools to pass on that gift of nature. She speaks of such things as teaching children to enjoy the outdoors. Sometimes she tells of fostering their love of nature by letting them bring dirt into the house—to make a terrarium. She writes of picking blackberries—the juicy kind that stain their faces and hands purple, or of keeping a wooly bear caterpillar for the winter. And she writes of her son, who worked for two summers straight using plastic yard tools to dig out a rotten stump, hoping to find a frog.

**In Karrie's words…**

*Regardless of who or what made the dirt, I live and mother with the idea that dirt is wholesome, and what is wholesome is good. Climb in the trees. Swim in the creek. Eat the blackberries and drink the rain. Sleep under the stars. Dig in the dirt. Every night that I need to hose my children off is a good day.*

*At ages four and five, my son worked tirelessly to remove a giant stump until one day last autumn, he finally pulled it out. We all cheered— even the neighbors congratulated him. When we asked what he's going* to do now, he simply shrugged, picked up his shovel and started digging. "Maybe a pond," he said. "We could get some frogs."

When I'm in the woods, everything becomes clear. The outside problems of my life dissolve and fade away and I can focus on what really matters in my life, what really means something to me. I become a part of what's around me and I really feel connected to the dirt and the trees and it puts the world in perspective.

There's just this glowing warmth that comes up inside of me. It kind of comes up my throat and everything is heightened. My senses are heightened, my emotions are heightened and it's a buzz. I carry it with me.

Watching people not let their kids get dirty and not let them jump in puddles and climb trees just drives me crazy. They should go out and play.

I lead hikes for young children in some of the local parks. I have a theory that if you're going to be a tree hugger, you have to be a tree climber, and to be a tree climber, you have to be a tree lover. So when I take kids into the woods, I really try to show them the magic of each tree, of each rock, of each leaf-seeing animal. That's a gift that I really try to give, to teach them what a gift nature is.

The joy of nature doesn't always come naturally. You have to recognize and appreciate it. Maybe it's just the act of stopping to look, of stopping to notice. Sometimes you have to work for it. Last year I planted probably 100 seedlings trying to grow a sunflower house for my kids, and either the toads got them when they were in the pots or the rabbits ate them.

This year, I was bound and determined, and my kids were, too. It's just a ring of sunflowers, about 10' in diameter, something I read about in Sharon Lovejoy's book, "Sunflower Houses: Inspiration from the Garden." You plant big sunflowers and little sunflowers, alternating. It's small, but wonderful. The idea is that when it grows, you can walk inside and be in a room constructed of sunflowers.

When I think of happiness, I think of my grandparents. They're retired and have nothing particular they really need to do, but they're extremely busy doing nothing. If it means they spend all day digging up one of their shrubs, and thinking about where they're going to transplant it, and the rest of the day transplanting it, that's what they do. It gives them happiness and joy and they'll talk about it for three days.

My husband and I both look at my grandparents and we recognize that they're old, but we can see how much joy they have in their lives. We know that if we want to live to be their age, and be that happy every day, that we really need to enjoy these simple things and find joy in everything that we do.

................................................................................

*I love that quiet time when nobody's up and*

*the animals are all happy to see me.*

*—Olivia Newton-John, singer, performer.*

................................................................................

### Food for Thought

*Actually going out* and finding the sweet spots of the Earth, uncovering its sense of place, its element of peace, of beauty, may be the best part of our life's journey.

*Start with the smell* of the honeysuckle, of pine needles, fresh cut hay.

*Take the detour* that leads to the lake.

*Be willing to wade*, to meander with the river, to follow the tracks of a fox, the path of a deer. Wait for the elk to bugle, the loon to call.

*Lounge* on a great and beautiful boulder and eavesdrop on the world around you.

*Rest in the woods* and listen to its surround-sound.

*Take in a concert* of katydid calls and beetle clicks and whirs.

*Detect the scurry* of a chipmunk, the splash of a frog.

*Mimic the voice* of a mockingbird. Hear the grass grow.

*Finger the finery* of tiny queen-of-the-prairie flowers and gain a new understanding of soft. Observe the silken scaffolding of a spider's web and learn the meaning of strong.

*Spot the splash* of a butterfly wing in a field of autumn gold and get high on its jolt of color.

*Be present* to send the wild geese and songbirds off on their migratory journeys.

*Watch for the sun* to grow flowers on the desert.

**Abandon** yesterday's indoor plans.

CHAPTER TWO

# The Sea

❀

*The Sea, once it casts its spell, holds one in its net of wonder forever.*
*—Jacques Cousteau, undersea explorer*

When I was maybe five years old, my grandmother, who lived in Florida at the time, filled an empty cigar box with layers of cotton and the most beautiful shells I had ever seen. Cowries and conchs, whelks, tulips, cockles and coquina, angel wings, shark eyes, limpets, sand dollars and my favorite little sea horse—I carefully set them out where I could see them, study them and admire them.

Today, many years and many moves later, this gift from the sea remains in a place of importance. The original collection of clean and showy sculptures and shapes is intermixed with a number of scruffier cold water cousins collected as I have walked along the rocky New England beaches where I live. Never minding their source and varying degrees of beauty, all provide a continuing connection to the sea and its net of wonder.

No one really knows how many shells exist for our pleasure. The *Book of Shells, A Life-Size Guide to Identifying and Classifying Six Hundred Seashells,* tells us that their selection represents only a small fraction of all known species of seashells, a mindboggling number considering that some say it is less than only one percent of the known. Worldwide, the number of mollusk species, including the likes of the single shell abalone or the whelk, the bivalves, such as clams and oysters, and the cephalopods—whose name literally means "head-feet"—is huge, far greater than that of fish and exceeded only by the vast armies of insects.

## Make Yourself a Promise

But numbers, while intriguing, do not explain the ability of shells to please us. In one sense, considering their seemingly fragile but remarkably impenetrable architecture of cones and spires and whorls, shells are a geometrical pleasure in their own right. They cause us to ooh and ah with delight. We promise ourselves that if we've never seen, let's say, a *harpa amouretta*, commonly known as a lesser harp, with its intricate and visually stunning markings, or the *murex pectin,* a most exquisite predatory sea snail with delicate spines and long tail, we will, at the very least, find ourselves a photo of its likeness, and admire its creation.

In another sense, it is what we don't see or know about shells that makes us pick them up and set them in our living rooms, where they may remain to brighten our days. We study their intricate sculptures and polished walls, admire them for the "who created these?" intellectual mystery they bring, and wonder where they have been.

## Preserve the Enjoyment

For Paul Valéry, French poet and philosopher, the sea shell stands out from the common disorder of perceptible things. "It delights my eyes and fingers; I stop to look at it as I would stop to listen to a melody." Shells intrigued him to the extent that he tackled the question of their form and origin in a meditative essay, "Sea Shells."

Shells, Valéry determines, "present us with a strange union of ideas: order and fantasy, invention and necessity, law and exception." He considers the mystery of the shell's presence, noting that since neither mankind nor chance are responsible for their construction, we need to invent something he likened to "living nature."

As a poet, Valéry described the force of nature well. As a philosopher, he fittingly portrayed its precious gift—its ability to "enchant our eyes with the tender richness of its iridescent bands." His musings are, in their own right, a delightful and thought-provoking probe into the broader mystery of lasting beauty. He marvels over the mollusk gathering all that is needed from its environment to create such a delightful object as a shell—"what perhaps, some day in the future, will be a fragment of the foundations of a continent." After the mollusk's death, Valéry continues, the beauty it formed in the course of its life "will break the sun's rays into their wave lengths, and will enchant our eyes with the tender richness of its bands."

Even now, such a tiny fragment of our world may sit there in the midst of that collection sent years ago by our grandmothers or found on our own shore walks, still maintaining, in its inexplicable, but timeless way, the living light of nature. It is a gift to experience each time we view our collections of cowries and conchs and—just as Valéry promised—find our eyes and our souls enchanted.

> There is, one knows not what sweet mystery
> about this sea, whose gently awful stirrings seem
> to speak of some hidden soul beneath.
> —Herman Melville, American author

### Connect to a Larger Presence

Anne Morrow Lindbergh, author of the widely praised *Gift from the Sea,* was also enchanted—in her case, by the shells of her summer visits to the island of North Haven off the coast of Maine. She writes of her observations and delight: of the little hermit crab who ran away, leaving his shell; of the moon shell, with its mysterious single eye, staring at her; of the perfect double-sunrise, each side like the wing of a butterfly, leaving her to wonder how its fragile perfection survived the breakers on the beach.

A noted writer, aviation pioneer and widow of aviator and conservationist Charles Lindbergh, Jr., Morrow Lindbergh spent her summers at the seashore, lying on its beach, drawing lessons from the shells that she turned in her hand, taking them home to bolster her winter spirits and musings.

The beach, she wrote, was covered with beautiful shells, shells that she greedily collected, unable to even walk with her head up looking out to sea for fear of missing something precious at her feet. But after all the pockets were stretched and damp, and the bookcase shelves filled, she came to realize that one can't possibly have them all. "One can collect only a few, and they are more beautiful if they are few. One moon shell is more impressive than three. There is only one moon in the sky."

Shells have a way of jump starting the music of falling and rising tides. This, in essence, is the true gift of the shell. Layered with the riches of their making, shells offer both a sensory and an intellectual experience. We look to their creation and discover loveliness, a beauty that sits in wait for us as we comb the beach for its fragments of summers and childhoods past, connections to a larger and eternal presence.

### Extend the Pleasures of Shelling

Thanks to their beautiful colors, shapes and fragile yet enduring designs, shells inspire one of the world's most popular amateur hobbies. Strong enough to outlast the creatures whose homes they are, these sculptures of the sea have been collected and used as tools, jewelry, currency, musical instruments, building tools and materials, spiritual symbols, soil conditioners, artwork and crafts of all manner and sort since the days of antiquity. Portrayed by artists and photographers, they are housed in museums and displayed in tourist shops. But mostly they are admired and pocketed by those who troll vacation beaches in search of take-home treasures.

- Set out when the sands are freshly washed and marked only with the tracings of crabs and shorebirds, before the tides—and other scavengers—beat you to the night's pickings.
- Fill your pockets with unspent sand dollars or silvery jingle shells—simply for the pleasure of it.
- Listen to the roar of the waves inside a spiral conch shell—and wonder where it has been.
- Fill your journal or sketchpad with the likes of their presence.
- Celebrate the full moon (or welcome the new) with an evening stroll at ebb tide. Tides are lowest around the full and new moons, exposing then the most treasures.

- See if you can outrun a ghost crab, estimated to travel at as much as 4.4 meters per second, while running sideways yet!

- Join with the young folk in building castles, digging tunnels to China.

- Stock up on sea glass.

- Rinse your feet in a tidal pool.

- Promise to return.

### Head to the Beaches

If you are looking for the largest seashell in the world, try heading to the shallow coral reefs of the South Pacific and Indian Oceans to find the giant clam, or *Tridacna Gigas*. A bottom dwelling bivalve mollusk, this behemoth specimen can weigh over 500 pounds and measure some four feet in length. However, seeing that such mammoth dimensions may not always appeal to the casual shell seeker, here are a few most popular—and manageable— beaches to explore:

*Calvert Cliffs State Park, Maryland:* A popular Chesapeake Bay haunt of shell lovers and fossil lovers alike. Scallop, oyster, clam, and snail shells, as well as beach glass, arrowheads and quartz, are among its treasures.

*Dungeness Beach, Cumberland Island, North Carolina:* This National Seashore barrier island beach is reachable only by boat. Coquinas, shark teeth, heart cockles, sand dollars, ark shells and moon shells are some of its more commonly found specimens.

*Ocracoke Island, North Carolina:* Take the ferry from Hattaras Island and share this beautiful beach with the gulls. Find whelks, sand dollars, cowry helmets and the occasional rare Scotch bonnet, a fragile egg-shaped shell with spiral bands and brown spots.

*Sanibel Island, Florida:* On the Gulf Coast of southwestern Florida, this barrier island with over 17 miles of beaches, is frequently cited as one of the best, if not the best, of United States shelling destinations.

Coquinas, scallops, whelks and sand dollars are just a few of its beauties.

**San Jose Island, Texas:** Visitors to the 21 miles of primo shelling beaches on this privately owned, but open to the public Gulf Coast island, may come home with lightning whelks, sundials, shark's eyes, olive shells and wentletraps. Gather them at night and enjoy the sight of phosphorescent plankton.

**Shipwreck Bay, Lanai, Hawaii:** Given its many reefs and powerful currents, this remote eight mile beach along the Kalohi Channel is more of a beachcomber's than swimmer's delight. Violet snails, sea slug shells, leopard cones and imperial cones are among its treasures.

**Silver Strand State Beach, Coronado Island, California:** The Silver Strand is named for the silvery oyster shells that litter this seven-mile long windswept sand spit off San Diego Bay. Other shells found include cockles, Pacific moon snail shells, limpets, scallops and an occasional sand dollar.

**Tunnels Beach, Kauai, Hawaii:** Though there are many beautiful shelling beaches along the north coast of Kauai, Tunnels Beach stands out for its abundance of puka shells. The Hawaiian word for hole, puka stands for the naturally occurring hole found in the middle of rounded fragments of cone snail shells. Popularly used for necklaces, bracelets, earrings and hair jewelry, they are traditionally thought to ensure a peaceful and safe voyage.

---

The happiness of the bee and the dolphin is to exist.

For man it is to know that and to wonder at it.

—Jacques Cousteau, undersea explorer

# Case in Point

### Learn from the Dolphin Spirit

VICTORIA IMPALLOMENI-SPENCER
Key West, Florida
*Charter boat captain, spiritual retreat leader. Best way*
*to experience joy: Draw on the energy of the water.*

Dolphins are arguably the most recognized and popular of all the residents of the sea that we have come to know. If we are lucky, we might see them catching a ride on the bow wave of a ship, or running across the water in a series of leaping dives. Those of us who have the good fortune to witness them are certain to be charmed by their natural playful spirit or to fall for their seeming smile.

Characteristically very social creatures with a seemingly remarkable ability to learn and imitate behaviors simply for the sheer pleasure of doing so, dolphins are, in fact, small whales, or cetaceans. Unlike their larger whale cousins, many live in fairly shallow water, often no more than seven feet deep, rising to the surface to breathe.

Victoria Impallomeni-Spencer, herself a being of boundless curiosity, spends her days on the warm waters of Key West as a charter boat captain and leader of Dancing Water Spirit Retreats. As such, she shares the energy of the water not only with her passengers and retreat-goers, but with the dolphins. Each trip is a magical and unforgettable day, due in part to the dolphins that come to play. They are, after all, her friends and source of joy.

Knowing that communing with nature can prove uplifting for the spirit and bring peace of mind, Victoria is apt to ask her retreat participants to lie in the water with the dolphins and let themselves be carried into a relaxed meditative state of being. Or she might invite them to move into another dimension by blowing into a Peruvian whistling vessel with its high pitched sound—a sound that never fails to get the dolphins' attention. Connection with the earth and the sea is at the heart of much of what she sees and shares in life.

Affectionately known as the Rose Goddess of the Sea, Victoria follows a spiritual path to healing known as Mother Earth Spirituality. Based on the belief that humanity is rooted in a living, feeling earth, this essentially Native American path seeks to reestablish a nurturing relationship with nature. It does so by drawing on Mother Earth, or Gaia, as the divine center and source of all life.

In part, Victoria attributes her appreciation of the water as a healing source to the work of Masaru Emoto, Doctor of Alternative Medicine and founder and head of the I.H.M. General Research Institute in Tokyo, Japan. His writings, *The Hidden Messages in Water* and *The Secret Life of Water*, present his theory that because water is able to absorb and even retransmit human feelings and emotions, we can heal our planet and ourselves by consciously expressing love and goodwill. It is a theory that Victoria turns to during times of extraordinary need, such as during the Gulf Oil crisis, when she sprinkled drops of especially dedicated water into the sea.

**In Victoria's words…**

*I think of the dolphins as intermediaries between the worlds. To commune with nature in God's paradise, and revitalize your being in the dolphins' playground, is truly uplifting for the spirit and brings peace of mind.*

*The dolphin has a joyfulness, a playfulness in experiencing humans, and you can bring that facet out in you if you can just lay still and be calm and get your breathing comfortable and quiet. I tell people to just lay there, just let your muscles relax and enjoy the feeling of water on your skin all around you like an envelope, and then let your mind move into being a dolphin. You've got to turn your thoughts off and just go into the sensations of feeling, which is a big part of the dolphin's life.*

*The water here is pretty warm and the skin disappears and the water inside and outside the body seems to move back and forth, and you're just a semi-permeable membrane as you lay there and move into a state of meditation. So with this guided meditation, you're being carried deep into yourself, deep into the ocean, and you're going there to receive a gift* and you're going to see this beautiful clear pool. Then I guide the person to seeing different things in the pool, inside themselves.

Something happens in our brains when we're in joy. It's a measureable endorphin and it floods the brain when it's in total joy. It's that feeling of being in love. "I don't know why I'm crying, but I'm crying," is not an uncommon reaction.

I play music while I'm out there. The music that I play most often has recordings of the dolphins and whales and I play it because it puts people in the space that I want them to go to. The dolphins really love it. They're very much sound animals. When I first started doing this, they would come to the surface with their heads out, with their rostrums pointed straight at the boat, and observe. They seem to feel that the sound we're doing is something that's important to them, to the world, to each other.

Color is probably the one thing I really want to get people into. To me, it is color therapy. I ask them to remember the color, to use colors to get into that peaceful place where they were in such joy. Color is the one thing that you can wrap around yourself, even by simply wearing the colors of the sea and of Mother Earth. Look at the hues and gradations here—from our feet, up into the sky, hues and tints of blues and greens and yellows.

You might not be by the sea. But no matter where you are, when you're in nature and you find colors and sound that you can bring back into your life regularly, that is the way to experience joy more often.

The cure for anything is salt water: sweat, tears or the sea.

—Isak Dinesen, Danish writer

## Wash Away Troubles

Water has a rather mysterious facility for clearing the mind of its logjam of thoughts and worries. Whether by the lull of its tranquil and calming sound, the draw of its eternal presence, or the cleansing wash of its waves, it has a remarkable ability to lift our spirits and refresh our bodies and souls.

We read of the early Egyptians bathing in their sacred Nile River, of the ancient Persians and Greeks building grand public baths, of Emperor Charlemagne holding court while relaxing in a warm bath. Hippocrates, the father of modern medicine, advanced the healing properties of water in his prescription of the bath as a therapy that "soothes the pain in the side, chest and back…soothes the joints and the outer skin, and is diuretic, removes heaviness of the head…."

Advancing to twenty-first century Hawaii, we find a group of surfers and a foundation known as the Mauli Ola Foundation making a connection between cystic fibrosis and the healing power of the ocean. Mauli Ola means "breath of life" in Hawaiian and is the motto of the Foundation's Surf Experience Days. Building on studies that show patients who inhaled a specially mixed saltwater solution at least twice a day significantly improved their ability to clear mucus from their lungs, the Foundation has paired professional surfers and instructors with young patients to experience what salt water's natural therapy can do for their lungs.

Witnessing the exercise and fun the kids experience during these events is satisfying in itself. But it is the way in which they respond to the salt water environment—in which they receive their own "breath of life" from the sea—that is most rewarding.

# Case in Point
## Know the Healing Powers of Water
ED NICHOLSON
Port Tobacco, Maryland
*Founder, Project Healing Waters Fly Fishing. Best way to
experience joy: Use love of fishing to help others mend.*

When U.S. Navy Capt. Ed Nicholson (Ret.) observed our nation's
service men and women struggling with their injuries at Walter Reed
Army Medical Center, he turned to his own lifelong love of fishing as
a passion to share with others. Sparked by the thought of how great it
would be simply to get a couple of guys out fishing for the afternoon,
Project Healing Waters Fly Fishing, Inc. (PHWFF) was born.

Today, thanks to therapeutic benefits of the Project Healing Waters
programs, hundreds of disabled military personnel are able to adapt to
their physical disabilities and soothe their emotional trauma. Complete
with fly fishing instruction, fly tying classes, casting lessons, rod
building and fishing outings, PHWFF is a commitment that consumes
not only Ed's life, but the lives of legions of supporters throughout the
United States, Canada and Germany who make it all happen.

Ed and the program's associates are by no means alone in their
understanding of the healing powers of the water. Herbert Hoover,
popularly described as the Fishing President, even authored a book
about it: *Fishing for Fun—And to Wash Your Soul.* "To go fishing," the
thirty first U.S. president once said, "is the chance to wash one's soul
with pure air, with the rush of the brook, or with the shimmer of sun
on blue water. It brings meekness and inspiration from the decency of
nature...."

For Nicholson, seeing a twenty two-year old with no legs able to
stand in a river on his fittings and cast for a fish is as good as if he
were standing in the river himself. "You don't just put the demons of
war aside. But once you get out on the river, the serenity is incredibly
healing."

**In Ed's words...**

*It was kind of a simple-minded thought, I guess. What if I could share my outdoor pursuits with some of these recovering wounded warriors, as they are want to be called. And guessing that many of these young men and women probably grew up in rural environments, I thought maybe they'd like to go out. So when I retired for good, I started probing around and asking questions, getting some support from organizations like Trout Unlimited and the Federation of Fly Fishers.*

*With the help of people like Colonel Bill Howard in Walter Reed Occupational Therapy Clinic, and the prodding of some of these wounded warriors who didn't know a fly rod from a fly swatter, we got them to give it a try. We ran the whole gamut of what it takes to be a fly fisher, building their confidence as casters of fly line, teaching them the elements of fly fishing, using the fly rod, tying flies. That's not to dismiss the real important issue of taking guys and ladies fishing, getting them out of the hospital environment, getting out with nature.*

*It's that special feeling of standing in a beautiful stream with the water gurgling around, knowing that there's a fish under that rock over there. And now because you've been trained, you've been taught, you're able to deliver the fly, and you put that fly in the right place and the next thing you know, you have a big trout come up and grab it and you're up for a ride.*

*Our relationships are built over time. I've known Mark for three to four years. He's one who was helped by PHWFF in Maine and is active now in the program in Augusta. Mark wrote in a letter how he went from complete paralysis to a wheelchair to a makeshift walker to leg brace, walking, over the past nine years. "I was originally told I would not get out of a wheelchair and now I'm standing in the river, with supervision, with a fly rod in an adapted holder, bragging my ass off! ... One more time, thank you!"*

*That's what this program is all about. It's offering hope—hope that their lives have meaning, no matter what their physical, or even their emotional, frame of mind. In a lot of cases, their emotional frame of mind is changed dramatically, which is just as important.*

*It's a healing experience, just being out there on the water. That's maybe what makes it so magic. It's hard to describe. It's an element that we all feel.*

*It's not as if I took some guy down and took him by the hand and stuck him out in the river, and said "feel the river."*

*But let's teach him how to cast a fly rod, tell him all about how to catch, say, a trout. Put on a set of waders. Give him a fly rod, put him out in the water and say there are fish out there, put it all together and catch that fish. There's a connection in our program of fly fishing to that joy.*

*Considering what they've been through, the trauma involved, they don't use the word* joy *very often in their everyday language. But what they do say is much akin to that. Sometimes, when you're working with these tough young Army and Marine Corps guys and ladies, they express to me either personally, verbally or in written testimonials, that it brings joy to their heart*

*Fly fishing is something that I enjoy so much. It brings joy to my heart, much like for these guys. But ratchet it up a notch, think of them, think of yourself as them. I'm reminded of a young man that I've become very close to as he has gone through the program over the years—double amputee, just above the knee, never had a fly rod in his hand and now he's about to be discharged from the Air Force. He's a Special Forces guy, and he wants to be a part of our organization, to help Project Healing Waters.*

*That he can do these things affected him in such a positive way— reaffirmed that he's a young guy with a wife and a young boy, that he hasn't lost everything. There can be times, and hopefully more and more times, that he can be in an environment where he has a great time and a joyful experience.*

*I'm just one individual in this program. There are volunteers all across the country that hear things like this all the time. When I'm asked about Project Healing Waters, I tell them it doesn't really matter what the process is, or what the program is. It's the whole idea of giving, volunteering of yourself to help others have a better life.*

*Since 2004-2005, this essentially has been a full time job. It's been a labor of love. But the rewards are great. The fulfillment is there and I just keep plugging along. I sneak away every so often. I was up in Michigan last month with my bird dog and my fly rod and with friends. But a good deal of my enjoyment on the rivers is received vicariously—just watching the warriors and disabled veterans that we help.*

..................................................................................................

A river seems a magic thing. A magic, moving,

living part of the very earth itself.

—Laura Gilpin, American photographer

..................................................................................................

### Running Waters to Love

Some quarter of a million rivers, running roughly 3,500,000 miles, distinguish the terrain of the United States. Their precise numbers and miles are difficult to determine, as they change over time. But here are just a few particularly known to be loved:

**AuSable River (Michigan)**—for its ranking as one of Michigan's top brown trout streams and for the chance to paddle in solitude along the pine and cedar-lined banks of the Huron National Forest.

**Beaverkill River (New York)**—for its legend and lore as the standard by which trout streams are judged and for its sweet-as-spring water that passes through a narrow rocky ravine between two mountains deep in the Catskill forest.

**Cahaba River (Alabama)**—for its 131 species of fish, said to have more per mile than any river its size in the country.

**Choctawhatchee River (Florida)**—for its broad floodplain and old growth bottomland hardwood forests that draw ornithologists in search of the elusive ivory-billed woodpecker.

**Green River (Utah)**—for its average descents of thirteen feet per mile as it tumbles past soaring red rock walls, forming clear pools of greenish depth.

**Henry's Fork, Snake River (Idaho)**—for its prolific aquatic insect hatches and rainbow trout fly fishing.

**Kickapoo River (Wisconsin)**—for being a favorite among canoeists and for living up to its "crooked river" name with its meandering 125 mile course that covers only 65 miles as the crow flies.

**New River (North Carolina)**—for the anomaly of its name and portrayal by geologists as the oldest river in North America and for its lazy and scenic course as it flows north through the Iron Mountains of Virginia and into West Virginia.

**Wailua (Hawaii)**—for being the only truly navigable river in all of Hawaii; kayakers have their own lane on the right side of the river. Starting at Kauai's Waialeale Crater, the slowly meandering river makes its way to the ocean, where several large stones with ancient petroglyphs carvings may be viewed depending on the amount of sand present.

**Yellowstone River (Wyoming and Montana)**—for being the longest undammed river in the lower 48; its nearly 700 miles flows through grizzly bear country to Yellowstone Lake, before plunging over a 380-foot-high waterfall, the highest on any large-volume river in America.

---

*Rivers know this: there is no hurry. We shall get there some day.*

*—A.A. Milne, author, Winnie the Pooh*

---

### Speak the Language of Water

In the tradition of classic Japanese haiku poetry, the spiritual path of nature is expressed through moments of intense observation preserved through words of poetic imagination. Haiku is an art form, a meditation, a way of seeing. Haikus can be addictive, both in their making and in their thoughts.

They speak, typically in just seventeen syllables, written in three lines of 5-7-5, of things like quiet lakes and ponds, of the no longer singing frog, of rain, of hearing simply the water's own sounds and language.

*Spring rain fills the cup*
*of the just opening rose—*
*puddles of sweet wine.*

*The fish filled brook*
*runs along the mountain's side,*
*singing as it goes.*

*With a single splash*
*the frog jumps into the pond—*
*the night becomes still.*

# Case in Point

## Make the Streams Yours

STEVE GRANT
Farmington, Connecticut
*Environmental journalist. Best way to experience
joy: Be intimate with nature.*

Exploring the peace and beauty of a river or lake can be a form of
relaxation for Steve Grant, as well as a kind of runner's high. It calms
his Type A tendencies and feeds his sense of wonder. But then again,
so does fly fishing—or yoga, or snowshoeing, or photography, or
reading.

In many ways, Steve might be likened to an earlier American
essayist and naturalist of note, John Burroughs. Burroughs tended to
haunt the farmlands, streams and lakes of the Catskills, but chose the
meadow brook as a favorite. His words are rich with description of
the meadow's love of the willows and of the willows' love of it, of the
bobolinks and the starlings and the meadowlarks, always interested
spectators of the angler.

As a modern day chronicler of the joys of the natural environment,
someone to whom rivers and trail guides are the raw materials of dreams,
Steve echoes the soundness of Burroughs' words and thoughts.

**In Steve's words...**

*To some degree, all rivers draw us into their seemingly separate world,
though it may not always be so apparent. A river, a healthy river, creates
an aura, as if it existed within a grand bubble of its own making. I don't
think it is an overstatement to say that when we enter a river's realm,
we are in another world, one where stresses wash away as briskly as the
flow.*

*Water, whether it's the sea, a lake or river, can be a terrific place for
contemplation and reflection. I find this when I go out alone, if I go to
some big lake that's quiet. I'll go up to Maine sometimes and I'll be on*

*Mooselookmeguntic Lake, which is a huge lake, like eight or ten miles long, and there are very few boats on it.*

*I've been out in my kayak there sometimes for several hours, hardly seeing anybody, and it might be a gorgeous day, and you're just paddling along. You just fall into a quiet rhythm and it becomes almost, I think, meditative. My mind just soars. It's a very peaceful, soothing kind of thing that can happen—a kind of runner's high on the water.*

*When I'm out on a river or a lake or on the ocean in my kayak, part of the joy is just relating to all the rest of nature. A river can be a kind of a vehicle to see the forest and to see the birds, butterflies, animals. You paddle along a stream and it's nothing to see beaver. I've seen countless mink, just running along. They love the little rocks along the edge of the stream. You see all kinds of wildlife and you'll see them in ways that often you otherwise can't, especially from a car.*

*Part of the pleasure of being out in nature is coming to understand it better. I think the more you understand it, the more satisfying it is to be out there. The good thing about a kayak is that you can get into almost any kind of water. If you've got three inches of water, you can get your kayak in there. You can go at any speed you want, and the other nice thing is that you can go ver-r-r-y quietly. If you want to bluster through the water and work out, you can do that. But then there are all the times that I just paddle very quietly, not very fast, and I'm just kind of looking and being happy out there. I have found myself sometimes smiling.*

*You just sort of get into a little reverie out there. You catch one of these beautiful days and you'll be paddling around and it's just so pleasant. Sometimes, I will paddle right up to shore and there might be some wildflowers and I check them out. As the seasons change, you're going to see different things flowering along the banks of the river.*

*I just find it very relaxing to be out there, which is its own kind of joy. I think, to some minds, joy could be an exuberant happiness. But I think there also is something more subtle. In my mind, I still think of joy as something that I quietly find in nature. Although, it's not always quietly. I've had some times with friends on rivers, long canoe trips, just having a grand old time being together, that I would consider joyous. I like to be with people on water. But at the same time, I also like to go on a river or a lake by myself.*

*I can see joy both ways, as exuberance and the more subtle, quiet, or quieter, joy. I think that's what we're all looking for in our lives. If you haven't tried canoeing or kayaking, give it a try. Go out with some people at first and find a safe place. There are places right on lakes in state parks where you can rent a kayak or a canoe for the morning and just go out and try it.*

*One of the nice things is no motor, no noise. You're going to be using you own body to move this thing along. You choose the speed that you want to go. That's part of the pleasure of it. I don't want to rush. I want to savor each sunrise and sunset at the water's edge.*

## Food for Thought

**The Sea is a body**…with powers to soothe and to calm. How it does so is a mystery. Its eternal rhythm, the way it moves us to places and times beyond the souls of our feet, do not explain its wonder.

**The Sea is a source**…whose gifts are enjoyed not so much through possession as through obsession with the stories behind its polished stones and sea glass, unbroken houses of hermit crabs. Its joy is in watching gulls swoop and dive, in breathing the sea air with its salt of happy tears.

**The Sea is a force**…that connects, both by its ageless presence and its tomorrow's hold. But mostly, its strength resides in the powers that pull it and us from one horizon to the next, that cause sailors to stand and to face the sea and the purple sky, and salute.

CHAPTER THREE
# The Sky
✸

*Only from the heart can you touch the sky.*

*–Rumi, Persian poet*

When the world with its plants and the animals was created, a sea gull flew up and formed the dome of the sky, like a spider weaving its web. This, according to one Marshall Island legend, was the origin of the sky.

Egyptian mythology offers its own sky creation story. In the beginning, as the story goes, only the ocean existed. Then, out of an egg that appeared on the surface of the ocean, Ra, the god of the sun appeared. Ra had four children, making the four pillars of the sky. Geb became the earth; god and goddess Shu and Tefnut became the atmosphere. Together, they raised the goddess Nut up to form the vault of the sky, the firmament to which Ra then attached the stars.

In a pictorial rendition of Nut, found on a circa 1102-952 B.C. papyrus of Tameniu, we see her body arched over the world. Goddess of the sky and all heavenly bodies, Nut was a symbol of protecting the dead when entering the afterlife. During the day, the heavenly bodies of the sun and moon would make their way across her body. Then, at dusk, they would be swallowed up, pass through her belly during the night and be reborn at dawn.

Today, the medium of papyrus is supplanted by cyberspace and mythological persona are displaced by scientific discovery. But the influence of ancient Egyptian understanding may still be seen in our definition of the sky:

Sky\skī\ n, *pl* skies
1.  the upper atmosphere that constitutes an apparent great vault or arch over the earth
2.  heaven
3.  a: weather in the upper atmosphere
    b: climate < temperate English skies

### Enjoy the Show on the Big Screen

Weather, for many of us, fascinates simply to the point of our wanting to know whether it will be sunny or rainy, too hot, too cold, a good day, or not. Thanks to the likes of weather satellites and computer models, not to mention the up-to-the minute reporting of zip code-specific forecasts, we find ourselves being more aware of and attuned to the sky and its never-ending artistic performance.

Featuring a screen that rivals the grandest of any IMAX venue, the sky provides a 24/7 display of sound and light. Lightening, snow and thunder— all put on shows that astound the senses and arouse our emotions.

One of the sky theater's most popular performances is that of the rainbow. An optical phenomenon of refracted sun rays reflected in airborne droplets of water, the arch of the rainbow intrigues meteorologists, artists and leprechauns alike. It is viewed, painted, sung about, thought of as a symbol of renewed hope. Rainbows tell us a storm is over, a clear day is ahead—or, for the wishful thinkers and idealists among us, that there is a pot of gold at its end.

*And when it rains on your parade, look up rather than down. Without the rain, there would be no rainbow*

*—G. K. Chesterton, English writer*

Reaching that gold by crossing under or over the rainbow's bridge is, of course, an impossible achievement, given the laws of physics. Seen by the human eye only when the sun behind us reflects on water droplets suspended in the air, rainbows are always positioned in front of us. Try to catch them and see what happens.

Michael Jones McKean, artist and professor at Virginia Commonwealth University, goes a step better than trying to catch these elusive gifts from nature. He creates his own. Using high-powered jet pumps and custom fountain nozzles to spray recycled rainwater into the air, he fashions a screen of water that mimics a rainstorm and then lets the sun do the rest. Each rainbow is different, depending on its angle, the amount of sunlight, atmospheric conditions, and other factors.

Commissioned in the summer of 2011 by the Bemis Center for Contemporary Arts in Omaha, Nebraska, McKean created a daily display of two, roughly fifteen minute long rainbows that visitors were able to walk through. Measuring up to 200' across and 200' high, they were produced in the hopes of stirring the imagination of visitors and to take them out of the everyday world for a moment—maybe even to determine whether or not there really is a pot of gold at the end of a rainbow's arc.

Rainbows, as it turns out, are all about sun and water, as well as all about color—three primary (red, yellow and blue), four secondary (orange, green, indigo, violet). The sky, with its own palette of blues, reds and yellows, is a canvas of never ending color, a backdrop for clouds known as mare's tails and mackerel scales, a place for comets with tails and for stars that streak across the night. Some say the sky is full of dreams. Others know that its dreams are simply the prelude.

*Exploration is in our nature. We began as wanderers, and we are wanderers still. We have lingered long enough on the shores of the cosmic ocean. We are ready at last to set sail for the stars.*

*—Carl Sagan, astronomer, author*

# Case in Point

## Fuel Creative Spark with Aura of Sky

JOSH SIMPSON

Shelburne, Massachusetts

*Glass artist. Best way to experience joy: Explore and push the limits.*

Josh Simpson creates, among other things, glass planets. Not just ordinary glass planets, but planets packed with more information than the naked eye can possibly see. To make them, he uses a variety of ancient traditional Venetian glass techniques, such as filigree and millefiori, a technique involving the production of glass canes or rods, all with multicolored patterns that are viewable only from the cut ends of the cane glass. But this is simply where he begins.

The last thing Josh does before he goes to bed is walk out to his studio to check the furnaces. Seeing an aurora borealis, watching a thunderstorm develop down the valley, or just looking up at the sky on a perfect summer night inspires him to translate some of the wonder of the universe into glass creations. That wonder, he says, comes out in his work, not in any purposeful way, but evolving slowly.

Blowing glass is far from an everyday way of finding joy. But for Josh, it's not just his work as a glass artist that fulfills him. Intellectual curiosity, challenge, pushing the limits, creativity, big picture vision and even a slightly self-deprecating humor all contribute to the *joie de vivre* that takes him beyond the state of stress to the realm of creative accomplishment.

The core of each of his planets is full of bubbles, threads, and kaleidoscopic patterns evoking unseen landscapes and underwater worlds. He knows he succeeded in his creations when viewers look closer at one of his little worlds and lose themselves in its textures and color. But for Josh, the excitement and the intensity comes from trying to compel, or to coax, this impossibly ridiculously hot material into some shape—to do something with it that is pleasing.

To him it is a continuing challenge to find a way to master this demanding material, one that is "as frustrating and difficult and as cruel a mistress as you can imagine. It laughs at burning you. It laughs when it drips on the floor, and laughs when it shatters." But he keeps on, always finding pleasure in having people look at what they first see as merely a simple object, a simple sphere, before realizing that it's just impossibly complex.

### In Josh's words...

*There's sort of a funny kind of pleasure in being creative—and in the stress of being creative. It's when I'm thinking this is going to be really cool, and I wonder if I twist it in this direction and if I heat it in this way, what is it going to do? Will it be intriguing to whomever is viewing this? Will this look like outer space? Will it be underwater?*

*I find that I am at my absolute most creative when I'm not trying to be, when nothing is contrived. It's a natural extension of curiosity and vision together.*

*I think another part of what I enjoy is a very peculiar meditative state that I sometimes find myself in when I'm making them. Not always, but sometimes when I make planets, I'm just so engaged and so concerned with the one I've got in front of me, plus the one I'm thinking about doing next, that I kind of lose track of myself, and certainly lose track of time. For me, it's sort of the act of satisfaction and engagement.*

*I watch my nine-year-old building Legos or disassembling a hard drive and there's really no sense of time there. There is a sense of "what will happen if I take...what is in this thing...how does it work? Oh, look at this!" And he'll come running over to me with the guts of this poor thing and I don't expect it to ever go back together again. But it's just that joy of discovery. For me, I get the joy of discovery in construction, in making things.*

*I seem to take a great pleasure in just the concentration of trying to add minute amounts of chemistry to the first batch to get interesting colors. The whole point is to make an object that ultimately is satisfying— satisfying in that it's an object that you can live with and derive great pleasure from over a vast amount of time.*

*When I originally moved to my home in Massachusetts, someone gave me a bag of daffodils. Then in the fall, I was outside the kitchen digging to plant the daffodils and discovered several handmade marbles that had been lost by kids, maybe 50 years before. I brought them in and cleaned them up and they were just as bright and beautiful as the evening they were lost.*

*It got me to thinking about all of the ancient glass that one sees in museums. All of that glass wasn't saved by collectors; it was found by archeologists in the ground where it was left or dumped. So at the time, back in 1976, there were no museums collecting my work, barely any galleries that wanted anything to do with me. And so I thought, you know, I should just hedge my bet here. If I really want to be thought of as an artist in the far future, maybe I should just hide my work for archeologists to find.*

*So as I traveled, I began to take these planets with me and hide them about. Then a friend would say, "I'm going somewhere, the Great Wall of China," or whatever, and I'd say, "Can you take some with you and hide them somewhere?" I will often take several planets with me when I go to a city and put one or more in the grate around the trees in the sidewalk and some kid will be looking down and see this beautiful thing.*

*They're not signed. But just to find something that's interesting and beautiful to look at, I think would be wonderful for someone separated from me by the time or economics. I mean there are many people who would never imagine spending money on art glass. And I like the idea that I can give someone something, someone I don't know, and they don't have to feel obligated—they found it.*

*I've hidden thousands of little planets around the world. The interesting thing is that only twice or three times I've learned that somebody found it. And every single time, it's been amazing because the people that found them were just dumbfounded. "Oh my God, what is this thing? I was 103' feet down in a cave in Cozumel and how did it get there?" I had to bite my tongue to keep from saying, "Oh, I did that."*

.....................................................................

For my part I know nothing with any certainty

but the sight of the stars makes me dream.

—Vincent Van Gogh, Dutch painter

.....................................................................

## Seeing Stars

Where do stargazers go to most enjoy the astounding astral sights of a night sky? Try on a mountain top. In the desert. In truly dark areas, away from urban lighting, smog and air pollution. Here are a few favorites to visit:

**Adirondack Park, New York**—One of the few places in the country known as a "dark puddle," Adirondack Park and its Tupper Lake area is a popular gathering spot for amateur astronomer star parties. Both the Adirondack Public Observatory and Kopernik Observatory & Science Center take advantage of the area's high altitude and little light pollution to explore the wonders of the Universe.

**Bryce Canyon, Utah**—On a clear dark night, it is said that visitors can see 2.2 million light years or 527,000,000,000,000,000 miles to the Andromeda Galaxy, the largest and most distant object visible to the naked eye. On any given night, those with telescopes may be looking at the Andromeda Galaxy, the ring nebula, 1,500 light years away, or at Jupiter, 48 light minutes away.

**Chaco Culture National Park, New Mexico**—One of the most important archeological sites in North America, this 1,000 year old Anasazi settlement provides several large telescopes and an opportunity to view the same stars the Anasazi looked upon a millennium ago—in a remote environment with clear, dark skies, free from urban light.

**Cherry Springs State Park, Pennsylvania**—Recognized by the International Dark Sky Association, the park offers visitors 48 acres of land on which to view a totally uninterrupted night sky. Its darkness sets off the nucleus of the Milky Way, rarely visible elsewhere on Earth.

**Cypress Hills Interprovincial Park, Saskatchewan, Canada**—One of the largest, darkest and easily accessible preserves, Cypress Hills is the first park in Saskatchewan and Alberta to become fully recognized in North America as a Dark Sky Preserve. Its annual Summer Star Party draws members of astronomical societies from all over each August to scan its dark skies, creating one of the largest gatherings of stargazers in Canada.

**Eagle Harbor, Michigan**—Located on Lake Superior in the Keweenaw Peninsula, Eagle Harbor's northern latitude, clear and dark night skies, and across-Superior vistas are perfect for Northern Light viewing. As viewers look north towards Canada, with nothing in between but water, star gazing is at its best, especially when the Northern Lights put on their outstanding show.

**Flagstaff, Arizona**—With clear skies, high elevation, and humidity often below ten percent, Flagstaff is a mecca for star gazing enthusiasts. Boasting three observatories, including Lowell Observatory, where Pluto was first discovered, Flagstaff was designated as the United State's first "international dark sky city."

**Joshua Tree National Park, California**—Joshua Tree is about as far from civilization and city lights as you can get in Southern California. With its 794,000 acres of open space, Joshua Tree is also a wonderland of boulders, cacti and shrubs allowing unobstructed views of the open night sky. Joshua Tree is loved for its clear sky views of such celestial beauties as the constellations of Sagittarius and Scorpio and the star clouds of Cygnus, the swan.

**Mauna Kea, Hawaii**—Those who attend the nightly stargazing program at the W. M. Keck Observatory find themselves not only 9,200 feet above sea level but above the clouds. Telescopes are pointed at attractions of the night sky, including open clusters, globular clusters, double stars, nebulae, planets, galaxies and supernova remnants.

**Natural Bridges National Park, Utah**—The night sky is so dark here that stargazers are able to see both the Milky Way and the whitish glow of the zodiacal light, sights that are virtually invisible from most backyards. Designated as an International Dark Sky Park, its starry skies are recognized by the National Park Service as part of the park's scenery.

········································································

*I have long thought that anyone who does not regularly—or ever—gaze up and see the wonder and glory of a dark night sky filled with countless stars loses a sense of their fundamental connectedness to the universe.*

*—Brian Greene, physicist, author*

········································································

OF THE B·L·U·E · M·O·O·N

FOR NEIL ◦ LAID TO REST THIS DAY

8·31·12

# Case in Point

## Bring the Sky down to Earth

JUDY YOUNG

Amherst, Massachusetts

*Professor of Astronomy, University of Massachusetts Best way*
*to experience joy: Watch how the sun and moon behave.*

As a college professor of astronomy, Judy Young, or more properly, Joyous Judy Young, Ph.D., translates her curiosity about the sky and the universe into everyday lessons that create understanding of the sun, the moon and the stars. Bringing the sky down to earth is her goal. Making connections between science, spirituality and joy is her end result.

One of the things Judy most loves about the sky and astronomy is its ability to teach people about things they didn't otherwise know, to enhance their experience of the universe. She refers to her teachings as everyday astronomy, noting that it doesn't take physics and math to see it—simply curiosity, attention and your eyes. Beyond her award winning research and studies, it is probably that ability to excite people's curiosity and help them feel at home in the universe for which she is largely remembered.

One of her favorite teaching tools is the sunwheel or stone circle calendar. Basically an outdoor circle of stones designed to illustrate the variations in the sun's position on the horizon throughout the year, it offers an understanding of the cycles of the sun. Judy had one built at the University to show people what happens in the real setting of the outdoors, to let them experience firsthand how the sun and the moon behave. She sees it as a gentler means of helping people to connect with each other and with the sky.

### In Judy's words...

*We gather at the sunwheel no matter what the weather, as long as it's not raining or a blizzard, and we witness the sunrise and sunset. It's very peaceful, very beautiful. People are interested in knowing just what are those rocks in that field, what's behind the patterns and motions of the sun and moon and stars? What is the astronomy that I can see every day?*

*I understand the cycle of the sun and I am familiar with the extremes of the sun rising and setting from either location. So when I see the sun come up, it's at a place that's very predictable, scientifically. But I don't just watch the sunrise from anywhere. I watch it from a place where I'm connected to it in time and space. Because I return there over and over, I can predict pretty closely what I will see. The sun does behave just the way one would expect in terms of where it's going to rise and set, year after year after year.*

*The earth and sun are here. They're going to continue their patterns independent of what we as human beings do on the surface of the planet. This larger picture of sun and earth and moon, which will be here long after each of us has passed on, is something that you can interact with. And that's what I find great joy in—understanding it, interacting with it.*

*Watching the sun rise and set is an activity that one does simply to be present. It's about being totally present. It's about your experience. It's your physical body, your mind, intellectually trying to understand, and it's your spiritual essence, just being there. So it really is the mind, body and spirit all present together, and there are not that many things that we do in our lives on a regular basis where that's true.*

*Another practice I love is wandering. I started out at the sunwheel in Montana and watched the sunrise and then just turned around and pointed myself in a direction and strolled and observed what I saw. It's like walking meditation, but it's different because in walking meditation, you might be going back and forth on a certain path and really trying to quiet the mind.*

*I do find the time of going within to be replenishing, whether it's for a half hour in the morning or evening, or a day long retreat. It's that getting to know yourself, getting to be still, not having to do anything other than be with yourself. I learned how much fun I had when I was by myself, just being out in nature. Observing and listening and singing and praying all contributed to my sense of joy.*

*The science of astronomy provides the observational and theoretical basis for our physical understanding of the external universe, while spirituality involves our individual experience and inner universe. Our lives are greatly enhanced by a blending of both the scientific and the spiritual, rather than relying solely on one as a means of interpreting the universe.*

*A love of what we see brings us joy, awe, and inspiration. Whether it is a sunset, a meteor shower, a full moon, a beautiful starry sky, a solstice sunrise, an eclipse, or a shimmering display of northern lights, an astronomical understanding of what we see leads us to feel more deeply connected to the world around us.*

*Then there are the everyday workings of the sun and the moon that most people don't pay attention to. The sun rises and the sun sets—10,000 times in the lifetime of a human being. That's just so many times for people to not pay attention and really understand that it's mind boggling.*

*So what I love about the beauty that is held in the sky is that it's understandable, it's observable. I don't have to go on a field trip to the Grand Canyon to see those particular moments. Everybody can do it.*

*If you like gardening and have some space, another way to be connected to the universe is with an astronomical garden. In the broadest sense, an astronomical garden is a garden that has elements that connect to the sky. It could be that you have a garden of flowers with astronomical names—sun flower, moon flower, etc. Another simple form is a garden in the shape of a crescent moon, a sun with rays, a Saturn, a planet, a spiral galaxy.*

*The kind of astronomical garden that I call most elegant is one where you align something to the sky. I've chosen the stone circle form, where stones mark the rising and setting sun on the solstices and equinox. Then the fourth kind, which uses the sun, would be if somebody doesn't have a good view of the east or west sky, like in a residential neighborhood with trees and houses around. But if you have a sunny spot where the sun is out at noon, it's possible to create an astronomical garden simply by having, say, a bird feeder hanging from a tall metal pole.*

*If you look at the shadow that pole casts every two weeks at noon, and actually mark it by either a rock or by putting a little wooden stake in the ground, you can create a calendar because the sun will do the same thing the next year and the next year as seen by how long the shadow of the pole is at noon. You can turn this into an astronomical garden by having plants that bloom around the time that the shadow is a certain length.*

*I find a huge amount of joy in my connection to the earth, kneeling on the earth, creating color and patterns and just growing whatever will grow in my small residential neighborhood yard. I find joy in watching the seasons turn, joy in the color of autumn, in knowing exactly where all my red and white trillium grow and seeing the first bud peep up in the spring. My connection to the seasons began in astronomy, but I carry it into my daily life and my gardening and my living.*

*If there's a message that anyone could get from my life, it would be that you don't have to be an astronomer to understand the seasons. It would be to actually watch what the sun and moon are doing. But don't stop there. Let your connections with the seasons grow even more through your own garden, through your knowledge of the sky, something that you can observe every day.*

Silently, one by one, in the infinite meadows

of heaven, blossomed the lovely stars,

the forget-me-nots of the angels.

—Henry Wadsworth Longfellow, American poet

## Do as the Morning Glories Do

What is it about the solar dawn (the twilight period while the sun is still below the horizon) and sunrise (when the upper edge of the sun actually appears on the horizon), that makes it so peaceful and welcoming? Partly it's the soft light, partly it's the breath of freshness. But mostly, it's the brightness of new beginnings.

Early morning is a time when the tranquility of the earth and anticipation of the day collide. The trick is to store up at that moment as much as one can of the peace and hope that is part and parcel of the early morning, giving yourself a reservoir to draw upon as needed throughout the day. Here's what you can do:

Rise early to take fullest advantage of each day's light. Do as the morning glories do and get up with the sun. Along with many water lilies, California poppies, crocuses, ice plants and African daisies, these light and temperature sensitive blossoms unravel their petals during the day and close as the day ends.

Take a hint from hot air balloonists and begin your day's journey at sunrise. Balloon pilots count on the calmness and clear visibility of the early morning air, choosing to lift off before the earth heats up and thermal conditions occur on the ground. Hot air balloons offer seemingly infinite clear views of the earth. So, too, does an early morning stroll taken at ground level.

Walk silently and invite the day's light and its new beginnings into your heart. Look west toward the far horizon, be it mountain range or ocean shore, and let the soft illumination of the day slip into your soul.

## Food for Thought

*There is good reason* to look to the sky. No matter how one sees it, studies it, tries to bottle it, it remains a place where eagles glide on outstretched wings, where humans soar on open minds and dreams.

*Within its universe*, frontiers are defined as tomorrows, marked by the moments and years in which it takes to reach them. Its travels are logged as flights, as voyages in space, as sails beyond the setting sun. Maps are made from its stars and boundaries are not meant to be.

*Its morning* is a clean slate where darkness is displaced by day and the heavens preclude despair.

*Colored with the spectrum* of rainbows and lit with a sun and moon that know how to break through the clouds, it veils a rapture as far flung as the reach of thought and prayer.

# Tapping into Our Bodies

# CHAPTER FOUR

# The Vista of Sight

✳

*It's not what you look at that matters, it's what you see.*
—Henry David Thoreau, American author, naturalist

As the great master Leonardo da Vinci saw it, the eye is the chief organ through which humans can realize the most complete and magnificent view of the infinite works of nature. It is the window of the soul, edging out the ear as being the most important of the five natural senses—sight, sound, touch, taste and smell. Considering that his artist's eye allowed him to both see and create such masterly works as the *Mona Lisa* and *The Last Supper*, it is hard to argue such a positioning.

In da Vinci's thinking, the eye receives the appearance of objects and transmits them through the sense organs to the second chamber, where *fantasia* or imagination reside along with intellectual reason. Forms created in the imagination, which "cannot visualize such beauty as is seen by the eye," were described as inferior, ultimately fading and dying in the third chamber, the *memoria*.

Da Vinci penned these thoughts in the 15th century, noting that drawing is based upon perspective, which he saw as "nothing else than a thorough knowledge of the function of the eye. And this function simply consists in receiving in a pyramid the forms and colours of all the objects placed before it."

## When Light Reaches the Eye

Broadly defined, vision, or sight, is a sensation caused in the brain when light reaches the eye. The eye initially treats light in an optical manner, producing a physical image in the same way as a camera. It is, however, the brain that allows us to interpret the visual image in a psychologically meaningful way.

It is a process that occurs so regularly, so unconsciously, that we seldom stop to think about the basics of its functionality. But more likely, and more universally, we do stop to appreciate the wonders that it offers us.

At the heart of sight is light. Light provides contrast between an object and its surroundings, enabling us to see it, to make out its shape and its contours. When white light splits into its prism of component colors, we are able to see rainbows. When our eyes detect the various frequencies of light waves as they are absorbed and reflected, we are able to see the ocean as blue or as green, the desert sands as pink.

True to his artist's genes, da Vinci loved colors. He was captivated by the effect that moisture in the Earth's atmosphere has on the color of things, especially when viewed at a distance, even putting together what might be described as a recipe book for light effects. To an artist who wants to create "striking blues in the manner of sunlight's effect as it passes through a column of smoke," try this: "...paint a board with various colours, among them an intense black; and all over let him lay a very thin and transparent [coating of] white. He will then see that this transparent white will nowhere show a more beautiful blue than over the black."

........................................................................................

*A single hour can consist of thousands of different colors.*

*Waxy yellows, cloud-spat blues. Murky darknesses. In*

*my line of work, I make it a point to notice them.*

*—Markus Zusak, author*

........................................................................................

# Case in Point

## Make Color and Light a Medium for Joy

### BRIGITTE BRÜGGEMANN

Rowe, New Mexico

*Professional artist. Best way to experience joy: Be here, here and now.*

Brigitte Brüggemann makes joy out of color and light. She creates it for herself through her paintings in oil, watercolor and pastels. She presents it to others through the vibrations in the soul that her works give.

Her recipe for joy, if there is a recipe, includes spontaneity, inspiration from nature and being in the moment, here and now. She has a firm belief in the power of art to change life, one moment at a time. Spontaneity, even wildness and unpredictability, is a big part of her joy.

Brigitte discovered the power of art as a youngster in Germany when her mother took her and her sisters to see the art and architecture. She recalls standing in front of Gruünewald's famous *Isenheim Altar*, a particularly powerful 16th century painting depicting the crucifixion of Christ.

She remembers being struck by its power, not so much because of the iconography, which she recalls as being as cruel or as ugly as one could paint a person in suffering, but because it touched her soul. She saw how it could touch her and bring up an emotion, and decided then, as a young girl, that if a painting could have such a powerful effect, that was what she wanted to do.

Today, Brigitte is very clear in her purpose—"to be light and to paint light." Believing that the inner landscape of the self mirrors the outer landscape, she tries to make the visible invisible through color and lyrical abstractions, the symbolic abstractions being her own personal visual language. Her works, which usually draw from a conscious or unconscious source in her life, are noted for their rhapsodic use of color as well as for their brushstroke.

**In Brigitte's words...**

*If you want to describe what happens technically, color is light. It causes vibrations in the soul. There is actually a chemistry happening with color and the surface of it. The passion I have for paint—what paint can do—is the vibration, I think. I look at art and a lot of it does not touch me. But there is something about the paint and its surface and the color that brings up vibration, and that brings us right back to color and light.*

*In the process of painting, I am allowing higher light frequencies to come into the painting through color. I can feel my own state of being changing into one of peace and joy. Color works on our psyche like music; the vibrations of color reach our unconscious and can change our moods dramatically. My choice of color is based always on the direct response I feel if I think of joy or sadness or uneasiness. In my painting, I stay away from most of those colors that make me cringe.*

*Right now, I'm sitting in my studio and I'm looking at this yellow painting. So yellow is something right now, but there are days where I do three red paintings right in a row, very deep red. White is always important for me because formally it sets off the colors. But also it is light, pure light. And then there are periods where I'm blue, where I'm doing blues, so it's painting with whatever is happening.*

*When I start a painting, I look at the tubes lying there on the table and try to connect with my emotions, how I feel that morning. Then I pick three or four or five different pigments, like blues and a little orange and some yellows and some red and I squeeze them out on the palette and then I just watch the colors. So it's based on emotion and I never know what will come out.*

*I can never have a plan. If I do have an idea, I start with one thing and it almost always has to get overpainted. If I start feeling precious about something, like a special brushstroke or a little area, and try to make the rest of the painting go with it, it almost never works. I usually end up taking that precious thing out and basically having to surrender to the will of the painting The surrender is not just for painting; I think it's true for life.*

*It's kind of a hard thing to describe, but I think it's the dialogue. It's like putting something on the painting and then suddenly the painting is yelling back at me and it says, No! When I start to listen to the painting, it almost paints itself. That's the magic.*

*I live by the Pecos River. So I will walk down and sit on the bank and watch the water. It's one of my greatest, greatest teachers, just to watch the flow. That's another way I connect with spirit, just letting energy lead you along.*

*It's almost like a pagan or animalistic kind of spirituality that if I go down to the river, the river has answers. If I have a question, I just sit there and I don't know if the river actually tells me, but a tree would kind of wave at me or a bird would suddenly appear and it sort of brings me to a point where I realize that I'm a drop in the ocean to be part of all this. I feel separate in the city and so here I'm able to connect to that larger universe. It's day and night. I look at the stars and I feel like I'm one of them, one of the stars.*

*I get great inspiration from nature and particularly from my garden. It's like a paradise, a lost paradise that we found. It's been a theme for me ever since my thesis when I got my Master's. Nature is the greatest landscape architect of what naturally happens out there.*

*Here I live in the middle of New Mexico, which is considered wilderness or arid desert, and yet I have a beautiful garden. I have cultivated space and the wilderness is right outside the wall. A garden is cultivation—it's manmade. So there is this constant contradiction there, and I used to feel guilty about that. But I don't anymore, because I am who I am and creating beauty is my biggest passion in life.*

*The first thing I do each day—I get up and I treasure that ten minutes where I make my coffee and feed my cat and do those kind of morning things. Then I'll go out with my cup and sit outside in the summer and I'll just look around and listen. I have a little pond and I'll look at the pond and the water and the fish and that is very soothing, too. So I walk very slow. It's called the Zen walk, where you take very slow steps and try to observe everything and connect with it.*

It's like this loving touch and sometimes I'll actually touch a flower and sort of give it a thought or even speak to it. And I'll go down to the river. I'll just walk very slowly. Being rushed by having to go somewhere, like having to go to the dentist, is the worst thing that can happen to me.

Peace is sort of an abstract term and it means a lot of different things to different people. For me, there's almost a physical energy that moves through me that is just light and is untroubled and positive about what I can do and about what's here and now.

Being present, I think, is the biggest bringer of joy. Just be here, here and now. Be in the moment. It's about letting the past go, the stories go. Our thoughts for the future and memories of what has passed can so clutter up our emotions. It's like a meditation. You don't have to sit cross legged and on a cushion to mediate.

So if there is a recipe at all, or a program to get from point a. to b., I think the first thing is to create that space for the feeling of being at peace. Just look at that tree waving at you, or the flower, or whatever is right in front of you. Look at it and the thoughts will go. Empty the vessel, so joy can come in.

Purer colors...have in themselves, independently of the objects they serve to express, a significant action on the feelings of those who look at them...A certain blue enters your soul. A certain red has an effect on your blood-pressure.

Henri Matisse, French artist

### Color Me Red – or Blue – or Yellow

The psychology of colors has long intrigued artists and psychologists alike. It is an inexact science, more of a study of the subjective effects various colors can have on our moods and feelings.

Although meanings can tend to vary by culture and by circumstance, some interpretations are fairly universal. Colors in the red area of the color spectrum, including red, orange and yellow, for example, are commonly known as warm colors, generating feelings of excitement, celebration, love, anger, aggression. Cool colors, including blue, purple and green, tend to be seen as evoking feelings of calmness, sadness or hopelessness.

### What Do Colors Mean?

Red:    Stimulating—represents power, strength, passion, courage, danger, energy

Pink:   Brighter, hot shades are stimulating; paler shades are calming—represents sensitivity, friendship, romance and love

Yellow: Energizing—represents happiness, sunshine, joy, cheerfulness

Orange: Boosts self esteem—represents enthusiasm, fascination, creativity, determination

Blue:   Calming—represents healing, loyalty, depth, wisdom, faith, heaven, tranquility

Purple: Alleviates nervousness—represents royalty, spirituality, creativity, mystery

Green:  Relaxation—represents nature, serenity, healing, growth, fertility, hope, harmony, safety

Black:  Depression—represents power, elegance, formality, evil, death, grief, security, fear

White:  Tranquility—represents pureness, peace, light, goodness, purity, perfection, innocence

*While there is perhaps a province in which the photograph can tell us nothing more than what we see with our own eyes, there is another in which it proves to us how little our eyes permit us to see.*

*—Dorothea Lange, documentary photographer*

## See with More than Our Eyes

Author Richard Louv has a delightful chapter in his most recent book, *The Nature Principle*, in which he writes of talking, singing, sniffing the air, watching for tracks, even feeling the hair on the back of the neck stand up, as ways to sense the presence of bears. When we think of seeing, we tend to single out our eyes. But eyesight is a complex gift, one that joins with a long list of other human senses in the reception of meaningful images.

Most of us probably are not too worried about refining our ability to perceive the presence of bears. To be able, however, to experience other images to the fullest, to grasp and comprehend their meaning, to delight in the full phenomenon of their beauty, is undoubtedly a capability we want to make the most of. Sight serves as the window into some of life's richest sweet spots.

# Case in Point

## See and Enjoy Life Twice

### JOAN TUNSTALL
Lawson, Australia
*IT marketing, amateur photographer. Best way to
experience joy: Examine and share what you see.*

Joan Tunstall lives in the Blue Mountains, a huge and scenic wilderness area roughly 100 kms., or 62 miles, west of Sydney, Australia. She lives there because she likes being near nature, likes the four seasons' climate, the small town sense of community, being able to afford a large house and garden. But most especially, she likes it there because it fuels her love of photography and allows her to share what she sees with others.

As one who rarely goes anywhere without a camera, Joan finds her life is enriched when she looks through the eye of a lens. She may, for example, see a landscape, an old house, a garden. But when she zooms in on some individual detail within, tries a different angle, seeks out light to illuminate it, she opens her eyes to a new dimension—details and images she might otherwise have missed. It's a practice she finds works throughout life.

Although Joan enjoys puttering away among the blossoms, weeding is not her top priority and she depends on nature to do most of the work of gardening. This frees her to focus on marrying her twin loves of writing and photography. She regularly photographs the colors and faces of jonquils, azalea and fox gloves on the woodland path and posts them on her *Burnbraejournal.com* blog along with an inspirational quote or scripture verse. She invites site visitors to join her in a moment of quiet reflection and recollection as she posts.

**In Joan's words...**

*There are several ways in which photography enhances things. The first is in seeing the detail. It's about slowing down. It's also about seeing the frame. Good photos have a lot to do with composition, how things are placed within the frame. There is a sense in which I often look at things as if through a view finder. So it's also about boundaries and balance.*

*Truth is, I am quite happy to capture and collect the beauty of a thing just for the enrichment it gives me. But the blog brings the discipline that delivers the twice-lived experience I find so valuable, as well as the practice that develops my skill. It pushes my boundaries. I find the viewers' thoughtful comments challenge me and that's good.*

*Another is in seeing the focus. Sometimes you want the background blurred, sometimes not. It's about showing what you want to show. It's also in seeing the light. The more you photograph, the more you love light. It's about the interplay of light and shade. A good photograph takes both. I believe a good life does, too. The joy—or the light—gives us the wellspring to understand and cope with the shade.*

*Lastly, it's in seeing life twice. When I spot something I want to photograph, there is that little leap of delight. As I get set to photograph it, I get to see it again. When I process the photos and blog about them, I live it again. I do enjoy going back over my blogs and reliving the moments. They are there as an imprint on my life that I carry with me always.*

*Seeing life twice is what writing and poetry are about. When you put effort into capturing the experience in words, you live the experience over again, and the experience is richer for having done so. It's as if the emotion of that moment is frozen in time, true to the time. This does a couple of things. You can go back and look at it—the photograph, the poem, the journal entry—and see it as it was.*

*However, I also find that it imprints more deeply into the "me" that walks around every day. I carry it with me more clearly than the blur of other things that go on in a busy life. If those things have been good things, then my life carries with it a deeper joy, a well of delight that can be tapped into without the photography or words before me.*

*I love words. I know my Bible well and have a pretty big store of poems sitting in my head. So when I have a photo, a theme usually presents itself. That is the fun of matching the right recollection with it. In most cases I don't know chapter and verse of scripture and certainly know very few poems by heart, but I know what I want and where to look. One quick web search, or diving into one of the many poetry books on my bookshelf, suffices.*

*Although, this is not always the case. Sometimes I have a theme and my mind turns up nothing. That's when I Google away and see what comes up. Often I will know that a poet—Robert Frost, Emily Dickinson, Les Murray, Judith Wright or whomever—is a good bet and I start with them, rather than empty space. Likewise, in the Bible I've got a good feel for where the theme will be addressed.*

*I guess I also read with a view to building up the treasure chest. One beautiful piece of writing is inspirational even when it has been selected because it's descriptive. Sometimes it is simply the memory, e.g., a childhood rhyme that is valuable. It's more about my personal response from which I derive joy and inspiration, rather than being deliberately inspirational.*

*I find beauty is a fleeting thing, a brief gasp of pleasure, unless I slow down and really take it in. Only then does it "keep a bower quiet, and a sleep full of sweet dreams, and health, and quiet breathing"—and become a joy forever, as the poet Keats found a thing of beauty to be. On the subject of beauty, I have discovered with my photo-blogging friends that beauty is a subjective thing. My beauty is not necessarily yours.*

*The reason I love photography so much is it makes me "see" the world: the detail in the garden, tiny differences in the forest, slowing down to capture the essence of a country town instead of just letting it whiz by, the beauty of subtle changes in the light that make the difference between a snapshot and a WOW photograph. When I see, it talks to my soul and I am happy.*

## More than a Thousand Words

It has often been said that pictures are worth a thousand words. In truth, it is the memory they prompt that gives them both their worth and their meaning. Cesare Pavese, Italian poet and novelist, once said that the richness of life lies in the memories we have forgotten. We do not remember days, he said, we remember moments.

Look at any photo album and that is exactly what we will see—a collection of moments. If we were to position and sequence them properly, we could animate a movie or cartoon with all those moments. Most likely, though, we want them more for their powers of revealing the substance of weddings, of births and celebrations, of portraits and vacations. Photos may be said to reawaken the momentary riches that have defined our lives.

# Case in Point

## Showing the Beauty of Each Moment

ERIN WALLACE
Damariscotta, Maine
*Collector of images and inspiration from the everyday. Best way to experience joy: Love the whole process—of photography, of life.*

Erin Wallace works everyday to make her and her family's life as simple as possible. She does so with the belief that when life is simple, you are able to see the joy and beauty in everything. So at the end of the day, she finds joy in their togetherness, their way of living, their simplicity. They live a life, she says, with intention and purpose, and enjoy every bit of it.

As a photographer, Erin has learned that she "really, really" loves being behind the camera. She loves its process, the ability to capture, edit and show an image. But most particularly, she loves portraying someone in a beautiful moment. Every moment she sees is amazing and wonderful and one of a kind, something she will never get back. Capturing that moment makes her heart sing.

### In Erin's words...

*To me, happiness is this thing that we all try to achieve. We want to be happy all the time. It's something where you can put on a smile and look like you're happy, but you might not feel it. I think joy is something that's really deep inside of you. You have to truly feel it to be able to express it.*

*I think that the word happiness is something that is thrown around a lot more; you can kind of fake it for a while if you need to. To me, joy has a kind of deeper meaning. It means that you're living from a place deep inside of you.*

*Joy can grow out of an accumulation of all those things that you do or focus on to be happy. If I lose that kind of joyful feeling, I try to focus on things that initially will simply make me happy. Happiness is a kind of fleeting thing—something will make me happy but it won't stick. Joy, on the other hand, is there for a long time. It's not like eating an ice cream cone or having something that makes you feel good—the feeling lasts just until you're done. But I do think that having all those little tiny things that make me happy stimulates some kind of joyful thing that goes on inside me all week. So I focus on the little things that make me happy and then I'm able to find that larger joy.*

*When I started the "Thirty Days of Happiness" series on my blog, my marriage was ending, I was separated from my husband, I was in this place where I was, like, what am I going to do. You know, for some reason, depression, or just dealing with depression, can be attractive enough to humans where they want to hold on to it, they just want to stay there, and it's really hard to get out of it. So I knew I was kind of on this edge where I could fall into that and say, "I don't know what I'm going to do, how am I going to get by, I don't have any money, I'm leaving with nothing." It was just so easy to be consumed by all these thoughts.*

*Basically, I had been at this space in my life where nothing seemed to be going the way I would have chosen for it to go, and I was feeling really lost. So I said I can either choose to get stuck in this or I can try to do something about it. Figuring if I can't control these bigger things, I decided I just wanted to know the little things that can at least make the days easier to get through.*

*During my pregnancy, I started a blog for family and friends. After Elizabeth was born, she had colic for a very long time and was a really challenging child. So I wrote about that, hoping that someone could help me. It was a very depressing blog. I was always complaining, "I haven't slept in three weeks," stuff like that. It was actually the complete opposite of the way my Bluebirdbaby blog is now. So it's funny, but just trying to focus on more positive stuff in my life really just switched my whole way of living.*

*When I photograph, I try to just catch a spirit in the people being photographed. Photos can pick up a beauty that we don't see.*

*There are things that are just so beautiful that people don't even notice and I think that being a photographer, it's almost like my eye is trained to kind of look for it. It's not necessarily physical beauty. It's just that moment and that flavor and emotion. That's what I want to capture. When it comes to having their pictures taken, most people are like "Oh, no, don't, I'm so ugly." I try to coax them out of that mindset because that's not how other people are seeing them.*

*The things that bring me the most joy in my life are my daughter and my partner. Growing up, we never really did anything together as a family. There was a lot of loneliness and bitterness and anger, so I never thought I'd ever have that family unit. So now, I just feel so fortunate that I have a partner whose life and everything that he loves revolves around Elizabeth and myself. That is my source of joy.*

*Making joy a part of your life is something that you need to choose to do; it's not something instant. It does take work before joy really settles with you. I've had days recently where I don't know if I can make it through the day and wonder what I am going to blog about. I guess the blog has been something to motivate me to keep doing what I'm doing. I want to be able to say, oh this is what I did today, and it made me so happy and I had a great time, instead of just sitting around all day moping, which is so easy to do.*

*When I began the Thirty Days of Happiness series, I was reading through people's blogs and saw how some would say they had a great evening and this is what made them happy. But then there was this one who felt nothing turned out right that day, that she couldn't even look at the sky, that nothing made her happy. Finally, at some point she said, "I guess that's not what this is about, I guess it's really about being able to look at something and just find some happiness in it." I think she kind of expected something big or major had to happen that made her day, or made her happy or joyful. But it was really just the opposite. It wasn't about the big things, it was about the little things.*

*For me, photography just kind of captures the feeling of the moment. I can look at pictures of Elizabeth that I took when she was five months old and still feel what I felt when I took it. That's my goal—to capture that moment and everything about it—not only what it looked like.*

## Many Ways to See

Capturing images through the lens of a camera so that we may study them, share them and replicate the emotions associated with them, is one way of exercising our sense of sight. Journaling is another.

*The summer I learned to draw wasn't anything special at all, it was just the first summer I ever really saw.*

—Hannah Hinchman, author, artist

# Case in Point

## Preserve Moments of Delight

PAM JOHNSON BRICKELL
Bluffton, South Carolina
*Artist, nature journal workshop instructor. Best way to
experience joy: Look carefully at a little something.*

Pam Johnson Brickell defines herself as a nature artist, nature journal
workshop instructor and calligrapher. The list of interests on her blog
covers the gamut of nature's creatures and passions, from raptors and
dragonflies to star gazing and crepuscular walks. But most important
is one seemingly simple directive—to not let the day slip by.

For Pam to see fully, to take notice of all that is around her and
then capture those images and details with watercolor sketches and
notations on the pages of a field journal, is not just a way of life; it's
almost a kind of therapy. It goes beyond exploring and creating and
has become an important extension of her life.

Pam has journaled since college, making it a pastime that served
as a comforting constant as she moved throughout the country during
different times of life. She journaled every day and feels it actually kept
her from getting that seasonal depression that can come with the long,
cold and dark nights of winter. Today, recognizing what it has done
for her life and its therapeutic possibilities, she reaches out to others,
teaching the joy that can be realized by using the process of creating
one's own nature journal as a means of seeing.

One of the greatest satisfactions she finds when teaching is in
helping those who don't believe they have any artistic capability to
overcome their hesitance. As Pam sees it, the value of journaling is
not in having the feeling that it must be perfect, but in knowing that it
can—and should—be done just for the fun of it. That said, she typically
begins her workshops with exercises on seeing.

## In Pam's words…

*It's important to me to be a part of the earth, and to not just dance on the surface; I want to know what kind of tree I'm looking at, what kind of bug, what kind of flower, animal or bird. I want the satisfaction of having said I lived on the earth, that I know the names of and something about the flora and fauna that surround me, that I didn't just gloss over and take nature's daily wonders for granted.*

*It's a pride thing with me to be able to walk down a wooded path and know as much as I can about what surrounds me. To notice if the anoles have had babies, or how a bird positions its legs when it lands, or the changing of leaf color in a garden—it's simply that it takes time to look at your surroundings.*

*I focus my nature journaling workshops on teaching my students how to see. Many adults want to draw but are so ticklish about picking up a pencil. Many have had a bad experience with art in grade school and over time lost the natural gift that they could have nurtured. So, we do some fun exercises, and by the end of the workshop they are absolutely amazed at the art they've created.*

*I use a tried and true recipe for viewing and sketching an object. I'll place seashells, leaves, bark or anything small in front of each student and have them start drawing by using the blind contour sketching technique. In other words, I have them draw their subject while looking only at it and not at their pencil and paper. They are also instructed to not lift their pencil off of the paper. We practice this technique quite a few times and then move on to modified contour drawing, where they can peek at the paper every now and then, but still can't lift the pencil off the paper. They have to look more at the object than at the paper.*

*Warming up like this is wonderful. The right side of the brain kicks in and students really start to notice the character of the item before them instead of channeling left-brain symbolism. I get so many that will draw a computer clipart type of leaf and I'll gently say, "if you take another look at the leaf, you'll see little tiny notches that run along its outside edge." They start to really notice the shape and contour and that's the ticket. It's all about taking the time. When we take time to look at an object, all of a sudden an hour's gone by and we lose ourselves in it.*

*Watercolor pencils are so much fun—they are just like using crayons. However, once you add water... voila—you have an instant watercolor painting. Another favorite tool is the waterbrush. It's a synthetic brush that has an empty handle that is filled with water. It dispenses just the right amount of water and when used in combination with watercolor pencils, the results are phenomenal—especially for a beginner. I've had so many students who say, "I've always wanted to try watercolors but it's such a difficult medium, and now I'm doing it!"*

*I try to sketch or make a written note about what I see almost every day. But, sometimes life interrupts and my journal entries ebb and flow. Sometimes I'll set aside fifteen minutes a day to journal, other times take a day trip, and then there are times when I'll go on a walk with the dogs and see something wonderful and upon returning home, do a memory sketch. One of my journal entries—I've titled it "A Discombobulated Day"—took about 15 minutes for the plein air pen sketch. I chose to add the color on a different day as I was feeling off kilter. There's no hard and fast rule that you have to finish a journal page in one sitting. When the mood strikes is always favorable, as you'll get better results when your heart is in it.*

*Taking time to draw something creates ownership. When I notice and sketch a new-to-me wildflower, I don't care that it was named long ago, it's my discovery and I own it. It's that sense of ownership that makes sketching what is in front of you stick with you forever. I can go back to a journal from 1974, look at a page and be transported back in time to that very moment. Priceless!*

*I call it therapy, because there have been many times in my life when I've needed an out, a diversion—sketching and painting in my journal lets me go to another place. Keeping an illustrated journal helps me remain centered and able to tackle the crazies that come my way, and always allows me to celebrate the wonders of nature!*

> To go into the dark with a light is to know the
> light. To know the dark, go dark. Go without
> sight, and find that the dark too blooms and sings
> and is traveled by dark feet and dark wings.
>
> —Wendell Berry, farmer, writer

### Food for Thought

*"Three Days to See"* is an essay by Helen Keller telling what she would like to see if given the use of her eyes for that short period of time. Having contracted an illness at the age of just 19 months that left her blind and deaf, unable to see and to hear in the usual manner of most, Helen is known worldwide for her unrelenting efforts to realize the joys and miracles of these two important senses.

Published by *The Atlantic Monthly* in January 1933, "Three Days to See" speaks of the many everyday and glorious things on which, if she were able, she would have let her eyes rest. Just reading about her vision of a life that she could not literally see has a way of opening our eyes to so much that we may simply have taken for granted. Helen wrote, for example:

of seeing friends, knowing that surely they possess some outward evidences of the beauty that is within;

of opening her eyes to the panorama of light with which the sun awakens the sleeping earth, just one small aspect of Nature's constantly unfolding splendor;

of being able to see not only by the rays of the sun but by artificial light, created by human genius to extend the power of sight in darkness;

of the color, grace and cadenced motion of a play, a movie, or of the pageant of mankind's progress as displayed in the city's museums;

of the spirit of Egypt, Greece, and Rome expressed in their art, treasures through which she would probe into the soul of man;

of the lacy structure of steel that spans the East River and
that she understood would offer a new and startling vision
of the power and ingenuity of the mind.

The few thoughts encapsulated in these pages barely begin
to cover the full depth and beauty of this beloved educator's
understanding of the gift of sight. They do, however, serve as
a perceptive and telling reminder to all who see to make full
use of the gift of sight—to use our eyes and our senses as if
tomorrow we might no longer see or hear or feel, to glory in
all the facets of pleasure and beauty the world reveals.

# CHAPTER FIVE

# The Pulse of Sound

*Music and rhythm find their way into the secret places of the soul.*
*—Plato, Greek philosopher*

At the ripe old age of twenty three days, the human fetus is able to feel sound. At roughly four months of gestation, it is able to hear, and by five months, to respond by blinking or moving to the beat of music or to the smallest unit of sound spoken by the mother. Of all our sense organs, the ear is the most fully developed at birth.

To simply dissect the role of the ear in hearing, start with the external ear. That's the portion that we see and from which sound waves are funneled into the ear canal. As sound waves bounce off the sides of the canal, they are channeled through the middle ear to the ear drum, which begins to vibrate when contacted by sound waves. The resulting vibrations are converted into neural signals and sent to the auditory center of the brain where they are interpreted as recognizable sounds.

The power of sound to influence and enrich our lives becomes clear when we listen to its voice. Hearing helps us to take care of ourselves, to distinguish the alarm or celebration of a bell, the pleasure or anguish of a moan. Thanks to sound, we avoid danger. We rest. We dance. We hear the call of a meadowlark, the first cry of a newborn, the whisper of a child's secret.

Sometimes we call the sound to which we listen, music. Other times, we think of it as noise. Other times, simply silence.

........................................................................................................

*Everybody should have his personal sounds to listen for—sounds that will make him exhilarated and alive or quiet and calm....One of the greatest sounds of them all—and to me it is a sound—is utter, complete silence.*

*—Andre Kostelanetz, Russian orchestral leader*

........................................................................................................

### The Symphony of Silence

The American composer, John Cage, is probably best remembered for his 1952 composition of silence—four minutes and 33 seconds performed in three movements, all without a single note being played. This is not to say that the piece, 4'33", was four minutes and thirty three seconds of silence. Rather, it was a composition of found sound, of noise and alternative instruments. Consistent with his belief that there is no such thing as an empty space or an empty time, Cage saw 4'33" not as silence, but as the unintended sounds of the environment that listeners would hear while it was performed. For Cage, listening is the principal act of musical performance.

Environmental sounds in their natural state can bring us remarkable pleasure. Possibly because we equate nature and peace, we tend to think of their whisperings, their lullabies, their voices, as sounds of silence. But they are, in fact, music, notes of silence that we have come to increasingly appreciate in these days of technology and its seemingly perpetual noise.

One author, painter and educator, John Lane, writes in *The Spirit of Silence: Making Space for Creativity*, that silence touches us in many different ways. It offers sanctuary and tranquility, puts us in touch with the inner depths of our everyday lives. Silence, Lane tells us, is a source of joy—an inspiration for art, literature and music. Perhaps most importantly, it awakens us to the present moment. Encounters with silence "can be the source of a wonderful clarity." We want to seek them out and savor them.

*The three great elemental sounds in nature are the sound of rain, the sound of wind in a primeval wood, and the sound of outer ocean on a beach.*

—Henry Beston, writer, naturalist

## Nature Is a Sound Machine

Mother Nature carries her own sound machine with her, positioning the dial and turning up the volume to match the weather, the setting, the rhythm of life. Her sound tracks consistently score at the top of the popularity charts. Whether rated according to genre, artist, performance quality or overall popularity, the music of nature is sought out and listened to world round.

A rock by the sea, a mossy log under the forest's canopy, even an old blanket spread under the stars, all can work as prime front row seats for nature's most popular concerts. But in truth, it's not so much where we sit, but what we hear, that matters. We listen to the ripple of a wave, the sigh of the wind, the voice of the lark and are soothed by a lullaby, to a love song and hear the voice of a soul.

Mary Webb, an English romantic novelist and poet of the early 20th century, sees nature's music as never being over—"her silences are pauses, not conclusions." In many ways, it is this lingering, almost haunting aspect of nature's music that positions it so well as a healing soundscape of meditation.

Built around holistic integration of mind, body and spirit, the practice of Zen yoga is noted particularly for its use of music—popularly known as Zen garden music. Subtle musical sounds of nature are used as a way of helping to awaken the subconscious mind and allow a deeper exploration of one's spiritual body. They become a sort of ecosystem of sound, a perfect resting place to sit in meditation as stillness is achieved.

## Case in Point

### Listen in a Quiet Place

GORDON HEMPTON

Port Angeles, Washington

*Acoustic ecologist and sound recordist. Best way to*
*experience joy: Listen to the voice and music of nature.*

When Gordon Hempton finds joy, he records it. He finds it by listening—by listening to and for the sounds of nature that bring with them a measure of peace and quiet. It is our birthright, he says, "to listen, quietly and undisturbed, to the natural environment and take whatever meanings we may."

A botany graduate of the University of Wisconsin, Gordon was struck at the age of 27 by what he refers to in his book, *One Square Inch of Silence,* as the "magnificent, deep, primordial, soul-shaking sounds" of thunder, sounds as he had never heard them before. Since that time, listening to natural sound or, more accurately, listening for the vanishing sounds of nature, has been his passion and inspiration.

An acoustic ecologist, Gordon records the sounds of nature in their most natural state. Fondly known as the Sound Tracker, he treks around the world in pursuit of quiet places of solitude, spaces where the lost sounds of nature are yet to fade away—the waking breaths of dawn, the sweep of beach waves, the concert of a stream, whine of a winged insect, the vibrating tongue of a winter wren.

Protection of sounds such as these, he firmly believes, is as necessary and essential as species preservation, habitat restoration, toxic waste cleanup, and carbon dioxide reduction. It is a task that he tackled by issuing a challenge of his own—to protect and preserve the natural silence of one square inch of natural soundscape deep within what is arguably the quietest place in the United States, the Hoh Rain Forest in Washington's Olympic National Park.

Designated as a sanctuary for silence, the forest park embodies those natural soundscape characteristics that are increasingly difficult to find and to manage. It also anchors Gordon's hope that just as we protect a single square inch of land from noise pollution, so too larger areas of the park will benefit. The rationale underscores the goal of his One Square Inch challenge—to introduce the first No Flight Zone for all aircraft, basically ensuring that the back country of Olympic National retains its natural state of quiet.

But to Gordon, One Square Inch is more than the challenge of conserving a seemingly miniscule plot of silence for others and for tomorrow's world, more than the preservation of nature's tone and voice so they may be heard by others on Gordon's Emmy-winning documentary soundtracks and CDs. It is the knowledge that he is helping to preserve an endangered species—the sounds of silence.

### In Gordon's words...

*When we're in a quiet place, we are free to let our senses simply take in what the body craves: beautiful sights, nature sounds. When you really take it all in, in a quiet place, you are no longer listening to what's 100 feet around you in every direction, you're listening to miles in every direction. You're listening to the summary of all the sounds, not just the sound of that songbird singing. You're letting your attention go and you're taking it all in. You're listening to the ambiance of nature and clearly that is experienced as music.*

*I'm not saying that it's musical. I'm saying that it is music. When I say music, I mean something that you at times feel inspired to dance to, something you're going to recall and hum along with as that summary tune and sound of nature.*

*The quiet place is the think tank of the soul. It reaches deeply. By going into nature and letting go, and reaching that deep spiritual level, quiet is quieting. It is also medically healing in that it's lowering your blood pressure and taking those stress hormones out of your blood stream. But it's also in the peace of mind. How often do we use the words peace and quiet together in the same breath?*

*Now here is the troubling news, that there are no quiet places left in nature. So where do you go from there? Well, there are "quieter" places* in nature. The modern measure of what I call silence—and when I say silence I mean periods where it's natural ambiance only, without noise pollution—is called the noise free interval. For just about everything east of the Mississippi, there is not a noise free interval that exceeds 15 minutes during daylight hours. In all of the United States, I've only been able to locate a dozen places, and just recently I've identified a thirteenth location which I think has a very high probability. Fifteen minutes is not much to ask for. But 15 minutes is considerably better than in other parts of the country.

A trick that I've learned when it comes to listening to nature is that you're not going to listen for some thing. You're simply going to listen to the place. Not to the birds, not to the insects, not to the wind through the trees. Listen to the place. Take it all in.

The defenses that we've built up from so-called listening in noisy areas are thick. Words don't penetrate that layer. They're just ricocheting off the surface and the mind is busy filtering out what's important, what's not important, pretty much arbitrarily.

Go to something as simple as a stream. There are lots of different streams and many people will admit that different streams make different sounds but are all pretty substantially the same. You can stop at any part of that stream, take five steps, listen again, five more steps, listen again, and it will all be basically the same. Right? Whoa—new discoveries!

The stones in the stream are the musical notes. A stream tunes itself over time and become more musical. So what I have students do is find a place on the stream and just sit down on the edge, take time and study the rocks. The mind begins to quickly sort out different sounds and not just hear it as water, a stream, but hear it in all its different parts, coming from different directions. That sonic image is beginning to develop in fine detail.

And then I have them reach into the water and pull out one of the notes and listen to how the stream sounds differently. Now, put the stone back in the water to try to get it to sound the way it did. You can't. You can't because the stream has tuned itself, and now you have retuned the stream.

*I built my life on listening. Listening means everything to me and if you read my book, you know I also lost my hearing for a short period of time. But there's a big difference between losing your hearing and remembering what it's like to hear, and growing up where you don't have the contribution that sound offers into your life.*

*Rebecca, the woman with whom I share my life and love, is deaf, never going to even guess at what I hear. But she is—and this is an important point—a great listener. And so that is our common ground, that above sound is listening. She reads lips very well and she observes. I asked her about this because we're now working on a project called Lip Reading Nature.*

*She doesn't listen to nature; she's never heard a bird song. She now has a cochlear implant and the cochlear implant just is so different than listening. All birds sound the same, all water, whether it's rain or a stream, sounds the same. All sound is annoying to her.*

*What she does in her listening is she puts the context together. Like one time I was telling her that I was going to the garage. She thought I said I was going to the greyhounds, because those are the same lip movements. But she later figured out in my following sentences what the true meaning was. So now what we are doing is I am developing a program with her where she can observe the visual patterns in nature. I can describe how those effects sound.*

*Our goal is that she will be able to give a guided tour of Olympic National Park and all its sonic wonders to a hearing group to help them explore and discover for themselves the wonders of listening. She absolutely loves Olympic National Park for its visual splendor. So through her explanation of how she reads lips and understands so well what people are saying, I'm taking that knowledge and then applying it to listening to Olympic National Park. Now she's going to have all these other great discoveries, so a new kind of joy is on the horizon for her.*

*I often listen with my eyes closed. But while I'm on location during a recording session, it helps to listen with my eyes open. Generally, there's not much transparency, translucency, in the environment, so vision* delivers one kind of information in one direction. Sound comes from all directions. The sound really tells the story.

You have to listen and give it time and I think a lot of people are too impatient to really listen; the listening process is now being treated much more like vision. So when I'm listening, and it takes time, I notice how much more I also see. And while I'm taking those 15 minutes just to make that sound recording and to take it all in, I'm also taking 15 minutes of looking at what's right in front of me and I see so much more.

If you know a preschooler, if you have a young child, hoist them onto your shoulder and go for a night walk. They'll tell you everything you need to know about being a better listener.

### Listen to that Bird's Song

Did you know that most songbirds need to learn their language? The need to sing is instinctual, but for some species the process of singing and knowing the song to sing is taught. Like human infants learning to speak, baby songbirds babble softly before advancing through phases of practice singing, copying the songs they hear. Most species learn their songs as juveniles, beginning as early as ten days in the nest, though they don't start fully singing until the next spring when they are mature.

The song of a bird tends to vary with age and gender and generally is used for a very specific purpose, whether to attract a mate, signal a domestic duty, or warn of danger. There are many variations in both the technique and the sound of birds' music. While such songbirds as wrens, sparrows, thrushes, and warblers rely on their bellows-like air sacs to produce their melodic sounds, hummingbirds produce their telltale hum through the rapid beat of their wings, woodpeckers drum with their bills and "voiceless" birds, such as storks and albatross, rattle or clap their bills.

We tend to be fascinated by birds' songs, recording their notes and even describing them through the use of such mnemonics as the *pleased, pleased, pleased to meetcha!* ending of the Chestnut-sided Warbler, or the Northern Cardinal's *birdie-birdie-birdie.* The Cornell Lab of Ornithology has a fascinating website, *www.allaboutbirds.org,* that walks us through some of the basic tips for learning calls and songs, even showing us how we can "see" the sound of five common bird songs. Using its spectrogram demo, try comparing the simple, clear whistles of a White-throated Sparrow to the chips and trills of a Song Sparrow. Then look at the whistles of a Northern Cardinal and a Red-bellied Woodpecker's harsh *kwirr* call before finishing up with the aural smorgasbord of an American Goldfinch's twenty five-second song. It makes for a delightful visit.

...........................................................................

*Hearing is a form of touch. I could hear less*

*through the ears but more through the body.*

*—Evelyn Glennie, Scottish percussionist*

...........................................................................

## The Tricks and Marvels of Sound

Although most mammals typically hear by way of sound waves transferred through the ear canals, there are a few puzzling as well as interesting exceptions. In whales and dolphins, some studies suggest that sound is channeled to the ear by tissues in the area of the lower jaw. One group of whales, the Odontocetes or toothed whales, uses the process of echolocation, or the emission of sound and reception of its echo, to hunt and to navigate.

Whales, dolphins and porpoises are not alone in using the echolocation— or ultrasonic sonar—process to see the world around them through hearing. Another celebrated user of this nifty trick is the bat, of which more than half of the roughly 900 species rely on echolocation to navigate and forage for food. Most accomplish this by contracting their larynx or clicking their tongues, emitting the resulting sounds through the mouth.

A most delicate and complicated process that begins with origination of the sound itself, hearing involves far more than the ear; our whole body plays a role in determining the manner in which we hear and experience sounds. As shown in research by the Anstendig Institute, if we want to hear the nuances of sound, such as voice inflections, emotions, or other expressive content, the whole body must vibrate in the patterns of those nuances. We are vibrating bodies living in an environment in which every part is vibrating, even those things that seem to be still.

Sound and music are found to be so intimately connected to movement that British dance music therapist Caroline Frizell describes life as beginning with a rhythmically orchestrated dance *in utero*. Referring to literature by psychotherapists Lloyd deMause and Margareta Wärja, she describes the rapidly developing foetus as testing a range of movement as it explores space—grasping, floating and kicking at boundaries while surrounded by the pulsating rhythm of the heart beat.

..................................................................................

*Music has been my magic carpet to the world.*

*—Paul Winter, composer*

..................................................................................

## Case in Point

### Making Music Speak

JUDY DWORIN
Bloomfield, Connecticut
*Professor of theater and dance, professional dance/theater artist.*
*Best way to experience joy: Be open to the discoveries of play.*

Judy Dworin sees and enjoys dance as just one piece of a larger creative vision. It is a vision built on the interconnectedness of the individual arts. It is also a matter of faith—a belief in the ability of dance, performance, words, song, music and spontaneous creativity to connect with and create change in our individual and collective worlds.

Delivered through the Judy Dworin Performance Project, Inc. (JDPP), a nonprofit company of performing artists who use the rhythm of the arts to address issues of social concern, Judy's work is based on her conviction that art can speak. It can comment on the world in which we live, engage and ask its audience to reflect and to experience, give voice to the unheard and inspire change. Its voice speaks stories of freedom and justice, of hope for a greener, kinder, more conscious world.

Working, for instance, with inmates of a women's correctional institution in Niantic, Connecticut, Judy and the JDPP professionals have created multi-arts performance pieces that capture the complex tapestry of feelings experienced by women behind bars—anger, pain, regret, fear, loneliness, despair and glimmers of hope—and brought them to the public outside.

"This," said one reviewer, "is as close as most people will ever get to hearing the voices of incarcerated women, of seeing the world through their eyes, and of experiencing how they feel."

**In Judy's words...**

*The way we first know about the world is through our bodies, through our senses, picking up the rhythm of life around us. This is what tells us we are alive. But as we grow up in this culture, as we begin to be able to speak, to write and to read, we often lose that connection to our physical selves. We move away from having that immediate awareness of the world, that sensory awareness. We are taught to become distant to our bodies.*

*I think that the joy of dance or movement is in coming back to that place in ourselves that is really where we started. It's rediscovering that place and allowing ourselves to receive all of that information that has been coming unconsciously, that we just haven't tuned into. It opens up a new world for us in the process.*

*There is an inherent joy in being in the moment, in feeling that moment, in being able to translate it into movement and just letting your body tell you what to do, as opposed to telling your body what to do. It feels to me that in movement, we learn or receive essential foundational tools for living. This kind of engagement with our movement contains such important values as trust, cooperation, listening, allowing, awareness, problem-solving and spontaneity—it helps us to identify ourselves, express and communicate.*

*Movement reconnects us to our own authentic self, as well as to the sensory world that exists around us—and to energy. We communicate through energy and we're always getting what you might call energetic messages.*

*When someone tells us that everything is fine but is sitting there all huddled up—a body that feels all scrunched together—we sense a contradiction. We intuit that the verbal message doesn't really feel right, but consciously we may not be able to determine why. Understanding the movement signals takes us back to that kinesthetic place of understanding. The experience of being connected to one's body and to one's physicality and to the energy of the universe is a joyful experience.*

*Dance, for me, always brings joy—in all of the residency work at York Correctional Institution, in the schools and in my teaching at Trinity College. At the college, I am bringing these students—most of whom have been deprived of movement knowledge in the same ways that everybody else has—to a place where they open up and express themselves. It's a wonderful unlearning process—to get back to that more basic level, to start to get to know oneself at age seventeen, eighteen, nineteen, or whatever, and to express and communicate through the body.*

*My approach is always one of discovery, of offering certain skills and structures, but using them as a base from which one can explore and go beyond. It's allowing someone to feel a measure of trust and comfortableness within his or her own self as well as with everyone else in the room. Once that environment is set up, each person can really explore and find that place and listen to what they want to say.*

*So many of the women at York [Correctional Institution] go through deeply painful moments along the way in our work. But it's pain that they are able to begin to process at that point, pain that is critical for them to process in order to progress. There is enormous release in this that produces great joy and self satisfaction. It's not self satisfaction in a complacent way, but a sense of self and a satisfaction in the achievement of self that comes out of that. I think that joy moves through the sadness inside of it and that brings them—or anyone of us—to a much better place.*

*Since my childhood, dancing was always a huge center of my life. In recent years, a chronic inner ear problem has caused me to have more limited ability to do the movement that I used to love so much. To have that piece taken away was huge, even though by that time I was much more interested in making work, or creating, than in performing. It was a big adjustment. But then again, it brings me back to the simple joy of being able to walk across the room. And the sort of creative energy that I have, and it hasn't diminished at all, just keeps expressing itself in whatever way it can.*

*Performance pieces that I made earlier were more extensively movement-based and less textual, and now they are more of an integration of the narrative and text. Song has also become very much a part of it. The form that I'm working with contains the elements of a musical, but works with those elements very differently in creating a statement about the world in which we live.*

*The process for creating the piece "Dreamings" went back to the work with the women at York sharing thoughts about their dreams, not only their actual dreams but also their dreams and aspirations for life. There was a growing sense of community among the women evidenced in that piece—a trust that developed as they shared their stories and realized* that they each had a bond—an understanding of and with each other based on the arts engagement process they shared together.

We later did a piece called "What I Want to Say." I asked the women to think about the idea that if there was one story they wanted to tell, and one person that they could tell it to, what would that story be and who would the person be that they would choose to tell it to? I emphasized that the first story, the first person, might not be the one, so to do a lot of journaling along the way. I find that more and more of the women are starting to write. There is a rawness and truth to their work that is just so beautiful. This piece has a totally different flavor; some of it is more painful but really speaks to who they are and what they want to say.

I think that movement connects us to an essential place in ourselves that allows us to move forward in life in a very different way, and this is an inherently joyous process. I think that there is no pure joy. We live in a continuum and the flavor of joy changes with our experience and the more experience we have. Sometimes that's painful, but the moment of joy takes on a kind of richness as we go through it.

I think that everybody is a dancer. I firmly believe that, because I think that some of the most beautiful movement comes from people who haven't learned how to do it but who find their own way of expressing themselves that is unadorned and real. It is about freeing the body to have the broadest expression that one can have, and that doesn't mean that you have to be trained and do it a certain way.

There's a very healthy child inside of each of us that we all need to preserve in ourselves. We are often afraid to show that, or even to acknowledge that it's there. So it's about getting back to that place in ourselves where we are open to playing. I think that so much creative activity comes out of playing around and realizing all of the richness of what there is to discover in our play.

........................................................................

*The truest expression of a people is in its*

*dances and its music. Bodies never lie.*

*—Agnes de Mille, dancer, choreographer*

........................................................................

### Dance to the Music of the Soul

Music and dance are fundamentally inseparable, both in their power to move us through life's rhythms and events and in their ability to build community. Michelle Parma of Dallas, Texas, began dancing at the age of five; at the age of eleven she wrote that dance was everything. "It is my air to breathe, my will to live, and the water to quench the thirst in my soul to express myself. When I am dancing, my life is in order; without dance and my ability to free my feelings, my world is chaotic and confused."

Michelle danced through life until a tragic accident claimed her at the age of twenty seven. Following her passing, Michelle's mother looked for a way to ensure that the legacy of her young daughter's dancer's soul might live on and so created the Dance to Live charitable fund. With a mission to perpetuate Michelle's love and understanding of the broad reach of dance, the fund awards grants to nonprofit organizations that provide dance therapy programs designed specifically for children dealing with debilitating health issues. Michelle may no longer be present to delight the world with her talent, but youngsters who might otherwise not have been able are now helped to free their feelings through the music and tongue of the soul. May it be a language that we all come to speak and to understand.

# Case in Point

## Speak with a Common Language

ADJEI ABANKWA

Boulder, Colorado

*Co-founder, producer, BaoBao Festival. Best way to
experience joy: Let yourself go with the energy of music.*

In traditional African societies, music is instilled into a child's life
beginning with cradle songs at birth, continuing even while being
carried by their mothers and family members at work and at festivals
and other social events. As diverse as the land's rich heterogeneity
of beliefs, values, religions and artistic expressions, African music
traditions are universal in their ability to speak with a soul that keeps
on chanting, keeps on searching and finding.

As a dancer, musician and choreographer, Adjei Abankwa works to
recreate the musical and dance experience of his native land of Ghana.
To do so, he drums up the image of a tree—the baobao or baobab tree.
Commonly called the Tree of Life, its massive size and out-reaching
roots provide a protected space for people in his homeland to gather
and celebrate the occasions of life.

Co-founder and producer of the annual Boulder, Colorado, BaoBao
Festival of drumming, dancing, storytelling and songs, Adjei easily
attests to the *joie de vivre* found under the legendary baobab tree. But it
is the music and dance performed beneath its branches—the clapping,
stomping of feet, the song—that he places at the heart of the joy found
in African culture.

Adjei believes that music and dance are very much languages in
their own right, languages with the power to break down boundaries,
to express how one feels, to soothe and to inspire joy. Today, more than
6,000 miles from the nearest baobab tree in Ghana, it is this sense that
he works to convey.

Adjei brought that language of his native music to cities across
Colorado in 2004 with the launch of the BaoBao Festival. Featuring three

days of artistic performances by local and international performing artists, the annual Festival builds on Africa's age-old community theater experience of gathering under the baobab tree for the purpose of celebrating life. The result is a colorful and moving mosaic of stories told through dance and music and song, costumes that paint the rich histories of early cultures, and musical instruments that turn to nature for their healing and spiritual sounds.

**In Adjei's words...**

*African music happens naturally. It's not like something we have to read, to do. What we do is listen and just go with it. We can be someplace where people are getting together and having a party—then sitting and hitting on cans and singing. It doesn't really matter whether you know the song or you don't know the song. But the moment you hear it, you follow it.*

*When you are doing Kenyan dance, you've got to get every part of your body to demonstrate exactly what you are doing. You've got your hand movement and your facial expression, so the people who are sitting there can read what you are thinking through the dance movement. What you have to do is just move. And if you get an aggressive movement or a jumping movement, which would be more like energy, have fun with it.*

*Most of African music is about joy—it's upbeat music. We have a slow music, too; all the music we have is helped by different kinds of tempo. With different kinds of tempo, like upbeat, we can play the Kpanlogo music. Kpanlogo is really upbeat, so it's not about technical movement, it's more about enjoying.*

*Music can be used to soothe as well as to bring joy. Adowa is a dance which is performed mostly in funerals. Adowa expresses how you feel from your feet and all the hand movements. The body language tells exactly what you feel, so when you're sad in Adowa, you find you can do the dance. Most people wear black and red because you lost someone. So that's part of the dance. Music and dance is very much a language in its own right.*

*The BaoBao Festival is trying to tell people how our culture is in Africa and show them how we tell stories and drum and sing at the same time. I grew up listening to all kinds of music and it looked like here in this country people have their specific music they want to listen to. But my advice is to just open up and try all kinds of music and you can get the sweetness from the rhythm of this music.*

*When you listen to music, you can get any kind of thing you want in that music. It doesn't have to be one sort of African music. It can be drumming, it can be some other instrument, some other culture. When you listen, there's one sweet thing in it that gives you more expression— it's the rhythm. So I would suggest putting all kinds of music into your life and enjoying it.*

## Food for Thought

*Music is a language* all its own.

*Its tongue speaks* through our feet, our ears, our heart, every miniscule stretch of our soul. Its voice is one of dreams, of hope.

*Its words are written* with tempo and pitch and timbre, spoken in tones that generate sadness and joy, refrains that soothe, rhythms that restore.

*Understood by old and young*, well and infirm, its notes rally the soldiers of battle and open the heart to love.

*Its messages make us dance*, clap our hands, smile, cry, sing. It never lies, never fails to evoke the truth.

*Music is a language* that is always present, if only in the blood of our veins and recesses of our memory. If we are quiet we will hear it in the flowers in the grass, in the wind— even in the moon and the stars in the sky.

# CHAPTER SIX

# The Essence of Touch, Taste & Smell

✺

*And if you see me, smile and maybe give me a hug. That's important to me too.*

*—Jimmy Valvano, basketball coach*

S upported, it could be said, by its own holiday celebration of hugs, touch edges into the winner's circle when it comes to deciding which of the five senses is the most important—or the most treasured. Observed annually on January twenty first, midway between Christmas and Valentine's Day, National Hugging Day is positioned as a festive spot on the calendar at a time when people tend to be at an emotional low. Created in 1986 by Reverend Kevin Zaborney of Caro, Michigan, the day advocates the emotional benefits of hugging by encouraging people to feel less reluctant to show emotion in public.

Perhaps such hesitancy began back around 270 A.D. when Emperor Claudius II set the stage to short circuit recognition of the pledge of love and marriage, and by association, the public hug. Believing that bachelors had fewer distractions than those who were married and therefore made better soldiers, Claudius outlawed marriage for young men. His order was defied, however, by the Roman priest Valentine, who recognized the emotional strength of love and continued to perform the forbidden marriage ceremonies. Executed for his treacherous behavior, Valentine went down in the journals of history as a martyr for love.

Today, more than 1,700 years later, researchers offer support for Valentine's belief in the value of a hug. Studies at the University of North Carolina-Chapel Hill, School of Medicine, showed that more frequent hugs favorably influenced how happy and relaxed its study participants were. Scientifically, the power of a hug boils down to the levels of oxytocin in the blood, which we increase each time we hug. Known to stimulate contractions of the uterus during labor and the release of milk during breast-feeding, oxytocin triggers a "caring" response in both men and women.

### Substitute Hugs for Handshakes

The practice and frequency of embracing, especially as a greeting, varies significantly by culture and ethnic origin. In many cultures, hugs are reserved for close relatives and friends, and practiced only in a private place. In others, it is more spontaneous and all inclusive. A poll in Great Britain, for one, reports that two out of three United Kingdom adults have a hug at least once a day. 26% of the Scots hug more than five times a day, with 24% of Londoners enjoying at least five per day. 10% of the Welsh report never receiving hugs.

U.S. couples aren't very "touchy-feely" in public, at least according to the Touch Research Institute at the University of Miami Medical School. Its studies, conducted in Parisian and U.S. cafes, show that French couples spend about three times as much time touching as Americans. But to the extent that National Hugging Day catches on, such numbers might be changed. Suggestions for observing National Hugging Day are simple: substitute hugs for handshakes, hand out hug coupons, offer a hug to anyone and everyone you want. Have a happy Hugging Day!

# Case in Point

## Make Treasures that Touch

TAMMY HENDRICKS
Blanchard, Oklahoma
*Soft Sculpture Artist. Best to way to experience joy:*
*Give something back to one who is hurting.*

Tammy Hendricks touches the lives of others by making memories tangible. Working with snippets of special pieces of clothing, maybe a favorite sweatshirt or well worn house coat, this former mental health counselor brings back moments of comfort and love in the form of Furever Friends and cuddly memory bears and babies.

She works from pictures to create them. Her goal is to turn each picture into feelings that touch the heart and connect with the soul. Tammy created one little teddy baby in memory of her great nephew, Bentley, who lived only seven hours after birth due to a rare heart condition. She hand-painted Bentley's footprints on the pad and weighted the bear to be Bentley's weight. Made from soft fur and a blanket in which Bentley was held, he is dressed in Bentley's jammies.

**In Tammy's words...**

*The bears that I create are all made out of memorabilia. People send me their loved one's personal things, so they are all special. I've also made dogs if it's in memory of their little dog that has passed on.*

*Infants are definitely the more difficult ones. They're hard because I get these little bitty baby outfits, these little bitty onesies, to create them with; it may be the only thing that they have, something that their baby maybe had worn following birth. I want to make certain that I take care and make it just right, because it's completely irreplaceable.*

*Sometimes I'll make the bears the exact weight and length of their little baby. I had someone tell me that just to be able to hold it was a way to feel and know what their baby had felt like. Because even though* they're never going to forget their baby, the feel of touching and holding that actual weight, 7 lbs 2 oz, 4 lbs 3 oz, or whatever, is lost. So just to hold that bear, the same weight of their baby, helps. Those things you can't forget.

I have had a few requests from military parents and those are hard ones, too, especially when they send me their story. I never ask about the loved one that has passed; they share what they want to share. Sometimes I get a whole three pages and I know that's part of their being able to share about their loved ones. But sometimes I never know what happened to the person. People have different ways of grieving.

I absolutely experience joy and a sense of fulfillment in creating a teddy bear from something that was so special and in knowing that I'm able to give something back to someone who is hurting. Being able to touch something that was part of someone's loved one, something tangible that they can hold onto, brings a sense of comfort.

Touch is so important. For me, it's a connection. When I hold my mom's teddy bear that I made from her coat, knowing that it once wrapped around her and kept her warm, that she was once so close to it, that is a connection for me.

Before I launched the memory bear business, I worked at the community mental health center with people who suffered from major depression, anxiety, bi-polar disorders, schizophrenia, which I enjoyed doing at that time in my life. So when this really started taking off, I realized that I'm still doing therapy, just in a different way. It's without words; it's in the touch and the feeling, the expression.

It also helps my customers out. I ask them to let me know about their loved one, whatever they want to share, and that gives them an opportunity to share if they want to send a picture. 85-90% of the bear itself is made from the clothing and with little things like buttons, hoodies, colors, etc. I incorporate as much of the garment as I can.

I save e-mails from people who share with me how they felt when they received their bears. I keep them in a special folder that I can read from time to time when I need to feel encouraged or blessed. Whenever I need a lift, or need to feel connected to those I don't get to meet, I read *their letters. They bring me a joy that sometimes brings tears. But they're good tears being able to remember in a good way.*

*I worked really hard when I was in counseling and I work even harder now because it's not just for myself, but for all the people who send in their orders. I'm just so grateful that I have this and that people find it worthy of sending in such priceless items for me to make these things for them. The joy I receive from having my own business is absolutely priceless. You can't buy joy. I could have nothing and still have more joy than someone who has everything. If you put a monetary value on it, I'm a millionaire.*

Hands are the heart's landscape.

−Pope John Paul II

## Experience the World through Touch

Laura Bridgman was born in the year 1829, in the small town of Etna, New Hampshire, a "delicate plant of a girl" with eyes as blue as cornflowers that seemed to take everything in. All this changed, however, when she was barely into her third year and scarlet fever left her deaf and blind.

Left to see the sun as heat on her face, mountains as sloped, uneven paths to climb, Laura turned to her remaining senses to guide her through life and her surrounding world. As told by Sally Hobart Alexander and Robert Alexander in *She Touched the World*, Laura "felt the soft muzzle of a calf and giggled when he touched her fingers....As her hands worked, her mind stirred."

The skin is the site of thousands of sensory or nerve receptors by which we feel or experience sensations of hot and cold, of pain and pleasure, and is the primary basis of our sense of touch. Receptors in the skin vary in number and sensitivity. Our backs, for example, are far less sensitive to tactile activity than our lips, tongue and fingertips.

Our skin and the sense of touch affect more than our ability to determine what we are holding, seeing, experiencing. Since the days of the famous Roman Caracella Baths, a grand and most elaborate third century bathing complex with accommodations for as many as 1,500 bathers at a time, people have been going to spas for herbal massages, body wraps and mud baths, aromatherapies and mineral water treatments. They go for relaxation and stress relief, for their cleansing and revitalization benefits and their healing magic.

## Heal with the World's Best Mud

A combination of soil, silt, clay and water, mud is an in-demand gift from the earth. Used to heal, to cleanse, to soothe, it is harvested from the sea, the moors and volcanic eruptions. Here are three of the world's most popular therapeutic muds and where they are found:

*Dead Sea Mud*: Drawn from the waterbed of the Dead Sea, the lowest point on earth and the most saline of all natural lakes. Known for its therapeutic properties, this black clay is enriched with healing minerals and organic remains of plants and animals. It is used to revitalize the skin by removing dry cell tissue.

*Karlovy Vary Mud*: Said to have a different curative effect each spring, varying from digestive healing agents to vascular and metabolic aids. The Karlovy Vary spa, also known as Karlsbad, is located in a Czech Republic valley of the river Teplá (meaning Warm). The river's thermal water infects the earth surrounding it, lending curative properties to the high-in-mineral-salts mud.

*Moors of Austria Mud*: Formed as a result of plant matter deposited thousands of years ago beneath the earth. Known for its magical healing properties, it has been used in European spas since the 1800's.

> The pressure of the hands causes the springs of life to flow.
> —Tokujiro Namikoshi, creator of Shiatsu Therapy

### Popular Since the Days of Antiquity

Massage therapy, of which there are some eighty to one hundred known modalities in use today, is a highly popular means of nurturing relaxation and well-being through manipulation of the body's muscle and connective tissue. Inferring from Egyptian tomb paintings showing people being massaged, it may actually be one of the oldest forms of releasing tension and enhancing bodily well-being. Hippocrates, the father of western medicine, was seen to prescribe rubbing in the 5th century B.C. as a means of loosening muscles or other organs that were too tense or stiff.

One form that is used throughout the world and is widely accepted as the official form of massage in Japan is Shiatsu massage therapy. Developed in 1912 by Tokujiro Namikoshi after pressing with his thumbs and palms to relieve his mother from her sufferings of rheumatoid arthritis, Shiatsu takes its name from the Japanese words "shi," meaning finger, and "atsu," meaning pressure. It continues to be used today as healing therapy to adjust natural energy flow and recover from conditions caused by day-to-day stress.

Massage therapies vary in approach, ranging from Shiatsu and the common Swedish massage with its long smooth strokes, kneading, and circular movements, to hot stone therapy, where heated, smooth stones are placed so as to warm and loosen tight muscles and balance energy centers in the body. While conclusions of effectiveness and outcomes vary, observations of such positive effects as diminished pain and enhanced alertness and performance are commonly cited. One such encouraging outcome for the Shiatsu system was noted in the 1950s after Marilyn Monroe was said to be successfully treated by Namikoshi for an unknown illness, furthering the popularity of his Shiatsu therapy in Western society.

*There is no substitute for feeling the stone, the metal, the plaster, or the wood in the hand; to feel its weight; to feel its texture; to struggle with it in the world rather than in the mind alone.*

*—William M. Dupree, sculptor*

### The Expressive Therapy of Clay

Touch, or tactile contact, plays a leading role in the development of human sensory response and communication. Just think about an infant and the importance of both oral and skin contact between infants and those who care for them.

A favorite medium for both sensory response and therapeutic communication is clay—that soft, earthy material formed as a result of the weathering or erosion of mineral containing rocks. Found throughout the ages in both functional and sculptural creations, clay delights both artists and anthropologists with its non-verbal language of expression. Watch a simple lump of moist earth take shape through a synergy of mind, hands and the earth with which the artist works, and the language of its intense and powerful therapeutic process will be heard.

# Case in Point

### Be in Touch with the Earth

JIM SUDAL
Scottsdale, Arizona
*Ceramic artist. Best way to experience joy:*
*Create something beautiful for others.*

For Arizona artist Jim Sudal, joy found its beginnings in the desert. It grew there and blossomed there. It was also tested there. Joy doesn't always come without pain, without a struggle.

Ralph Waldo Emerson once said that "most of the shadows of life are caused by standing in our own sunshine." Ironically, it wasn't until Jim created a blooming Prickly Pear Cactus ceramic wall mural for a client with life changing difficulties that he realized how healing it can be just to get in touch with the earth.

Jim fell in love with the desert when he vacationed there as a youngster and saw his first saguaro. It intrigued him and he wondered how something like that with its "bizarre form, something from another planet," could grow without water.

The saguaro and the desert landscape with its big sky made an impression that never went away. Eventually, Jim returned to Arizona for college, beginning as a business major before giving in to an unshakable lifelong interest in the arts and enrolling in a ceramics course. It was a leap, but he threw his first pot, and was hooked.

The leaps, creatively and professionally, have always, it seems, led Jim to a continued exploration of new and ever increasing challenges. But life is more complicated than the twists and turns of careers and avocations, and feelings of joy or personal well-being don't necessarily follow. So when Jim unexpectedly found himself dealing with the emotional and financial entanglements of a longtime relationship break-up and a declining national economy, he lost his hold on that positive feeling that comes from within, that adrenaline that comes with joy.

In retrospect, he isn't sure just how he managed, other than that he found some comfort and purpose in his persistent realization of having "so much more to create before I go." What he does know is that it was the invitation to submit a design proposal for an original ceramic wall sculpture for a prominent Paradise Valley couple that began to move him back to center, to fill his mind with something other than all that he had been dwelling on. The piece, as it turned out, was for the home of Mr. and Mrs. Muhammad Ali, who for three years had been looking for something "bold and beautiful" to hang over their fireplace.

Jim agreed to do it and within nine months, spending over 400 hours, using some 325 lbs. of stoneware clay, iron, wood, concrete board and ceramic glazes, Jim conceived and created "Butterflies and Bees." Settling on the theme of a blooming prickly pear cactus plant with multiple buds and two large golden colored blooms as its focal point, he designed the 61" x 61" piece as a comment on life's challenges faced both by his client and himself.

Wanting the mural to have an overall healing and calming effect for its viewers, Jim drew on his lifelong enjoyment of and familiarity with the desert and chose its colors to harmonize with the room in which it hangs, as well as for their ability to soothe. Glazing on the blossoms was applied to emulate a watercolor effect, enhancing the delicate and elegant nature of the flower petals.

But it was the center of each flower that turned out to be the real showstopper. Sculpted with over 100 tiny clay butterflies and bees set in the delicate and fragile beauty of a flower against the austere desert background, it categorically captured the poignant meaning of Ali's iconic phrase, "float like a butterfly, sting like a bee."

Today, Jim thinks of the piece as having healing powers. Given the extent to which it enabled him to recharge his life with the revitalizing energy of joyful creativity, and the fact that Mrs. Ali tells him she will be sure to stand in front of it to catch its healing rays, one might well agree.

**In Jim's words...**

*The feel of a lump of wet, cool clay is very sensual to the touch. But the greater sensation is more in my mind and heart than just my finger tips. Sometimes I can close my eyes and see the endless energy of creative freedom and its possibilities unfold before me. I use the colors and images of the desert that I love in my work, and that in itself is soothing. But it's also a diversion, a relief from whatever the day's distractions might be. It's surprising what healing grace and beauty can be found among what may initially seem harsh, bleak and hopeless.*

*For me, pottery was always something that was inside of me. Maybe I didn't see it early on and maybe was a little fearful. I was trying to force other things, thinking this is supposed to give me joy, these should give me joy, I should be in the corporate world. I should, should, should, when all the time I knew what was giving me joy inside. Sometimes it's the simplest thing, right there in front of your face. Looking back, I would say don't be afraid to follow your heart. Don't be afraid to trust and take a chance on your passion. Your life depends on it.*

*With ceramics, I'm sort of self taught and I'm glad it is that way. I've sort of fumbled my way through without any one telling me that this is the right way, the wrong way. I think that's why my work looks so different from anything that any other ceramic artist does, and in that sense I learn something every day about what I'm doing. It's absolutely a part of me, it never goes away. I'm inspired by anything and everything, wherever I go. I'm out in the desert, in nature, looking for something to spark.*

*The agave plant and its life always intrigued me. It has a lot of common names. One is the century plant because it was believed that it lived a hundred years. That's not necessarily the case, but they do live a long time, with an end result of sending up this beautiful stalk. It takes so much energy to do this that it actually kills the plant. So its whole purpose is this one bloom. But I always looked at it and thought, boy, you're spending your whole time on this earth to send up this one beautiful bloom for all of us to enjoy and then you go away.*

*I credit the opportunity and challenge to create something so extraordinary, greater than anything I had ever done, as the main reason for having survived that time of anxiety and depression. I continued, of course, to deal with much pressure, but thanks to that driving creative force—a force that kept me in touch with the desert that I love and the drive to capture its beauty for others—personal pressure was relieved a bit. I became so obsessed with stretching myself creatively and technically that the Ali piece moved to the forefront of my thoughts and the other stuff slipped to the not-too-far background.*

*This opportunity to create the greatest piece that I absolutely could gave me the greatest joy in my life—that of saving my own life. It was the joy that came through my looking at what life is really about, searching deeper than I ever had, realizing what's most important and what really is trivial.*

*With clay, you've got this lump of, in essence, earth, and I look around at what I've done and what I can transform it into. In that sense, there is a lot of joy that I can find and can give, just in the material. You know, you can hang anything you want on the wall. But unless someone comes in and finds joy in what you've done, I wouldn't call it pointless, but I believe we need to produce something that the rest of society can use.*

*I think of one of my early-on pieces, sort of a mark of my transition, the point at which I was hooked and new on my path. It's one of those that is so beautiful and with such detail that only I would know what was involved to get it to that point. It was a small vase, maybe 12"-14" high, with agave images and a lot of detail. It just came out so wonderful and could never be duplicated again—not the clay that was used, the way it was done, where it was fired—it was something that I could not reproduce here in my studio.*

*But I thought that people should be able to enjoy it every single day. I had my start at the Desert Botanical Garden, which is truly a living museum, and was inspired by its beauty. So now my vase is in their permanent collection, on display under glass, and has been since 1996. One hundred years from now, people will still be looking at it.*

*People are doing their part to sustain us; we need to do our part to sustain them. My part is in shaping the earth to bring joy to people. I believe that art should be beautiful and should contribute to every day and every person's life.*

*Smell and taste are in fact but a single composite sense, whose*

*laboratory is the mouth and whose chimney is the nose.*

—*Jean Anthelme Brillat-Savarin, French author, gastronome*

### Sensing Memories and Feelings of Joy

The average human nose can discriminate between 4,000 and 10,000 different odors. Given our ability to sniff out and identify a substance through often miniscule trace amounts, some in the range of parts-per-trillion of air, smell is often said to be the most fascinating, if not the most important sense in terms of its role in our behavior, emotions and memories.

Looking back in time, we see a wide variety of species using their noses to identify food and dangers, locate prey, navigate, to recognize kin, mark territory and to mate. Many animals are known to have a greater sensitivity to odors than humans. Think of the way we turn to dogs to help detect explosives or drugs, or to find missing people.

Smell and taste are intricately linked through gustatory or taste nerve cells, all clustered in the taste buds of the mouth and throat, as well as through olfactory bulbs or smell nerve cells, located high up in the nose. Gustatory cells react to food or drink mixed with saliva; olfactory cells are stimulated by odors and aromas around us. All transmit messages to the brain, which in turn identifies specific smells or tastes.

As an added bonus, the pathways of the brain that analyze smell and taste are closely associated with parts of the brain responsible for emotions and memories. Thanks to this connection, this most important chemical-sensing system is able to turn the aroma of roasting chicken or the smell of leather into emotions and memories of the past.

# Case in Point

## Follow Your Nose

MICHELLE KRELL KYDD

Ann Arbor, Michigan

*Marketing communications specialist with a passion for all things olfactory and gustatory. Best way to experience joy: Pay attention to the flavors and fragrances of life.*

Michelle Krell Kydd is a "trained nose" and award-winning writer with a love of flavor and fragrance. Working in business worlds that depend on the senses of smell and taste, she knows that the back story of a favorite perfume or a saffron cake is often rich with history, myth and folklore, and that when all of these aspects are brought together, they tell a story of our common humanity, as expressed through the senses.

Her blog, *Glass Petal Smoke*, is designed to tell those stories. She tells them to those who are flavor driven, to those who are aware of the connection between the senses and memory. But mostly, she tells them to share with others, to convey the joy and the wonder that is there to be found in food and fragrance in hopes they may enjoy the same.

### In Michelle's words...

*One of the strongest food senses for me is the smell of crisped chicken skin when a chicken is being roasted in the oven. I'm seven years old again when I smell that. I'm immediately—in my mind—in the kitchen of my childhood. I can tell you where everything is, what my mother is wearing, detailed things, and it's mind-boggling.*

*Because they're connected, taste and smell evoke joy in a way that your other senses can't. When you put something in your mouth and you detect flavor, that's called retronasal olfaction. That's when you're pushing puffs of air up behind your nose to combine smell and taste*

*If we've been fortunate enough to grow up in a family where we had a mom or dad at home who was cooking and made sure we all sat together* at the dinner table, that creates a foundation. That's your compass for going back and forth in your memory for taste and smell.

I did an article on Chrism a little while back, and there was a time that I was trying to find a priest who would let me smell it, tell me about how it was formulated. I had no luck. Eventually, I connected with a monk at a monastery that produces Trappist preserves, but also produces fifty percent of the Chrism in the United States. I have a whole bottle of it, by the way. It is so beautiful and it has become one of my favorite smells. I love it. Though I was able to ferret out the ingredients in Chrism by smell alone, I was respectful when I wrote about it. I didn't want to disclose the ingredients because what mattered was what the ingredients did in combination with each other. When I asked the monk to share the recipe in confidence, he politely declined. I respect that. They make their living that way.

There's a quote in Exodus where Moses is commanded to make an anointing oil and specific ingredients are called out, but the exact number of ingredients are found in the oral tradition of Judaism (referred to as the Mishnah). This incense is called Ketoret in Hebrew, or temple incense in English, and it was made by a family called the Avatinas. The Avatinas were appointed by the Sanhedrin and the patrilineal line made this special incense that was used in the second temple for generations.

There was a secret ingredient that until very recently was not known; it is likely that it was derived from a particular type of grass that would send the plume of incense smoke straight up in a very high column. If you've ever seen incense burn, it sort of twirls and twirls, makes mesmerizing patterns. It rarely goes up in a straight line.

Smell and taste are ecumenical when it comes to their enjoyment; anyone can attain the insights and pleasures that these senses offer. To me, smell has hallmarks of the holy because, depending on what your experiences in life are, there are certain places or events in our lives that make us have a sense that there is a higher power.

The thing about essential oils and smelling them is that they are the pure essence of a plant—its lifeblood, its very soul, if you will. Essential oils have numerous constituents. So there is a level of complexity to them.

*Like a person, they take time to get to know, not just to memorize and go "oh, I'm smelling this or that."*

*I'm at a point now I can tell if the rose is from Turkey or Bulgaria. I know it right away. You have to exchange your essence with the essence of the thing you're smelling if you are doing this consciously. It's a bit like love.*

*Favorite scents? Well, saffron definitely is up there in the top five.*

*Leather. The smell of leather. It's so hard for me to choose because I like so many things.*

*Osmanthus, which is a type of flower from China that's used in food and in tea, which my gut tells me is going to make it into the olfactive vernacular here because of our trade with China.*

*What else? Chocolate. It's my kryptonite.*

*Vetiver, which is a fragrant grass of which the best quality grows in Haiti. I love that smell.*

*Back to leather. My father worked in the garment district. He worked six days a week, and sometimes on Saturday I would go to work with him. The sights, the sounds, the smell of that place, and the way he smelled were all bound up in the scent of leather. He would come home and he smelled like leather. His shirt, his hair, his skin were perfumed with leather. There are different kinds of leather smells. This was like the smell of a light-colored leather handbag, a new one that smells sweet, almond-like and floral. I just went nuts for that smell.*

*So leather is a very big smell memory for me. After my father died, I remember walking past a Harley-Davidson store and the door was open and I got a glorious waft of leather and for a moment I expected to see my father come walking around the corner. Smell can do that. It transcends time.*

*When I mentioned earlier that smell connects to the eternal, I meant it. Smell is holy. The Egyptians, who introduced the world to incense and perfumery, were burning incense to the gods with the hope that the smoke would carry their prayers to the heavens. Makes sense to me.*

*Now saffron, that's the smell and taste of pure joy. It's a scientific fact that components in saffron alleviate depression. I met this woman from Iran in the perfume business who introduced me to saffron. Before I really tasted saffron fully, I was talking to her about the ingredient. I was doing research on a fragrance project and I said I'd really like to get the good saffron from Iran. She looked at me and sort of chuckled and said, "Well, you know if you eat saffron, it makes you laugh. In Iran we always give saffron to people and tell them they can't be sad if they taste it."*

*A week after our conversation, she gave me a container of saffron from Iran that was harvested from a field blessed by an historical imam named Reza, who is long dead but revered in the Muslim tradition. I was quickly lost in its scent as it had a leatheric aspect, an animalic aspect, and an almond aspect—just layer upon layer of smell.*

*When I started using it, I could not stop. I made a cake with it. I started putting it in my oatmeal. I found every excuse to put saffron in my food and still do. It blew me away, not so much because I was told that saffron would make me happy, but because it woke me up to my senses.*

*What is it about the sense of taste and smell that the average person can attain? Well, this is how I look at it. Every day we have to eat and we go through our day where we encounter ordinary things around us. I think it's easy to take the sense of smell for granted. Everyone knows what the smell of snow is like, but we just don't key into it. If we allow ourselves to focus on the smaller more simple things, we can see how profound life really is.*

*If you want to experience joy, stop, slow down, and begin to pay attention to what you taste and smell when you're making breakfast, when you're in a restaurant, when you're having wine, when you're outside and it's the beginning of spring and you can smell the earth getting soft under your feet. Pay attention to those things happening all around you. You'll be amazed at what you discover.*

My favorite jellybean is the pink one with the flavor inside.

—Chester Bennington, American singer, songwriter

# Case in Point

## Flavor and Aroma Vie with Visual Appeal

### ERIC WEBSTER
Saint Helena, California
*Private chef, professional photographer. Best way to
experience joy: Capture the total essence of a dish.*

Eric Webster has spent much of his time in world-class kitchens, perfecting the techniques necessary to get the most out of the best in produce, meat, poultry and fish. He understands that great food, like great wine, comes from starting with the best raw ingredients and taking just the steps necessary to enhance their inherent flavors and then to present them in appealing ways.

But as a chef who also loves the art of photography, he knows that visuals can deceive you. When people get too caught up in the visual of a dish, they are missing the taste and smell, he says, which is really the essence of the dish.

Eric has spent much of his time as a chef in the Napa Valley creating dishes that capture that essence. His approach is simple. Start with excellent raw ingredients, use time-honored techniques, and match the food with the occasion, the season and the climate. Throughout it all, he remains conscious of a dish's visual appeal as well as its combination of flavors.

Listening in on Eric as he creates a simple butter lettuce salad with citrus vinaigrette is like watching an artist choose colors for his palette.

### In Eric's words...

*Maybe the most important thing I've learned is to not just cook seasonally, but match the food temperature to the setting. Food flavors are diminished when served at temperature extremes. Braised meats, roasted vegetables and hearty soups can comfort and relax in the cold of winter. Bright, vibrant salads, chilled soups and clean flavors can enliven in the heat of the summer. Simply marrying the elements of food with the weather can have a profound effect on their enjoyment.*

*If I was going to shop for a salad, I would pick maybe the taracco, because it's delicious. They're sweet, with not much acid and a great visual. Then, maybe one or two others that are sort of sweet or sweet tart, and then maybe a couple that are pucker-tart, that you wouldn't want to eat straight up.*

*And what I do is I make a citrus vinaigrette. In citrus season, I'll always have a variety in the kitchen. I basically want segments for the salad, so I cut the peel off and then instead of just throwing that skin away, I squeeze it so I've got some taracco juice, some clemenvilla juice. I taste it and it's going to be sweet. So I grab these pink lemons, or limes, or something tart, and squeeze that in there. Usually I've got three or four citrus in this mix of juice and then I usually just throw like a splash of red wine vinegar and champagne vinegar with a little bit of sugar and extra virgin olive oil; it makes a pretty amazing vinaigrette.*

*The final addition to the plate is maybe butter lettuce or something mild and then segments of the fruits that eat well, that aren't so sour. That's a simple, but hugely popular dish.*

## Eric's Citrus Vinaigrette

*Juice from:*
*2 Meyer lemons*
*1 blood orange*
*1 sweet orange*
*2 limes*
*champagne vinegar – 1 tablespoon*
*red wine vinegar – 1 tablespoon*
*sugar – 1 teaspoon*
*salt – pinch*
*pepper – to taste*
*extra virgin olive oil – to taste*

*For this vinaigrette, I use an olive oil that is light and fruity, rather than bold and peppery. Any combination of citrus is fine, I just use what is best at the farmer's market when I go. Just make sure you have some sweet citrus as well as some that is sour.*

*Mix together the juice, vinegars, sugar, salt and pepper until the sugar and the salt are dissolved. Slowly whisk in the olive oil. Taste the vinaigrette along the way and stop when you like the balance of sweet and sour. Normally the rule of thumb is about 1 part vinegar to 2 parts oil. This recipe will likely use less oil, as much of the vinegar is replaced with juice.*

## Food for Thought

*The senses of taste, smell and touch*, when considered in the perspective of vision and hearing, might be viewed as being relatively less important, less vital—albeit possibly more sensuous. But wait. Isn't life all about food? Isn't it the kitchen where we all congregate, the supper table where we gather around and share our day, our troubles, our triumphs? Isn't it comfort food that we bring to the sick, the downtrodden?

*Taste*—if we stop to think about it—dresses up the routine, adds panache to peas and carrots. Our personal preferences in taste influence us to the extent that we tend to eat foods that we love, but shouldn't, and to the point that political candidates' tastes in food influence the map of their campaign trails. Taste entertains our tongues, satisfies our bellies, stirs our minds.

*Smell* is another underrated sense, one we so often overlook and neglect to credit. With its discerning reach, its honesty in the way it absorbs and passes on what it comprehends, smell can be the embodiment of awareness. The sense of smell exchanges the fragrance of flowers and the salt of the sea air for memory and preserves the day for tomorrow.

*But mostly*, it is our sense of touch that is underestimated. Look at the way one simple touch fills us with feeling, shapes our lives. We love the dreams and promises of touch— intimate gifts of the hand and the heart. Touch surprises and holds us, signals a closeness, a connection, a power, a strength. Touch couples the soul with wonder, turns moments into happenings.

Stretching Our Minds and Souls

# CHAPTER SEVEN

# Frontiers of Wonder

*And above all, watch with glittering eyes the whole world around you
because the greatest secrets are always hidden in the most unlikely
places. Those who don't believe in magic will never find it.*
*—Roald Dahl, children's book author*

Wonder, in its own breathless, fantastical way, is far from ordinary when it comes to the senses. In the hierarchy of things, wonder is an emotion—and a most important one at that. We might think of it as an engine that fuels our ability to make the most of our five primary natural senses. It's tempting to call it our sixth sense.

But call it what you will—a sense, an emotion, a mindset—one way or another, wonder opens the door to the delights of imagination, of curiosity, creativity, intellectual discovery. Readily sampled in the pages of fairy tales and science fiction adventure, it adds vision to sight and aura to hearing.

Jules Verne, best known for his popular novels *Twenty Thousand Leagues Under the Sea*, *A Journey to the Center of the Earth* and *Around the World in Eighty Days*, brought a new level of interest to the traditional tale of fiction.

Often referred to as the father of the science fiction genre, a form of writing said to offer its readers a sense of inspired awe, Verne captured fascination well when he wrote about space, air, and underwater travel in a time when such adventures were still seen as fantasy. "Look with all your eyes," he said, "look."

Born in Nantes, France, in 1828, Verne ran away to sea at the age of eleven, simply to be sent home in disgrace, leaving his travels to the world of imagination. But in the end, after feeding his mind with the miracles of 19th century science and invention, he left a legacy of more than 50 stories and tales that were enjoyed as much for their fantastic adventure as their scientific prophesy of outer space flights, submarines, helicopters and guided missiles.

> I like nonsense, it wakes up the brain cells. Fantasy is a necessary ingredient in living. It's a way of looking at life through the wrong end of a telescope. Which is what I do, and that enables you to laugh at life's realities.
>
> —Dr. Seuss, children's book author

Nonsense literature, a writing genre that combines truth with incredulity to tell a story, positions the sense of wonder front and center in minds of all ages. As might be expected, children in particular fall in love with such whimsical characters as Horton, the elephant, Bartholomew Cubbins and his 500 hats, and the ever popular Cat in the Hat. But adults are known to be captivated, too.

In the world of the beloved children's book author, Dr. Seuss, "everyone's a pony and they all eat rainbows and poop butterflies." The thing is, nonsense works. It is, as Seuss sees it, a necessary ingredient in life. It wakes up the brain cells, balances logical reasoning with bits of absurdity, made-up words with contextual meaning. It lets us laugh at reality.

# Case in Point

## Books Lead Way to Dreams

MIRIAM EPSTEIN
Manchester, Connecticut
*Founder and Director, Books to Dreams, Inc. Best way to
experience joy: Watch a child turn the page into a new world.*

Wonder, whether in the nonsense of Seuss' world or the reality of the
place in which we live, has a way of stirring our minds to wander and
explore. We hear it in the cry of a newborn child, feel it in the whisper
of the wind—and are drawn by its words in a book. Reading can feed
our imaginations, spawn creativity and teach us to see with the mind's
eye. It helps us make sense of all that we behold and experience.

Miriam Epstein, founder of a grass roots literacy program that puts
books in the hands of children in need, can attest personally to how
the words and pictures of books bring the wonder and inspiration of
unknown worlds to life. Bolstered by the love of her father who always
took time to read to her as a child, Miriam became a sort of Pied
Piper of storytelling, arriving at soup kitchens and homeless shelters
throughout the state with bags of donated books.

This was the beginning of Books to Dreams, Inc., a nonprofit
organization that has now distributed well over a quarter of a million
books to children and their parents as well as to homeless shelters,
libraries and other community facilities. As for Miriam, she still carries
along with her today the very first book she ever owned, *Mother Goose*.
With its covers "loved away" from use, it is inscribed with her name,
just as every book given away in the program is personally inscribed
with the recipient child's name.

**In Miriam's words...**

*I didn't go to kindergarten, so I didn't learn to read at that age. But I was
what would probably be called a voracious reader from that point on.*

*I always felt at home with a book and I still do. That's a security that I didn't always have at home. But I had books and they were my friends.*

*That's always been a major thread in my life. Everything that I've done since I was little has led me to where I am today in some way, shape or form. I've used dance, I've used art, imagination. But the most important nugget or kernel was the book and reading.*

*In the beginning, I didn't have enough books to give each child a copy of the same book I read to them, so I figured I could do "Old McDonald had a farm..." and just collect any book about farms. I brought them in a big plastic bag that they couldn't see through, full of stuffed animals, farm animals. One of the reasons I did that is that a lot of children don't know what farm animals are.*

*I'd go into the room and I'd say, "I have a story to tell you today, but I didn't bring a book. The story is in the bag. I'm going to sing you the story and you are going to help me sing the story." So I'd reach in the bag and with each stuffed animal I'd hand it to one of them and they'd get to hold it while we'd do the whole song.*

*I'd act out the story or have them help me with it. But I think what I do first is what always touches everyone and touches me most of all. They're all in a circle on the floor when I come in. I get on my knees and go around and I'm really close to each child and introduce myself and talk with each one of them. I find out their names and thank them for smiling at me and for being my new friend. If I can only do one thing, that's what I need to do.*

*When I look at those children, I know what they are doing. They are looking and learning and taking things in and that is a very fragile moment in a person's life. Many, many things get formed then. So they are soaking in everything and I make sure that what they're soaking in is worth it. If I can give them an experience and enhance what their teachers do, but in an imaginative way, then they will remember that and will remember the book that was presented and the book that they get to take home that day. And that's all that I can ask for.*

*Many are now college graduates, and they still call and ask for books. Some are attending college now and one young woman went to law school; there are, as far as I know, four families out of those original ten who own their own homes now and have for some time. We played a part in all of that, but it was a little part. It all came out of the hope of a better future through books and education.*

The gift of fantasy has meant more to me than

my talent for absorbing positive knowledge.

—Albert Einstein, Nobel prize winning physicist

### Fiction Opens Doors to Happenings

C. S. Lewis, creator of the fictional world of Narnia, a place where animals talk and magic is an everyday occurrence, loved fantasy for its ability to give us experiences we have never had. His bestselling *Chronicles of Narnia* is generally thought of as a series of seven fantasy novels for children. But lest we begin to think that the content of fantasy—imagination, surprise, awe, and ultimately wonder—is the province of children, we may be relieved to know this is just not so.

We can read in Lewis' essay, "On Stories," that when he wrote, he spoke "to the adult, the child, and the child within the adult." Apparently, that's also what Rudyard Kipling, author of *The Man Who Would Be King* and J.R.R. Tolkien of *The Hobbit* fame, were doing. Whether they spoke to the child within or to the adult, who knows, but Lewis did know that when he read such stories as those of Kipling and Tolkien, he was affected by a feeling of awe.

It is that feeling of awe, coupled with limitless imagination and a quixotic longing for something more, that Lewis and others who write for the child within the adult tap into. It is also a world into which present day artists such as Tracy Kane enter daily and to which they invite both children and adults like us to join them.

# Case in Point

## Joy Has a Tendency to Hide, Just Like the Fairies Do

TRACY KANE

Lee, New Hampshire

*Author and illustrator. Best way to experience joy:*
*Indulge in moments of discovery and imagination.*

Tracy Kane builds tiny little houses in quiet places hidden away from the road. Passers-by, if they look carefully, might find them tucked into the base of an old gnarled tree, or possibly sheltered under a lichen-covered rock. Dry grasses, pebbles, bark and pinecones are her usual construction materials, though sometimes shells and seaweed might be used.

Building them takes her back to her childhood days growing up in Rochester, New York, where every day she went out exploring in the meadow and woods by her house, a magic world that she saw as a fairy land. It wasn't until years later when she actually came across a neighborhood of miniature wee folk houses hidden in the Cathedral Woods of Monhegan Island off the coast of Maine that she realized maybe the fairies had, indeed, lived in the meadow right next door as she was growing up.

With her imagination sparked by the Monhegan village, Tracy put her creative talents to work and launched her career as an author and illustrator of the popular Light-House Beams Publishing series of Fairy Houses books and videos. Children, she knows, have an enviable ability to let their imagination and creativity play—to enjoy the reward of a moment that adults are often too busy to take in. Working with illustrations and how-to instructions, Tracy invites children and adults alike to let their imaginations and creativity play and to share in the discovery of nature's magic.

**In Tracy's words...**

*A lot of joy comes from the natural progression of using our senses and going outside. The discovery of the magic in nature is a joyful thing, and building fairy houses is a way of getting children softly into it. When they discover a little visitor, a grasshopper coming to visit, you can see their eyes light up.*

*We have such busy lives, we don't give ourselves a moment to use our senses, to really smell the air around us, to look at what we're doing, to let ourselves just drift for a moment again. You just have to give yourself a moment.*

*In today's world, kids are missing that connection with their senses, a platform that children need to build from. If I have a two or three year old out there, every stone is like a new discovery to them. They pick it up, they touch it, they see it, they feel it. I don't know if it's the sense of discovery, but their imaginations start going off. "What if a fairy comes, would it choose my house?"*

*Part of the joy that I find relates to the delight of the magic that children initially see when you tell them an egg is going to hatch into a little baby bird, or a tadpole turn into a little baby frog. It's this amazing way that they take it in, and what their imaginations do with it.*

*Sometimes I feel that fairies could be butterflies in disguise. When I have one of those beautiful moments of nature with the sun breaking through, something so beautiful and magical, I feel it's a fairy moment. All of a sudden you feel bliss and joy; you're filled with that wonderful glow. That's a magical moment, and for me, it's usually just because I'm surrounded by beauty when it happens—when something special happens in nature, like when all of a sudden a little hummingbird comes whipping by just so close to you and then goes on its way.*

*I remember liking being six years old. I think that was when my most creative time was—when fairyland and everything was. I work with children from about three to eight, but six to seven is the middle of what I work with and I just feel that my most joy is working with that age.*

*But I'd say three to eight are the principal ages of building fairy houses. It's when they start to look around in nature and think of what's* out there and what they're creating. They go a step further and go beyond what's just in front of them, and their imaginations and creativity start to play. When I do an event, I feel like the Pied Piper, and all the kids say, "Mrs. Kane, Mrs. Kane, come see my fairy house!" It's fun to work with them.

Sometimes I'll come across parents who are building little houses and they'll look up and say, "This is fabulous! I'm just so relaxed, this is so meditative. I just love this!" It brings back all that childhood joy. The experience is still there, and this is another way to bring it out, even with fathers.

### How to Build a Fairy House

Tracy knows exactly how to build a fairy house—anywhere, any time of year in the woods or meadow, at the beach, even in our own backyards. Her Fairy House Rules are few, but important:

1) Fairy Houses should look so natural they are almost hidden. A location close to the ground is best.

2) You should use only natural materials. Dry grasses, leaves, sticks, pebbles and pinecones are just a few examples of materials to choose.

3) Be careful not to use or disturb any of nature's materials that are still living, especially flowers, ferns, mosses and lichen. Fairies do not like to disturb or destroy anything growing in nature.

### Read to the Child Within

It's hard to know if wee folk like to read, but now that we know what their houses look like, and where to find them, we might want to try peeking inside to get a look at some of their favorite story books. Make note of what they are and treat your own child as well as your own "child within'" with pages of delight and awe. Fantasy, with its predisposition of lightheartedness and mind stretch and indulgence is an infectious affair.

Speaking of infectious, it seems that half the popularity ratings of children's books comes from the delight of the adults who pick them out and read them— not only to their youngsters at bedtime, but to themselves. How many of these classic favorites have you read—either a long time ago or lately?

*Cat in the Hat,* **by Dr. Seuss**—Featuring a tall, anthropomorphic mischievous cat with a tall, red and white-striped hat and a red bow tie, this favorite classic is one of a series of six rhymed children's books that promoted the cause of elementary literacy in the United States.

*Charlotte's Web,* **by E.B. White**—This delightful story of the friendship of a pig named Wilbur and a barn spider named Charlotte was adapted for film and translated into 23 languages.

*Eloise,* **by Kay Thompson**—The story of a 6-year-old little girl who lives at the Plaza Hotel still causes kids and parents alike to giggle over her antics.

*Madeline,* **by Ludwig Bemelmans**—Written by the Austrian-born painter, illustrator, and author Bemelmans, *Madeline* is the charming story of a mischievous and precocious young girl who lives with eleven other girls in a home in Paris.

*The Tale of Peter Rabbit,* **by Beatrix Potter**—One of the best-selling books of all times, this British children's book follows the antics of mischievous and disobedient Peter Rabbit as he is chased about the garden of Mr. McGregor.

*Winnie-the-Pooh,* **by A.A. Milne**—Inspired by the author's son, Christopher Robin, and his stuffed bear, *Winnie-the-Pooh* is probably one of the most loved and quoted children's books of all time thanks to such lovable Pooh friends as Piglet, Eeyore, Tigger, Kanga and Roo.

The best way to help people to maximize their creative potential is to allow them to do something they love.
—Theresa M. Amabile, Harvard researcher

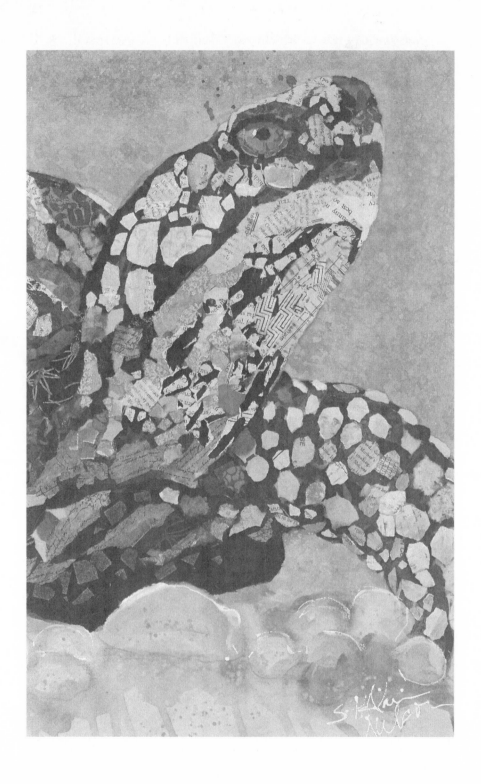

## Case in Point

### Spread Creativity on the Sidewalks

ROBERT (SIDEWALK SAM) GUILLEMIN
Boston, Massachusetts
*Artist and organizer of community art initiatives. Best
way to experience joy: Spread beauty in some form.*

The process of creativity, if it can be called a process, is one that appears to elude many. Doing something we love is an excellent way to begin. Think about it for a second. When we fully love someone or something, we tend to open our minds with abandon, with song, focusing on the image and idea of all that we see as good. There, in its essence, is the starting gate of creativity.

Robert Guillemin is one artist who goes through that starting gate almost daily as he turns the sidewalks of Boston, or any other city that he visits, into a vision of other people's joy. Acting on a sense that people are more joyous than they know, he uses the sidewalk, paints or chalk, plus his own infectious spirit, to inspire others to create their own better vision of existence.

Robert answers to the name "Sidewalk Sam." It is, in truth, simply a stage name. But for anyone who knows his story and has seen his work, the "Sidewalk" alias has become so synonymous with his persona that it totally eclipses his given name.

After receiving Bachelor's and Master's degrees in painting from Boston University, Robert began to follow a traditional artist's career path with numerous commissions and exhibits filling his days and portfolio. But still he worried that the art world's focus on a small, elite audience overlooked too many people in society at large. He decided to take creativity to the street and into daily life, crouching on the sidewalk, kneeling at the feet of people and having art look up at them for a change. And so Sidewalk Sam was born.

Encouraged by the positive reaction of those who took a moment to pause and enjoy, Sidewalk continued to delight viewers with his sidewalk art for some 40 years until an accident left him paralyzed and wheelchair bound. Even then he wasn't dissuaded from his purpose of making art a part of daily life. He simply began to invite the people on the streets to create for him. Working with corporations and civic organizations alike, he comes up with projects on sidewalks or some other appropriate community space, often involving 500 to 2,000 people at a time. Once he had some 40,000 school children join together on a work of art; his largest project topped out at 60,000.

Sidewalk feels strongly enough about changing people's lives through art that he formed Art Street, Inc., a nonprofit arts organization to perpetuate his vision of taking the arts out of the "culture houses" and into the streets. Its website, www.sidewalksam.org, tells how the contagious power of creativity has been used, time and again, to inspire and rally ordinary people around noble causes.

### In Sidewalk's words...

*Each and every one of us is inclined to express, to share, to give happiness in hundreds of ways. I decided to find art that can emphasize people's joy. I want art to serve people as a natural part of everyday life. I think art should bring people closer to each other and inspire people to a better vision of society.*

*My sense is that people are more joyous than they know. As you go about daily life, there are all kinds of things that teach us how to complain; everything is about correction of an imperfect state. But that's because nobody can make money out of our joy.*

*Nobody tells us that basically we're a good, happy, healthy nation of Americans who feel beauty and delicacy in daily life and find joy in daily life. But if we would just pause and realize that we have so much to be thankful for, so much to be happy about, it would change the way we went through a day.*

*With Art Street, we've done some giant artwork. We call up businesses and we say to invite your employees to come out and show joy in their daily life, pride in their company, happiness with their fellow* workers. Just do a simple little artwork like you were in third grade, feeling good.

They do artwork just to show that they are happy, that they care for themselves and for others, and that they have joy and happiness in their life. I kind of feel like a Johnny Appleseed of art, bringing joy to people on their daily walk of life.

When we think about joy, we think about peace, goodness, love, happiness, spirit. All these words are synonymous—they all support each other. It's a family of goodness. People don't realize it as they go about their day. I've been doing art at the feet of people in the public space for 40 years and I have found only a resurgence of goodness, of confidence, of love, of caring that exists between people.

The common denominator that makes the city work is this guarantee that humans offer every other human—that they'll behave decently, that they'll look on life positively, that they'll try their best to make life a good experience and they are basically happy, good, joyous people. And that's the character that makes the city work, that's the glue that holds society together, the reality we don't ever give credit to.

I'll talk to a CEO, a lawyer, a business exec, and say, trust yourself to be good and think of yourself as a third grader. Don't try to do great art. Try and do the art as a simple resurgence of your faith in the goodness of life and draw a flower. Draw a happy face, draw the sun, draw a bubble letter with your name, or the word joy or goodness and color it in and everybody will love it.

I had a chance to speak with the mayor of Boston and I thought why don't we just allow the children in the neighborhoods where the problems exist to express their joy, their spirit, their confidence in goodness? And so we did a thing called Paint for Peace. We painted doves on the sidewalks where killings had been going on, and instead of having an expression of evil on this street, we had an expression of peace, of happiness. The children painted doves that would last for a year. In the dove's talon was a banner, and the banner said, "Stop violence. Create peace."

You don't need to have a lot of skill. You can create beauty in some form, no matter who you are. You simply have to be a human being. If you are a human being, it means that you are, in a way, a poet, a dancer, a musician, an artist, an actor. These kinds of qualities are part and parcel of being a human being.

There are untapped solutions out there, relying on the arts and humanity. We've got to have the arts and humanity speaking out and finding a whole new solution for society. They provide a whole new path of peace and enlightenment and goodness and joy.

........................................................

*Memory feeds imagination.*

*—Amy Tan, novelist*

........................................................

# Case in Point

### See Beyond the Surface Image

ELIZABETH ST. HILAIRE NELSON
Longwood, Florida
*Fine Art collage artist. Best way to experience*
*joy: Learn and do something new.*

Elizabeth St. Hilaire Nelson knows that by combining snippets of color, torn photos, news clips and treasured keepsakes, she is able to bring memories alive with real time dimension. For Elizabeth, it is often the memory beneath the painted image that not only inspires its creation, but that gives it its soul.

When the mother of Elizabeth's late best friend, Suzanne, looks closely at Elizabeth's portrait of her daughter, she sees snippets of memorabilia saved from two friends' intertwined lives—keepsakes from Syracuse University, mementoes from their semester in London, memorial tributes following the fatal bombing of Pan Am flight 103. Thirty-five of Elizabeth's friends and fellow students died along with Suzanne on that flight.

Elizabeth's bewitching depiction of Suzanne touches the heart with its tangible bridges to the past. The minutia of its detail is eclipsed by a magical likeness in vibrant color and artistic spontaneity, simply demanding that delight be found in its joyful creativity.

But the three dimensional powers of Elizabeth's collage process extend beyond its depth of view. There's the joy she finds in the act of creating it; the satisfaction of seeing the final piece, and, thirdly, the pleasure of giving it to someone else and witnessing their joy. Then, for Elizabeth, there is a fourth dimension—the joy of simply doing what she loves to do.

**In Elizabeth's words...**

*That was probably the most traumatic experience of my entire life to lose all those friends, and at the age when you pretty much thought you were immortal, that you were going to live forever, get married and have babies and be a grandparent. The rug was just pulled out from under those kids; one of my roommates was only nineteen.*

*So I did a lot of painting of death and drowning and of the feeling of being overwhelmed. I kind of worked my way through that bereavement process with my art. I wasn't exactly getting joy, but I was really glad to have it to lean on at that time. I just worked and worked on all these images, which kind of got me through it. It was really hard to talk to anyone about it, so I felt like my art was my safe, happy place.*

*I've become very close to Suzanne's mother. I lived with her at one point, right after London when I was struggling with things, and she's been a joy in my life. And because she lost Suzanne, we kind of leaned on each other for a while. I had saved all these papers and stuff and incorporated it all into a portrait of Suzanne and gave it to her. It makes me feel good to do something for someone, for people, something that I know is going to make them happy.*

*After I got married and had my kids, I didn't have as much time for my art. But when my daughter was maybe five or six, I was able to start getting back into it. Once they were in bed, I'd go out to the studio by myself, and I'd listen to the music that I like and do my thing.*

*Sometimes, I look forward all day to going out there at night. If I have a bad day, it gives me my own space or place to decompress. When I'm painting, I don't think about anything that's in the area of my daily woes. Art removes you from all that stuff and just allows you to be in your own little solitude.*

*The first collage I ever did was the result of my father giving me this giant box of personal memorabilia that he'd had for 35 years. So I went through it and it not only had stuff from my childhood but also cards from when my mother graduated from nursing school and some of her personal memorabilia. So I figured if I incorporated that memorabilia into the artwork, I could hang it on the wall and look at it and enjoy it and it would become part of something bigger, rather than staying in that box.*

*I made it into a portrait of my mother, a collage that incorporated the care instructions they gave her when she gave birth to me in 1968. It was about six pages of what not to: don't drive, don't move, don't eat, don't sit up! Also my pediatrician's first bill for the office visit, my birth cards. It won best of show the first time I showed it.*

*Art is like the thing that I'm the best at, so when I have success with it, it really makes me feel good, just to be good at something. My friend Suzanne's mom always said that she has no artistic talent. But she took a watercolor class for years and told me how much she enjoyed it, even if her paintings didn't come out that good. She just enjoyed painting and meeting new people and going and taking the class.*

*I volunteer at our school with the kids and teach them art. You don't hear little kids say, 'Oh, I can't draw' or 'I'm not an artist' and 'I'm not good at that.' They all feel like they can be a wonderful artist when they're little. It's not until we're older that we start to say, 'I can't draw.' We don't start out that way; it's almost like a learned behavior.*

*I think if you ever have an opportunity, you can take a workshop and just kind of explore and play with new material. See if it might be fun to learn something new. Go in with no expectations and don't feel that you have to come out with a masterpiece. Give yourself permission to throw it out and just enjoy the process. What's most important is that you enjoy doing it; you shouldn't let someone else's opinion stop you from enjoying and doing what you want to do.*

**Food for Thought**

## WONDER
Sometimes—
when I watch the flight
of the swallows and the laughing
gulls and see the herons rising
as lords from their temple yard—
and when I listen
to the turn of the tide
and the leaves and the breeze
and feel the tease of the thistle's
head and the fullness that comes
with the doe-eyed gaze of a deer—
all of these—

I consider then
the nature of a world
where children may play
in concrete parks forever
in shadows of burned-out buildings,
watching and listening for fearless
and frightful rats, to junkies
and addicts playing with needles
and lives, to voices singing
the blues—yes, all of these—
and I wonder.

**Wonder is a heady state**, a full-bodied mix of passion, discovery, awe, magic, celebration. Its absence counters innovation, its presence is the threshold of wisdom.

**Rooted in memory**, in curiosity, in dreams, imagination, wonder is the gateway to creativity. Perpetuated by the sharing of its fruits, wonder is contagious, infectious, addictive. It bridges ideas and dialogue, action and invention. Adventure, art, greatness are fed by it.

**Forming the conversation** of meditation, wonder fosters understanding, compassion. Wonder is the hard part of sadness, the tipping point of joy.

# CHAPTER EIGHT

# The Heart of Giving

※

*Nobody has ever measured, not even poets, how much a heart can hold.*

*—Zelda Fitzgerald, novelist*

Considering its role of pumping life-giving blood throughout our bodies, allowing organs to function and the brain to act as the mind, the heart is one sure sweet spot in life. I love you with all my heart, we tend to say. Or, it warms my heart, breaks my heart, comes from the bottom of my heart. But to be fair to our brains, not to mention our nervous and hormonal systems, when we refer to such emotions as love and kindness, benevolence and caring, we're really speaking of a collaborative effort. Yet, somehow, it is the heart that reaps the credit.

Kindness, according to happiness expert and sociologist Christine Carter, Ph.D., at Greater Good Science Center, University of California, Berkeley, is a "terrific happiness habit, good for both our physical and emotional well-being." Helping others, she says, "protects overall health twice as much as aspirin protects against heart disease." Others, such as University of California, San Diego, economist James Andreoni speak of the "warm glow" of internal satisfaction experienced by people who give.

Simply stated, regardless of how we define it, giving makes us feel good. Whether demonstrated through the gifting of self or money or time, there appears to be a positive physiological and psychological effect from goodwill and generosity.

···································································································

*We give of ourselves when we give gifts of the heart: love,*

*kindness, joy, understanding, sympathy, tolerance, forgiveness...*

*—Wilferd A. Peterson, author, columnist*

···································································································

# Case in Point

### Draw on Talents and Instincts

MARILYN DOUGLAS

Simsbury, Connecticut

*Volunteer and hospice caregiver. Best way to*
*experience joy: Give of yourself to others.*

Marilyn Douglas enjoys giving gifts that don't come in boxes. She wraps them instead in music, or in a gentle touch. By looking inward and assessing her skills and passions in life, Marilyn landed on hospice care giving as a way of making a positive difference in the lives of others. Often, that difference is realized through the singing of calming melodies with the Threshold Choir at the bedsides of those who are stressed. Other times, it is delivered by a sloppy wet kiss from her pet-therapy partner, Ranger. Invariably, it is given in the form of a simple comfort that takes the recipient to a place of respite and joy.

When Marilyn began to think about retiring from her human resources and recruiting career, she looked inward and answered for herself that perennial question: What would I do differently if I had to do my life over again? She answered the question by becoming certified as a volunteer hospice caregiver.

For a large part of Marilyn's care giving work, she is accompanied by Ranger, her gentle and sensitive yellow lab. Registered with the Delta Society, an international association that governs the activity of pet partners, Ranger is trained in Animal Assisted Therapy Activities conducted in response to specific medical treatment plan goals, as well as in Animal Assisted Activities. Performed predominantly for socialization, the latter may simply bring patients a break in the routine, a light moment.

Marilyn and Ranger were recently re-evaluated for their roles as pet partners; according to registration requirements, both must pass. Ranger, as it turns out, scored higher than Marilyn. He always brings a smile.

**In Marilyn's words…**

*For me, joy has a few different components to its definition, but overall, whether it's in my personal life, my professional life, my family life, joy comes from my directly making a difference. From the time I was ten years old, I have been actively engaged every year in no less than two to three organizations where I can make a difference.*

*People say they'd love to do some volunteer work but don't know where to start, what organization to do it with. But I think it's pretty simple. I think if we just sit down and do an assessment of our own skills, personally and professionally, whether we worked outside the home in our life or were a fulltime mother raising a family, whatever those skills are, they identify what our passions are. Whatever your physical skill set or passion is, wouldn't it make sense to take what you've spent your life honing and use that as a natural springboard?*

*I should have been a nurse. But I did go into a profession that required a lot of the skills of nursing, such as nurturing, counseling, healing and making a difference. So one day, I saw an ad about becoming a certified hospice caregiver. I did my research and found out it was a five week course covering the ground from spiritual to clinical, something that would fill that void.*

*Hospice work basically deals with the five stages of the end of life— denial, anger, bargaining, acceptance and actual transition. Probably the most common response is an element of spirituality—a relationship or a diversion that helps take the suffering individual to a different place.*

*Other times, it might be simply the connection between two people linked by the need to talk and the ability to listen with an open heart. I use music; I use pets; I use reading; I use just plain conversation. Or if they can't speak at all, then sometimes just our gentle presence with massage and music is a diversion.*

*Quiet presence is very often the peace and the joy that a patient wants. There are different ways in which they let us know this. We could be talking, reading a newspaper, and they appear to be agitated. So we stop doing what we're doing and just have quiet presence. You can see the body start to relax.*

Music is another way of bringing peace and respite to the patient. The role of the Threshold Choir, which was started in California by a woman named Kate Munger, is in bringing joy through music to those who are struggling, sometimes with life, sometimes with death. Sometimes it is through just a single voice where I might go in by myself; other times it might be with two or three other choir members.

There's a pretty expansive Threshold songbook, but the music itself is written to replicate a heartbeat. Very often it's in repetitive rounds. Sometimes it feels like the body is swaying, rocking, and it's very soft, sweet, gentle, like lullabies, very quiet, almost under the breath, where you really have to be quiet for it. What it does is quiet the vital signs physically. If a person is very agitated with pain, which very often happens at end state, the music will relax the nervous system and the person will become very relaxed.

We know that the last two senses to leave the body are hearing and touch. So we will sing into the ear and touch the body while we are singing these songs and it just has a tremendous powerful effect, physically as well as spiritually.

Animals have that unspoken power of being non-judgmental and very comforting, of being able to take people to a different place, especially if they had animals in their own life. We have some documented cases with hospice patients that validate how pet-assisted therapy actually helps hospice patients clinically. Blood pressure goes down; vital signs go down; heart rates improve; this leads to relaxation.

One of my favorite stories is of one youngster whom Ranger and I met by chance in the children's medical center where Ranger regularly visited. In a coma for four weeks after having been hit by a car, he had been unresponsive to a number of stimuli tried by his team of doctors and therapists.

As they stepped off the elevator on the way back to his room from a therapy session, one of the women with him said, "Tanner, Tanner, look, the doggie. Look!" No response. "Tanner, look, the doggie, he's looking right at you." No response. So I asked if I could touch him and when they said yes, I put my hand on his knee, took Ranger's paw and put it on his knee. Then I took Tanner's hand and put it on Ranger's paw.

So we are sitting there with Ranger's paw on Tanner's leg. Then his mom, while his hand was touching Ranger's paw, said, "Okay, Tanner, turn your head, because Ranger wants to hold your hand. Tanner, turn your head!" His little head started to move, straight, straight, slowly. She says, "Keep going, keep going, keep going." His eyes are closed and his head's turning. "Keep going!" He's responding to her voice and she says, "Now, Ranger's looking right at you, open your eyes—open, open!"

He opened his eyes and it was like a child looking at a Christmas tree. His arm came out around Ranger's neck and he bent down and gave Ranger a hug. Can you imagine that mother! I put a treat in Tanner's hand and said, "Give Ranger the treat!" So he puts his hand there— Ranger's mouth is big, he weighs 87 lbs—and his tiny little hand went right inside his mouth. Of course, Ranger has a soft mouth, so his hand got all slobbery and stuff and he started clapping. We did the treat thing two or three times, through him laughing, through him making noise, through him clapping his knees together, through excitement, until finally they decided we'd better take a break from this as it was so emotionally charged.

We continued to work with Tanner and his team over the next four weeks to restore range of motion, eventually even taking Ranger for a walk on a leash. Tanner continued to improve and, last we heard, was happily back in school, playing baseball. Ranger received a national award for his efforts.

*Happiness doesn't result from what we get, but from what we give.*

*—Benjamin S. Carson, M.D., pediatric neurosurgeon*

## A Habit Worth Cultivating

Considering the positive effect of giving or sharing on our brain chemistry as seen in a number of scientific studies, kindness appears to be a habit worth nurturing.

Wanting to better understand the connections between brain anatomy and altruistic behavior, researchers from the University of Zurich observed the brain activity of volunteer participants when given different options for sacrificing money in order to aid another. Not only were marked differences noted in the brain activity of individuals focusing on different ways to use the money, but people who behaved more altruistically were found to have a higher proportion of gray matter in the particular brain region that is believed to influence our predisposition for altruistic behavior. As reported in *ScienceDaily,* the results showed a connection between brain anatomy, brain activity and altruistic behavior.

In other studies, University of Oregon researchers observed significant activation of pleasure areas of the brain when money given to the study's subjects was automatically transferred to a food bank account; an even greater effect occurred when the subjects themselves chose to make the donation. Even toddlers under the age of two were found by psychologists at the University of British Columbia to be happier when they gave away their goldfish cracker treats to monkey puppet friends.

> *It is in your hands to make a difference.*
>
> *—Nelson Mandella, South Africa president*

## Characterizing the Ultimate Mentor

Nelson Mandela will go down in history as an anti-apartheid activist and leader of the African National Congress (ANC) who was arrested and served twenty seven years of a prison life sentence. He will be remembered as the first democratically-elected president of South Africa, and as the recipient of over 250 awards, including the Nobel Peace Prize. But it was his prioritization of actions combating poverty and inequality in South Africa, of caring for the people in the manner that his popular name of *utata* or *father* suggests, that endeared him to many and became his legacy.

Archbishop Emeritus Desmond Tutu captured the essence of that legacy in July of 2012 on Mandela's 94th birthday when he called upon millions of South Africans, as well as others throughout the world, to do good deeds for others on that day and to take a few quiet moments to contemplate all that Mandela had given to his country: "Mr. Mandela taught us to love ourselves, to love one another and to love our country. He laid the table so that all South Africans could eat; we must ensure all members of the family are invited."

Mandela, in so many ways, characterizes the ultimate mentor. As one who is respected and admired, both demanding and supportive, willing to share knowledge and insight, and who cares about the success of others as much as they do, a mentor brings a whole other dimension to the meaning of giving.

> The greatest good you can do for another is not just to share your riches but to reveal to him his own.
>
> —Benjamin Disraeli, British Prime Minister

# Case in Point

**Turn Professional Experience into Life Skill**

LYNN WHITE
Willimantic, Connecticut
*Founder, Growing Stronger, Inc. Best way to
experience joy: Plant seeds of recovery.*

Lynn White works with landscapes to transform lives. Recipient of a college degree in landscape design, she started with a career in landscaping, a profession that she continued part time while raising four children. But when all the kids were in school, she found herself looking around for something that would allow her to mentor girls and maybe help them get a fresh start.

Observing that her community had a number of agencies to help people recover from substance abuse, Lynn figured she might help people through gardening, keeping them busy while possibly making them stronger and healthier. She began with an after-school group of teenagers, turning them into a landscape crew with the goal of re-landscaping a daycare center. It was when she saw how she could give a group of people vocational training while accomplishing something for others at the same time that inspiration struck and Growing Stronger, Inc. was formed.

Operating today as a mentoring service program that provides free vocational training in the fields of horticulture and landscaping, Growing Stronger is known for its projects that support a mission of transformation—or recovery—for both individual life and the environment. Transformation comes through a variety of joint efforts, one of the most visible being the Garden on the Bridge.

Initiated as a project of the Windham (Connecticut) Garden Club, it was created as part of a five-year town venture that transformed an historic stone arch bridge into a huge public garden. Today, the completed garden runs alongside the landmark "Frog Bridge" that was built as a replacement bridge. With over 25 granite planting beds, native trees and views of the Willimantic River, the popular Garden on the Bridge serves as a beautiful teaching tool for Lynn and her Growing Stronger participants.

As it turns out, regardless of the scope or size of a project, simply stopping to listen, along with a bit of spirituality and seeds planted in gardens, are all most important parts of Lynn's recovery program. She wrote as much in a personal development guide she prepared for girls coming out of correctional institutions. It opens with a dozen simple words: "It all began in a garden, and things were right and good."

**In Lynn's words…**

*I love mentoring and helping people to enjoy gardening. And I love doing things for folks that are disabled. So I got my courage up and combined the two. I called it the Growing Stronger Mentoring Service program and asked around to the people in the community whether they thought it was worth doing. And they said, "Please!"*

*So within a year or two, I started combining two loves: helping women transition from a bad place to a good place, while teaching them landscaping for a vocation or as a nice hobby. I like to think of it in the context of a reference made by a woman at the University of Arizona that just said it so well—that gardening soothes the spirit, calms the soul and brings peace to the whole being.*

*It's true; there is something so basic in gardening. Something is connected to the earth and satisfies you and brings you to a point where you can focus and let the other cares of the day take the back seat for a while. It's what you need to clear your head.*

*I think of one of the first women helped in the Growing Stronger program. She was HIV-positive, progressing into AIDS; because she was weak and tired, she did nothing most of the day. So I did the garden for her and then said, "Now it's your responsibility to come out and care for it. Do you think you can do that? And if you can't, at least sit out on your front steps and look at it."*

*She began slowly, but surely, and over a year's time, began to go out more, to get off her couch, get out of her house. She gave me increasing* reports of better health. Her blood counts went back to an almost normal level. I can't claim it's all from getting her up and about in gardening, but I do believe it was an element that helped.

In one project, I worked with a team of girls who were in recovery from substance abuse to create a Recovery Garden by the courtyard entrance to a behavioral health agency in the community, Perception Programs, Inc. It took three groups of volunteers to get in and pull out all the weeds, the bittersweet, the poison ivy, the layers of plastic and mulch that had been there for years. I was determined I was going to bring joy to the people who go in and out of that building, many of them people that need help on their way to the road to recovery and who had not seen beauty in their lives. The director of the agency told me that the best part of her day is walking by the garden.

We've worked on about four or five major gardens, as well as having gone to the homes of people who are ill or elderly. We do public gardens, which encourages the girls, as they get a lot of joy just from being encouraged by the passers-by. The Garden on the Bridge is probably the most well known.

So I bring the girls over there; it's a wonderful place to sit. People are comfortable talking. It's so calming, listening to the river gurgling underneath it. So if they want to take a little spiritual journey, I can show them how things can get good again.

Every lesson has a plant component starting with the seed. Put a seed in the ground. It has a seed coat around it, a hardness around it that protects it until it's ready to grow. But if we're going to grow and emerge from where we are and you want to listen to something better, you've got to let that part break open, take off that seed coat and grow. There are a lot of similarities between the healthy growth of plants and the healthy development of people.

..................................................................................

*Only when you give from the heart*

*does it make the giving whole.*

*—Stephen Richards, cosmic ordering practitioner*

..................................................................................

## Understanding the Power of Green

When we look at the centuries old Indian concept of chakras—specific energy locations that contain the keys to our physical, mental and spiritual well being—we see that the Heart Chakra bridges the gap between the physical and spiritual worlds and governs our compassion for others. It is the center of how we connect to humanity. A person with a balanced Heart Chakra is able to love more, empathize and feel more compassion.

The color of the Heart Chakra is green. An emotionally positive color, green is also the color of spring, renewal, hope and a generosity of spirit. It is a powerful color.

# Case in Point

### Add a Smiley Face to Hope

BONNIE WALDRON

Boston, Massachusetts

*Wife, mother, grandmother, empty-nester whose days are
full. Best way to experience joy: Ease the life of another.*

Bonnie Waldron understands the power of green. She recognized it as a
symbol of hope when her then 16-year-old daughter was being treated for
a tumor at the base of her spine. Neighbors and classmates began to tie
green balloons around their small Massachusetts town of Harvard and
outside Mary Kaye's hospital room to show their support and the image
of hope took on a life of its own.

Determined to honor and preserve the memory of their daughter
after her loss to cancer at the age of 22, Bonnie and her husband, Jim,
formed a charitable giving fund and launched a variety of initiatives
to help others in life. The fund's combination of hope and giving is
a contagious and infectious force, and through its gifts of support,
especially for children and young adults with disabilities, Mary Kaye's
spirit and community presence lives on.

Making someone's life easier is the prevailing thread of both the
charitable fund and the Waldrons' own philosophy. The fund plays
a part in helping many with specific needs. But, as Bonnie mused to
a friend, what about all those people walking around who need help
in less observable ways? Wouldn't it be nice if they were to receive an
envelope with a little cash in it, just to put a tiny spark of happiness into
a given moment of their day?

**In Bonnie's words…**

*The green balloons started when Mary Kaye was going to be having surgery
and I needed a raincoat and this green raincoat caught my attention. I tried
it on and thought that I needed this because green was the color of hope. I
came home and showed Mary Kaye the raincoat and said that I was going
to tell people to wear green, the color of hope, on the day of her surgery.*

*Leave it to the kids, word spread like wildfire through our little town of Harvard. It's been said that most of the kids at the school and the teachers all gathered. They all had green, the teachers prepared some green ribbons for anyone who forgot to wear green, and two women put green balloons around the whole center of town. Whenever we were in the hospital, I would always hang one outside the room—at that time you were able to use a regular latex balloon—so that people would know Mary Kaye was here. People would write a note and draw a little green balloon, and it just took off.*

*At the time of her death, we knew that there were going to be lots of people coming to the wake and so forth. There would be no place for flowers, so in lieu of flowers, we asked that contributions be made to the Mary Kaye Fund. It is now many years since her death on April 15th, 1995, and we still have donors.*

*At Oprah's tenth anniversary, I was watching her show and she had this penny collection that people used to do. So I thought, well that's an easy way and it's definitely all inclusive—children can collect pennies. So I sent out letters to our nearest and dearest friends with a little poem I had seen before, "When you find it." It was about a penny being kind of a little message from heaven. So I sent that poem and asked people to put it on a container of their choice and to collect their found pennies for others.*

*Contributions ran the gamut. One of the most beautiful stories was from a dear friend who teaches in the Bronx, at that time they were first graders. She had them memorize the poem and they all drew pictures and collected. At the end of the year they had collected $23.20.*

*What the fund provides seems to be mostly technology, new technology that's out there for children and young adults with disabilities— wheelchairs, adaptive wheelchairs, programs to get out in the outdoors. One time Jim and I went on a sail around Boston Harbor and there was a thirty eight-year-old man who was blind and had learning disabilities at the helm. We went around in circles—and I am a slightly nervous sailor—but talk about joy! We were laughing, saying, "I bet all these other boaters are wondering what's going on with this boat." Going back to just simple, simple, simple pleasures brings joy.*

There are so many more people walking around than just those with the assistive aids that really need help that we're focusing on. So I was just wishing that people on a given day could have a little spark in their moment and simply get an envelope with a little cash in it. I happened to tell my idea to my friend, Karen, and lo and behold, within a week an envelope shows up in my mail with a check. So that started the project.

I put a $50 bill in an envelope with a smiley face, a green smiley face. I had these stickers in the house that said "Green, the color of hope. Smile." I thought, this is perfect; it's kind of connected with green balloons. If I draw a little stem on the circle, on the smiley face, I've got a balloon. So I created a letter that just puts a $50 bill on it and says, "Hope the above cash adds to the smile you already have."

So what does joy look like? I think it comes with just having an open heart. It shows up in the most unusual places. It shows up when you're walking in the street and you're so focused and your face is somber and all of a sudden somebody walks by and smiles at you and says, 'Hi!' That really puts a smile on your face. So I think it finds you. Or maybe it's just putting a smiley face on the little word joy and putting it in an envelope.

..........................................................................

*A thing of beauty is a joy forever: its loveliness increases; it will never pass into nothingness.*

*—John Keats, English poet*

..........................................................................

## Giving Is an Ongoing Process

Oprah Winfrey, whose name is synonymous with the joy of giving, once said she doesn't think one ever stops giving. "I really don't. I think it's an on-going process. And it's not just about being able to write a check. It's being able to touch somebody's life."

Consistently rated as one of America's top and most well loved philanthropists, Oprah herself is remembered for such highly visible and successful initiatives as funding support for the rebuilding of Gulf Coast communities devastated by Hurricane Katrina and for her Angel Network. Launched in 1998 with donations from her talk show viewers, the Angel Network continued until Oprah's decision to end her show after twenty five years on the air. In the course of its existence, it raised more than $80 million for charity from nearly 150,000 donors.

The goal of the Angel Network was simple—to encourage people to make a difference in the lives of others. There, summed up in those few ordinary and doable words, is the source of the warm glow that comes from giving. It is, as it turns out, something that we see happening all around: everyday people doing everyday things to make even a tiny difference in the lives of others.

# Case in Point

## Preserve Legacy with Gifts of Help and Hope

HERB OUIDA

River Edge, New Jersey

*Co-founder, Todd Ouida Children's Foundation. Best way to experience joy: Share the life of one to make another's richer.*

Herb Ouida spent much of his professional career inside the offices of the World Trade Center. His work was in international business development with the Port Authority of New York and New Jersey and the World Trade Center Association. Yet when he speaks at community and civic events, he rarely mentions it—beyond, perhaps, in references to September 11, 2001. He speaks, instead, of the Todd Ouida Children's Foundation.

Established by Herb and his family following the loss of their twenty five-year-old son and brother in the tragic terrorist attack on the World Trade Center towers, the Foundation celebrates and perpetuates Todd's life by creating a legacy of help and hope. Born out of Todd's own successful struggle with childhood anxiety, it supports psychological services for children of families in need and promotes mental health initiatives for all children.

By charitable grant measures, the Foundation makes a significant contribution, with donations already awarded to over thirty different charities supporting such services and programs. But by gauges of emotional support and encouragement, it registers a more significant impact as it reaches out to the hearts and minds of untold numbers, bringing a feeling of healing and sense of encouragement to others who lost family, friends and fellow citizens on that momentous day.

For Herb and his family and friends who knew Todd, the Foundation carries its own personal measure of relief and happiness. It is a transfer of Todd's impact in life to the lives of those that it manages to help. Building on the words written by the poet Keats, it is the joyful continuation of a thing of beauty.

**In Herb's words...**

*It brings joy to my life, peace, some feeling of healing. Where we are starting from is the overwhelming feeling of pain. So instead of saying that Todd's ashes are in the dust of the World Trade Center, he's in our hearts and people talk about it more, which really helps us.*

*Some will tell me when I speak about Todd's struggle with childhood anxiety and the mission of the Foundation that they suffer from Anxiety Disorder and that to freely discuss it takes the stigma off. It's kind of like a burden that we carry around, almost the opposite of joy. People talk about their inner self. We tell them that children have an inner self and what we're trying to do is to help even children express those feelings. You get a lot closer to happiness and contentment and, I guess, joy if you're not carrying those burdens.*

*Joy has so many connotations. The truth is you start with the thought that you're not entitled to joy anymore. You're at a point where it's no longer in your life lexicon, and that is a very, very painful burden to carry.*

*If you say to yourself, I'm so-o-o depressed that the best I can think of is to never really feel great about being alive and appreciate the sun and the gift of every day, then you're also denying other people that you love the ability to share their joy with them. I think of the grandchildren right away, and certainly we are joyful about them. How can we say to our son and daughter, "We lost your brother, there is no more joy, there is no more celebration." That's really the most difficult part. I know that people feel guilty about feeling joyful.*

*And honestly, there are days when there is lots of pain—there will always be days where there is lots of pain. Things will come back and then there will be joy. You're mixing pain and joy all the time.*

*Even for us to get up and talk about the Foundation and 9/11, we don't know if we're going to cry or be able to go through the whole presentation. I have known so many people who have lived with this and continue to try and transform that tragedy into hope. It's an inspiring story and the truth is it is Todd's story and there may be someone in the audience who suffered as Todd did. By sharing his story, you're taking a risk every time, as you don't know whether it's going to be the joy part, the hope part, or the pain part—it's usually a blending. But I don't think you can ever have joy by denying the pain.*

*To be afraid when you lose someone you love that this person will be just in the dump of the World Trade Center, to say that's the end of the twenty five years of the blessing of having Todd with us, that is so painful. But that's not all there is. Though what you really want is your loved one back, what really matters is how that life makes other lives richer. That's the second part of the grief, the inspiration.*

*People talk about closure—that's a terrible word. But the Foundation perpetuates Todd's life. Through it, his life continues to touch other lives. That's the root of the Foundation. It's about trying to do good in Todd's name and spirit. It brings our family together and that's another very important part—that we don't wallow. The Foundation is a way for all of us to work on that, which is very important.*

*When people look at ways to work through the pain that may be in their lives, it might come through selecting or developing a foundation that will help them. One marker that I might give to people to help them select their giving is that it has to be meaningful to help bring joy out of pain, whether firsthand pain, or something you observe. The meaningful part is the key—it must relate to personal values.*

*I find that the real joy in this life is not in the accumulation of things or in taking, but it is in giving. I really believe that joy is in reaching out to other people and seeing how your life helps another person and changes another person. So it's in being a person that looks beyond oneself, and says "I am part of a community," or family, whatever.*

*One time we were helping abused children who live in a home called the Holly House and they asked if instead of sending them that year to a Yankees game, which we had done in the past, would we mind sending them the money instead so they could use it for barbecue equipment, tables and chairs. So we did and then they asked us to come to their first barbecue.*

*They took us back to see their garden. It had big stones, inscribed with love, joy, peace. And there was something written on the wall: "Todd's Garden, a place where hope grows." It was very special—they captured everything we are trying to do on that little plaque.*

## Food for Thought

*A friend wrote* on her blog that there are moments in life when she cannot find explanations—moments when searching for *why* becomes too much to bear. It's then that she walks off into the woods, where, instead of answers, she just finds peace.

*Finding the why of giving*—understanding why we give, why we feel good when we give, where and what giving is all about—relates in many ways to the message of my friend's post. To forget about the *why* and instead pursue the peace of a walk in the woods may be an unexpected way to understand the meaning of giving. But there, in its freedom from definition, is the true story of giving's heart.

*Giving is commonly* described as caring, helping, doing good. It is an act of benevolence, generosity, charity, altruism, self-sacrifice, endowment, philanthropy. Each covers some aspect of giving's multidimensional meaning.

*But my favorite*, and the closest to the metaphorical example of finding peace instead of answers in the woods, is love of humanity. It is there in that love where we find giving's defining thread. The unspoken answer to the why of giving, to the meaning of giving, to the reason we feel good when we help is found in that love of others. Giving, freely and spontaneously for the good of others, is the best peace-finding walk in the woods we can take.

CHAPTER NINE

# The Spirituality of Life

*Sometimes people get the mistaken notion that spirituality is a separate*
*department of life, the penthouse of existence. But rightly understood,*
*it is a vital awareness that pervades all realms of our being.*
*—David Steindl-Rast, Benedictine monk*

I f we think about spirituality simply in the context of life's sweet spots, we
might be tempted to plan a visit to Machu Picchu in Peru. Or possibly to
Wrangell-Saint Elias on the border between Canada and Alaska. Or maybe
the labyrinths of Glastonbury, England, or the conical marble mountain of
Mount Athos, Greece. Each, along with a curious mix of mosques, cathedrals,
temples, mountains, canyons and wellsprings, is commonly known as a sacred
place, a place where all the elements of a sweet spot dwell.

Sacred places are powerful and tangible examples of how cultures before us
pointed to the heavens, exalted the gods and searched for the indefinable. With
their associated legends and rites of being with nature, their worship, sacrifice
and meditation, all illustrate the diversity of ways in which humankind seeks
to connect to the divine. They are expressions of spirituality.

While difficult to pin down, definitions and practices of spirituality basically refer to what we do with our inner being, with our souls. Although distinct from organized religions with defined church doctrines, spirituality aligns with religion in its fundamental nature. Regardless of one's position on religious faith, spirituality is about how we nourish or foster the values and energies that influence our soul's inner journey.

### Sweet Spots Known to Be Sacred

Associated with mythological or religious events, sites of spirituality are significant for their celestial, cultural or ceremonial happenings. Some, such as Niagara Falls, where Charles Dickens felt near his Creator, or the town of Bethlehem—birthplace of Christ, resting place of Rachel and place of prayer for Mohammed—are places we might know of through lessons and images of history, geography or travelogues. Rebecca Hind, author of *Sacred Places, Sites of Spirituality & Faith*, takes her readers on a literary journey to such locations around the globe, places "that speak of the divine and the unknown, and which allow us to rejoice in the great mystery of our connection to the world and our place in it." A handful of these spots appear here on these pages as starting points to spiritual inspiration.

**Bungle Bungle, Purnululu National Park, Western Australia—** Once known only to the Aboriginal people who painted on its extraordinary rock walls and buried their dead there, the Bungle Bungle massif remains today a cultural wellspring of Aboriginal spirituality, treasured for its awe inspiring orange and black banded sandstone formations rising out of the arid landscape.

**Castlerigg Stone Circle, Cumbria, England—**Popularly known as Druid's Circle, this ring of 38 stones is believed to have been a place of ceremony, ritual and worship as far back as 3200-3000 B.C. Mysterious in its origin and in the understanding as to how the stones might have been placed there (the tallest being more than seven feet high), the site is a place of contemplative meditation.

**Delphi, Fokís, Greece—**Perched on the side of Mount Parnassus, Delphi was a major site for the worship of the god Apollo. It remains today as a major architectural site where visitors may visit the ruins of the Temple of Apollo, the Altar of the Chians, and the fountain house, where supplicants would bathe in the Castalian spring before consulting the oracle.

**Kii Mountains, Honshu, Japan**—Home to ascetic mountain dwellers since around the seventh century, this heavily forested mountain range was noted for its fusion of Shinto and Buddhist beliefs. With a network of shrines, temples and pilgrimage routes, the region represents over a 1,000 years of worship.

**Petra, Jordan**—Situated between the Red Sea and the Dead Sea and surrounded by mountains, Petra was half-built, half-carved into sandstone rock. Believed to be the place where Moses struck a rock with a stick to release water to quench the Israelites' thirst, it is one of the world's largest archeological sites of elaborate tombs, temples, altars and carved gods of lost civilizations.

**Rapu Nui (Easter Island), Southern Pacific Ocean**—One of the world's most isolated islands, this tiny island is famous for its enormous *moai*, iconic statues. Carved from volcanic stone by Polynesian craftsmen to represent a variety of deities and placed on platforms within shrines, most of the figures stand in a protective position facing toward the population, their deeply carved eyes often inlaid with coral to activate the statue's spiritual power.

### Sing within the Soul

Spirituality nurtures our soul and shapes our actions, our morality, our joy of living. But how do we feed it? What are the practices and encounters through which we can taste and see its graces and inspirations, even when we are not looking?

Letting our lives intersect with the natural wonder of the universe is one way. The late rabbi and theologian Abraham Joshua Heschel said that to be spiritual is to be amazed. Opening our eyes to nature's gifts of wonder—being amazed—is one of the finest nutrients we can come up with when it comes to feeding our souls.

Feeding the soul with amazement is something we enjoy so often through the words and creations of poets, authors and artists. Textile and mixed media artist Hilary Rice of Stirling, Ontario, Canada, for one, creates hidden messages in her art work. Art making, she explains, "is a way of connecting with the world, a way of connecting what is inside, with what is outside. My work touches and links me to the holy."

Inspiration for this award-winning textile artist comes from somewhere deep within, often in response to a piece of text, a beautiful melody or simply the natural world. Using a variety of intricately layered materials, often illuminated with metallic gold and silver threads and touches of jewel-like color, Hilary creates works of art that observe and preserve moments of wonder and amazement. Each creation encompasses reflections of all that makes her soul grow—moments spent "in the cracks between the stars… in the cooling of the sun." Stopping not only to look, but to let what we see impress, helps explain why we sing.

......................................................................................

*Let us be grateful to people who make us happy, they are*

*the charming gardeners who make our souls blossom.*

*—Marcel Proust, French novelist*

......................................................................................

# Case in Point

## Be Awed in the Wonder of the Flower

### CAROL KORTSCH

Radnor, Pennsylvania

*Psychotherapist and gardener. Best way to experience
joy: Be aware of God's presence in the garden.*

For many, the fruit of the garden is the pure and simple beauty of
its flowers, providing our senses with a heady pleasure of scent and
color, softness and luxurious splendor. But for gardeners such as Carol
Kortsch, it is the dimension of spiritual meditation, of making physical
and mental connections, that brings inner satisfaction.

A psychotherapist by profession, Carol complements her career
interest with the physical activity of her garden. Home is in an old 1750
farmhouse, situated on a two-acre property that had been let run down
into an old wisteria patch and a lilac bush in need of tender loving care.
Responding to what she figured to be her gardening genes, Carol began
to plant borders around the pathways and the house, turning it into a
place she loves.

For many, and Carol is no exception, water brings a symbolic and
spiritual focal point to the garden. Whether due to its aesthetically
pleasing movement or sound in an otherwise still environment, or
simply its reflective tranquility, water in a garden has been equated
for centuries by most Asian cultures with peace and joy. Given its
promise of serenity and peace, gardeners of all backgrounds commonly
incorporate water in the form of a waterfall, a pond or a gurgling brook
into their surrounding space.

Carol became hooked on water gardening when she first saw the
lotus flower while on vacation in Barbados and decided it was the most
gorgeous flowering plant she had ever seen. In the Buddhist tradition,
the lotus is said to represent purity of the body, speech and mind, as
if floating above the muddy waters of attachment and desire. Buddha,
himself, is often represented as seated on a pink lotus. After studying

up on this ancient and symbolic flower, Carol convinced her family that they needed to create a water garden so she could grow lotus.

Today, although she sees much of the lotus symbology as significant, it is the larger presence of the garden that is most important to her. Time in the garden becomes an active meditation, an expression in so many ways of who she is, who her soul is. It is a time in a sacred place, a place where she becomes aware of God's presence.

### In Carol's words...

*Gardening is a counterpoint to sitting and so it's almost like that's what my body needs, what my soul needs—to get out and do something in the natural world. It's just a very natural outgrowth of spontaneous pleasure to do something that brings life and that my hands can be involved in.*

*There's an ongoing creativity in finding something your soul longs for and then once you get there, it opens up a whole new venue of pleasure that is linked to work. It can be work in the mind, of energy. But you can only sit and look at lotus for so long without thinking, oh well, that's nice, so thanks. It evokes a whole journey that is full of surprises.*

*I think that has a lot to do with joy. You never know, there's an expectancy. What's going to emerge next? I have such a sense of that now when I garden and it has also taught me how to live for the rest of my life. I take my gardening experience and apply it in all sorts of ways.*

*Just the journey of all of our lives brings so much suffering and pain, for many different reasons. I was watching the news one day and I just didn't know what to do with the anguish I felt for people of Kosovo who had been ripped out of their land and could not farm anymore and couldn't sustain their lives and were forced into urban enclaves of different kinds. I felt that all I could do, in some ways, was to go out, and I literally dropped my spade in the middle of the yard and started digging these oval shapes.*

*I think I must have thought about it somewhere before, but I just began that day and that became my Kosovo garden. I thought I can't do anything else, but for me it felt like a prayer for others who could not do this very thing. My intention was a way, in some mystical sense, of bringing something back to people who are suffering.*

*You know there's a tremendous sense of purpose and joy that comes out of feeling like you can do something—that you do have a part to play. We are all in this web of life, in this community of life, and I'm really using that energy of compassion to transform the ground in my surroundings. It's been remarkably healing for me and for others.*

*That's a very personal inner kind of journey that is different for each of us. We are all sort of unique in this way. Rocks, for me, are huge symbols of beauty. They're one of the most long lasting things that we see in nature; they have been forever. I tend to have natural objects as sort of physical bones of the garden. Rocks are easy to come by, so I often will dig them up.*

*Sometimes we think a memorial has to be for someone we personally know. I firmly believe we are all connected in the invisible sense and we don't understand all those connections. We can influence and affect the world in very practical ways and in deeply spiritual ways that build beyond our own understanding. That's the nature of prayer. Creating the garden memorial feels like an act of prayer in that way.*

*It's a way of my body working out what my soul has known all along. It's the basis for pleasure and truth. The sense of nature and joy is so much of that. As a psychotherapist, I can't help but use gardening as a metaphor, as an inspiration. It is my life. Every time you turn around you can see some sort of application to us as creatures:*

> *Courage—When we first dug our water garden, we had this huge gaping room in the middle of the garden. It started to rain, and it filled with water and was a disaster for a while, but you just keep on going. Courage is that sense that you have to move into the unknown.*

> *Contemplation—Gardening has developed the spiritual contemplative within me. I can say I'm a born activist, but I have learned how to stop and be quiet and listen and learn in all of the spaces.*

*Consciousness—Being raised in nature as a child, I quote what Albert Einstein said: "Look deep into nature and then you will understand everything better." Consciousness, awareness—that's all been really significant for me.*

*Connectedness—My garden is a haven for all sorts of animals and creatures, half of them I don't even see because they come at night. But it sort of invites the whole web of life. Gardens are all about relationships. Everything is connected to everything else—connections around family, working together.*

*Creativity—Creativity comes out of change, out of just learning. The more I have learned, the more I have learned to be creative in the midst of these changes and not despair. The opposite of joy is, I think, despair. There is creativity in learning about the garden's color, space, form, texture and light.*

*Change—There is no finished product in gardening. There's always a new season, a storm that's about to arrive and knock something down, or beetles that will eat something. Everything is continually changing. Our life is like that, there's always something that's going to come, that teaches you. There's a lot of joy in trusting a process of change.*

## Follow the Winding Labyrinth Path

One block south of the 10 Freeway in Los Angeles is a mid-city oasis of flowering trees, fountains and a lily pond, a sanctuary to reflect and recharge in the calming surroundings of nature. Visitors are invited to sit and contemplate. They are also invited to stand at the threshold of their consciousness, ready to step from the exterior world into the interior world represented by the hand carved stone labyrinth of the Peace Awareness Labyrinth and Gardens spiritual retreat.

A labyrinth is an ancient path of pilgrimage, a place to explore the metaphor of the movement in life, to follow a path to the center. Labyrinths are known to have been followed since the days of King Nestor. The oldest positively dated labyrinth, circa 1230 BCE, comes from his Phylos, Greece palace, although evidence suggests that they date further back in history.

Classic labyrinths combine the function of meditation with the image of a spiraling path, symbolizing a person's path in life. By following a labyrinth's path to its center while breathing slow and letting the mind quiet, one is able to quietly clear the mind of thought and to simply *be* rather than *do*.

Although labyrinths may be as tiny as a finger labyrinth, held in the palm of one's hand while traced with a finger, the most common labyrinths are designed for walking and typically utilize a single winding path with many left-to-right and right-to-left turns as one moves to the center point. Labyrinths have enjoyed a revival in popularity over recent years and are as apt to be found in private yards as well as sacred and historic settings. Here are a few of note:

*Basilica of Reoperates, Orleansville, Algeria:* Likely the oldest known example of the pavement labyrinths found in many of the old Christian churches of France and Italy, this fourth century labyrinth measures about eight feet in diameter. At its center is a *jeu-de-lettres,* or play on the words Sancta Eclesia, which may be read in any direction, except diagonally, starting at the center.

**Chartres Cathedral, Paris, France:** One of the most famous eleven-circuit design labyrinths, it has the same dimensions as the great rose window over the Cathedral's west doors, positioned so that the colored light of the window and the darkness of the labyrinth are combined.

**Glastonbury Tor, Somerset, England:** Designated as an Ancient Monument, the Glastonbury Tor, or hill, is known for the terraces, one above the other, that spiral seven times around its sides, ending at St. Michael's Tower on the summit. Speculation has it that the pattern was created in the past for ritual purposes.

**Grace Cathedral, San Francisco, California:** Both indoor and outdoor labyrinths play an active role in the Cathedral's experience of life. In addition to being available for walking daily, candlelight walks, peace walks, walks with music, even yoga on the labyrinth are scheduled regularly.

**Ohio State University Chadwick Arboretum, Columbus, Ohio:** Modeled after the classic Chartres Cathedral Labyrinth, the Arboretum's labyrinth was dedicated in 2000 at the time of a worldwide revival of the labyrinth as a path for prayer and meditation.

**Sacred Garden of Maliko, Maui:** Run by the Divine Nature Alliance, this nonprofit nursery and healing sanctuary offers a medieval eleven-circuit labyrinth outdoors under the Kuku trees and a classical sevem-circuit labyrinth in the greenhouse.

*World Wide Labyrinth Locator:* To find additional labyrinths in the United States or worldwide, consult the labyrinth locator website at www.labyrinthlocator.org.

..............................................................................

*Every natural fact is a symbol of some spiritual fact.*

*—Ralph Waldo Emerson, essayist and poet*

..............................................................................

## Case in Point

### Feel the Rhythm of the Universe

ANNE ROWTHORN

Salem, Connecticut

*Environmentalist, teacher, advocate of eco-spirituality. Best
way to experience joy: Let nature just be part of your being.*

Anne Rowthorn connects ecology and spirituality in ways that tap
into the wonder of the natural world. Though she has traveled around
the globe to collect ecological literature from the great cultures and
religions of all time, she finds she needs only to look outside her home
to sense life's spiritual pulse.

When Anne was eighteen, she spent a summer with the Native
American Lakota people, an experience she feels probably changed
her life. As it was, even before Anne reached South Dakota, she had
made up her mind that she didn't enjoy the urban lifestyle she had been
experiencing in the northeast and wanted to move on.

After teaching English and history in southeast London, she
moved with her husband to New York City where they raised their
three children, and Anne earned a master's degree in recreational
therapy, followed by a Ph.D. from New York University. Eventually,
she returned to the eco-spirituality-friendly environment of her rural
Salem home.

There, inspired by her life's travels and exploration of the world's
great cultures and religions, she now spends much of her time writing
such books as *Earth and All the Stars* and *Feast of the Universe,* among
others. They are, as she describes them, books on spirituality and the
natural world, invitations to wander Ulysses-like through the world's
ecological treasures, to listen to the music of the heavens and feel the
rhythm of the universe.

**In Anne's words...**

*I suppose it began at a very young age. When I was very young, my mother would take me to the beach and she would help me explore tidal pools, the seaweed, the tides, crabs, just the winds and the breezes.*

*But probably what I enjoyed more was exploring for myself. Every afternoon after school I'd go with a next-door neighbor to one or another beach. It was before people worried about kids being safe and so we had beaches, we had woods, we had skating ponds, and we really grew up outside.*

*In the winter, when it was very cold, we'd always look for the snow days and go sledding. We had a few skating ponds around and so we used to go ice skating. I think winter is still my favorite season. I don't like to be cold, but I like the feeling of cold and I love ice. I like the smell of winter, the sound of the trees.*

*Joy—rather than happiness, rather than fun—is actually something that comes from inside, something that wells up from beneath. But, on other hand, it is fed by the outside. It's fed by these ferns, by that brook, by those hawks that are out there, by the scent in the air. It's not something that you can manufacture; it's something that I suppose evolves over time.*

*Joy taps into the deep roots within me. I think there is an aspect of joy that touches on authenticity. It can't be fabricated; it's real. It's there, or it isn't. Experiencing joy, just in the Zen way, is living totally in the present, being totally alive, totally here, totally connected with right now. I suppose there has to be a certain awareness, a certain openness.*

*When I was eighteen, I left to work one summer in South Dakota and I saw how people with very little had such a huge abundance. First of all, the rolling land was absolutely beautiful. My experience had really been with the sea, and so as I'd look out in the evening over the undulating prairies, watching the evening shadows roll in, it would be somewhat reminiscent of the sea.*

*With the Lakota people, I lived in a small village on the Rosebud Reservation and became very friendly with an old Indian lady called Granny Lambert. I used to sit on her doorstep every night and she'd just sit there; sometimes she wouldn't even talk. But I just felt a centeredness and authenticity about her. I think it was only later that I realized that*

*I kind of absorbed a way of life. I felt that I had absorbed a religion. I figured that if this was her way of life, I wanted a life like that.*

*I was, and still am, a social activist. I thought that people needed to know what we are doing, how we're trashing the environment, the land, the seas, the skies, everything. And so I taught an ecology and justice course called Caring for Creation.*

*I thought that if people knew the facts, it would evoke a religious response. The students said, "Wow, I never realized until I studied what we are doing to our forest that it causes the salinization of the rivers, the rise in temperature, etc. We need to address this; we need to have Biblical readings and readings from other religions." So we had a little time at the end of every class where we would address this spiritually with the resources that we have from our traditions.*

*I really feel—and it's not an original idea at all—that the wonder, the glory and the majesty of the holy one, by whatever name, is primarily revealed through the natural world. And so I experience God right out here, and I can be arrested by the sunbeams early in the morning.*

*Actually, my husband also likes to hike, and so on a regular basis we work in the morning and in the good weather take a hike every afternoon. Right now, when it's too hot, I have what I call my secret pond that I go swimming in. It's probably about a half a mile back and forth. Nobody's there; it's my pond. Sometimes in the fall, the Canada geese swim with me; I don't mind cold water. Sometimes a deer will appear at the other end of the pond; usually I disturb a few frogs that jump off the tree stumps when I go by.*

*I will just sit there and before I get in the water, I'll say, "Wow, it doesn't get any better. It doesn't get any better than this." And this is just a little pond. It doesn't take much. So I suppose that's how I practice spirituality. Now, do I bring that to conscious thought every day? I don't think so. I think that the natural world is just part of my being and it gives me a lot of pleasure.*

*I think it was Thomas Berry, the late Catholic eco-theologian, who said, "The universe is our teacher." Emerson thought so. Thoreau thought so. Muir thought so. I really don't think I can improve on that.*

*I honor the place within you where the entire universe resides;*

*I honor the place within you of love, of light, or truth, or peace;*

*I honor the place within you, where, when you are in that*

*place in you, and I in that place in me, there is only one of us.*

*—Mahatma Gandhi, Indian political leader*

## Appreciate the Soul of Another

*Namaste*, a combination of *namah*, meaning *bow*, and *te*, meaning *to you*, is the customary Hindu way of greeting others. To perform *Namaste*, one bows one's head slightly while bending the arms from the elbow upwards and facing the palms of the hands together in front of the heart chakra. In so doing, one is extending friendship in love and respect. Bringing the hands together at the heart is said to increase the flow of divine love; bowing the head helps the mind surrender to the divine in the heart. More than a mere word, *Namaste* is an acknowledgement of the soul in one by the soul in another.

Eckhart Tolle, contemporary spiritual writer and author of *A New Earth: Awakening to Your Life's Purpose*, expresses the equivalent of *Namaste* in similar words: "To love is to recognize yourself in another." Regardless of its basis—spouse, family, friend, neighbor, even enemy, personal relationships represent some of life's most significant spiritual connections. Thomas Merton, Trappist monk and author of books on spirituality, looks at the meaning of life with another and concludes that love is our true destiny. Reference to its importance is found dating back to the Bible scriptures and pronouncement of the second commandment: Love thy neighbor as thyself.

*I like to laugh and be with my family and friends. I like to think*

*I have done something good, a little good every day, even if it's*

*thanking someone for a service rendered, small acts of kindness.*

*Nature, green grass, animals, nature again, are very important*

*to me. And true love, people you surround yourself with.*

*—Anjelica Huston, actress, director*

### Grow One's Soul with Love

Spirituality is about what we do with our spirits, how we feed them, how we touch them. All of those things with which we surround ourselves—green grass, nature, family and friends, people, even those whom we have not met beyond the edges of our awareness, are ultimately tied to the sustenance of our souls. Philosopher and theologian Saint Augustine saw love as "the beauty of the soul"—a most fulfilling nourishment. To the extent love grows within, so grows the spirituality and beauty of the soul.

# Case in Point

### Tough Love Speaks Volumes

ABDUL MUHAMMAD
Newark, New Jersey
*Co-director, Comprehensive Center for Fathers. Best way to
experience joy: Learn, earn, return to the community.*

The story of Abdul Muhammad illustrates the meaning of spirituality
in the context of love and beauty growing; it is all about "tough love." It
is about a love that he describes in the context of having had a second
chance at fatherhood, and a joy that he receives from encouraging
others to nurture and give their own father's love and caring.

As a co-director of the Fathers Now initiative to help ex-felons
and at-risk men become engaged fathers and citizens, Abdul speaks
with passion when he tells how he turned his life around following
imprisonment for the accidental shooting of his brother. His hope is
that his story will serve as an incentive to others to change their lives.
Consisting partly of basic education and life training, the Fathers Now
program works to reunify families after fathers have been dislocated or
uninvolved in their child's life, as well as to place the men vocationally.
It does so by trying to intensify their relationships with their sons
and daughters, helping them to understand the deep importance of
fatherhood.

### In Abdul's words…

*Every day I wake up and look forward to motivating and encouraging
these men. It's the greatest feeling—it's like a touch. It's a feeling of
intense invigoration that's internal, that I can feel even as I'm sitting here
talking about it. Joy to me is like when you're talking about something
you're involved in so that you get happy in your soul and it radiates and
you get warmer. That's what fatherhood does for me; it gives me that
touch. It makes me happy in my soul.*

*I'm just thankful to God that I'm at this place in my life where I'm able to give. When people hear my story in the way that I convey it to them, it's a touch that they feel. You know, when other people are down and you've been down and you show them how you came out of it, that, I think, is the connection that I have been blessed with. It's for the men to say, "I can be like him!"*

*I come across to them with tough love. But intertwined with that tough love is love. And they see that, they feel that. I know that my guys know Abdul Muhammad is not a faker because everything that is going on in my life is reality. It's real and it's hope to the guys that are here; it gives them an incentive to want to motivate themselves to change their lives. It gives them joy that they take out of here, back to their environment and their home. They become more appreciative of life and that to me is what community service is all about.*

*For me, I figure what turned me around was more or less my compassion to want to prove to my family that I made a mistake, that I was sorry for the mistake that I made, and that I wanted to do everything in my will power to alter my circumstances when I came home. So it was more or less to make my mother proud of me, my grandmother proud—who I just lost recently—and my father and my grandfather proud, to let them understand that, yes, I made a mistake, I pulled the trigger and I admit it, but I made a mistake and I didn't mean it and I worked every day of my life that I was in prison to better myself and go back to school and do the right thing.*

*I had a daughter that was born in '87 and we named her after my brother. I missed her—I missed her growing up. But I now have a two-year-old daughter, so that's another aspect of my joy: my own personal fatherhood and responsibilities. I have shared parenting of her, so she's split between me and her mother.*

*But, wow, just hugging a two-year-old, just hearing her. I didn't get it from my oldest daughter because I wasn't there, but just hearing her say "Dada, I love you" and holding her in my arms, and my playing with her, and me being able to provide for her! You know her basic necessities and by just giving her love and just seeing her give it back to me in* return, she has really become the beacon of my joy. She's the shoulder that I stand on.

So Chavi is an especially neat young lady in my life and no matter what my circumstance has been, it's still incumbent upon me as her father to be in her life. And I'm learning, I'm really learning what it takes to be a parent, getting her up in the morning ready for school and day care and seeing to her—I'm really doing it! What gives you the most joy is experience. It's the things that you've been through and that have become unique in your life and allow you to transcend and evolve and become a totally different individual.

You know, there's a difference between knowledge and wisdom. I say most of us have knowledge, but most of us lack wisdom. It's wisdom that teaches you to use knowledge correctly. So my wisdom tells me through my experiences that you can't do certain things that you used to do. I think joy comes out of your experiences, because once you have been through some things, as tough as they may have been, you become a little bit wiser. So you learn, you learn.

When I was with the Street Warriors, one of the things that we used to say to the kids is learn, earn and return. And those three things simply mean you go to school to learn, and you go through life to learn through the experiences to better your circumstances, to gain the joy so that you can earn a decent way of life. And then it's to come back to your community, your family or society, our country, to give back to those that are less fortunate than yourself.

So I would say, learn, earn and then come back and return—give love, give caring, give trust, give honesty. And as much as possible, just be a good servant.

There is one thing one has to have: either a soul that is cheerful by nature, or a soul made cheerful by work, love, art and knowledge.

—Fredrich Nietzsche, philosopher, poet

## Case in Point

### Discover Who You Are and Nurture Relationships

WILLIAM RENZULLI, M.D.

Paducah, Kentucky

*Physician, artist, husband and father. Best way to*
*experience joy: Trust your instincts and dreams.*

William (Bill) Renzulli has successfully woven art and medicine into his life. Doing so, however, required a journey of many steps, many lessons. Learning to be centered in life through purpose, through engagement, to live life from the inside out, to trust instincts, to seize windows of opportunity, and to realize that love and friendship are one and the same were just a few of the lessons learned.

If you look closely at his paintings, you will see just two simple initials: W.R. No flourish, no M.D., just the simple signature of a man who chose to give up his successful practice of internal medicine in order to nurture minds and souls through art. Having purpose through his art is what makes him feel good. It tells him he is doing what he was intended to do.

Probably one of the first things that strikes people when they see his work is his frequent bold use of color. Initially, when he began the transition from medicine to art, he used pen and ink to create townscapes and urban landscapes, before moving primarily to watercolors. Eventually, he expanded to new media, utilizing liquid clay, pigments, pastels and fabric to create the startlingly bold and vibrant works that today define his studio and gallery showings.

It is these colorful visuals that Renzulli uses to distinguish the cover and pages of another component of his personal journey—a book written and illustrated for his three daughters and stepson. Aptly entitled *Have I Told You Today that I Love You – A father's words to his children*, the book developed out of a journal he began back when he was wrestling with what he felt was wrong in his life.

His reflections and the words he wrote came from a place deep within him, born in a spiritual awakening that literally transformed his life. The journey was a long and introspective process, not always easy, not always predictable. But over time, its experiences came together to form a central force that guided his life, enabling him to navigate a personal journey in which he found his soul.

**In Bill's words...**

*I became unhappy with what was once the reason for my life—practicing medicine. It took me a while, with several years of looking into myself and really discovering an entire interior life that I had been totally unaware of. I realized that I wanted to be an artist, to have the kind of life I thought an artist would live.*

*I think back to a biography of Thomas Merton in which the writer said, "never was someone so unafraid of his destiny." And that concept of destiny kind of grabbed me. We tend to think of destiny in terms of historical epic heroes, but in reality, that's something that each of us can shape.*

*I, too, had to learn not to be afraid. I didn't leave medicine completely but continued to work part time. I never felt like I was taking a courageous step, to me it was simply what I was supposed to do.*

*I think we all have these windows of opportunity. Sometimes they are very fleeting and the greater the opportunity, the smaller the window. It takes personal will as well as our circumstances to make that step. There are a number of factors that are in play.*

*There are folks out there who say we've got to think positively, that we can make everything happen. I think there's an element of truth to that. I think of joy as being honest with ourselves and living the kind of life we want to live. For me, it has to do with work. I think that work is at the root of all of our lives.*

*Right now, life is somewhat difficult. I am dealing with a lot of ups and downs, financial concerns in this economy because of the way I fractured my career. But I have never wavered in what I've done and what I'm doing and I am proud of what I've accomplished, proud of my children. So I'm very content. Joy is not about eternal bliss with no worries. There is a need to embrace the anxiety that comes with certain things, to accept it as part of the mix.*

*One of my daughters is an artist, one a doctor and one works in Internet marketing and makes jewelry. The son trains racehorses. I wrote "Have I Told You Today that I Love You" for them. I wasn't trying to shape their lives. They will shape them. I wanted them to discover who they were and to go with it and not be afraid.*

## Lessons from Bill's journey...

*Trust your dreams, imagination—I think that's important. Several things had to happen for me. One was not to dismiss the idea of painting out of hand as ridiculous. I could always paint on Sundays, etc. I didn't have to leave medicine, but I had to validate those feelings. They're mine, so they must mean something. That was an important step, to give them credence.*

*Nurture your mind and soul—I did a lot of reading. I went to the library and literally walked the shelves. I found reading biographies, Thomas Merton, Rilke, Aldous Huxley, helpful, not specifically for what they were, but to see how they grabbed hold of their own lives. If there's something you really enjoy doing, if you enjoy walking in the woods, or you're in the city and you love the vibrancy of the city, get in your car, take your camera. Don't just sit in your chair. Do those little simple things that give you pleasure, that nurture those feelings that you have.*

*Find God—That's what started me on this whole journey. I was not raised in a church but my first wife came from a family that went to church every Sunday, and so we did. For me, it was a hollow exercise and I decided if there is a God and this God is everything that people say he or she is, why don't I know it? Is he a secret? So I set out to see if I could find faith. In the end, I searched for God and found my soul. Since then I've come to accept that I don't know if there's a God, if there's not a God, if there's some supernatural being. To me, it's the mystery that becomes God. I guess the message is to not just take what you read and hear as the truth. Each of us will find it in a different way. No one knows more about God than you do.*

*Value and nurture relationships with others, whether a romantic relationship or with a friend. Caring about others is part of a relationship and it is in the relationships, I think, that people find joy.*

## Food for Thought

***Spirituality feeds life*** from the inside out. Shaped by the experience of the senses, spirituality draws from all that vision reveals and that intelligence explores. It is a mind clearing awareness that allows us to both listen and hear, to know not only who we are, but who we want to be.

***Spirituality is a recurrent journey*** and process of self-discovery, a search for true self, for values, for purpose and meaning in life. Gardens of meditation are a starting place. Connections with lives of others, a power greater than oneself, the essence of being, with divine reality, are its characteristics and fulfillment.

***Spirituality is nourishment of the soul***—the ultimate sweet spot of existence.

# Finistère

A usual and sufficient way to signal the conclusion of a book is simply to say *Finis*. According to the dictionary, *Finis* means exactly that: finish, end, termination, close. Yet none of these feels appropriate here. Given a choice of words that better represent the conversations of these pages, I prefer *Finistère*.

Derived from the Latin *finis terrae*, finistère literally means *end of the earth*—a place where pilgrims, tourists, artists and lovers of the tides stand before the sea and watch the sun set over tomorrow's horizons. In Spain, Cape Finisterre, as the country's westernmost point, is renowned as "the edge of the world." In France, the wild and rocky Finistère coastal area of Brittany points toward the Atlantic and is commonly referred to as the "head/end of the world," a moniker that it shares with Land's End of Cornwall, England.

Finistère represents an ending that is also a beginning. So, too, the words in these pages are simply starting points in a great and wonderful journey that reaches end points, but not an end. They are written in the hope that the stories shared, the thoughts and examples given, will serve you well, take you to new places, places that are both endings and beginnings.

That is the fun part of our continuing exploration of life's many sweet spots. Learning where they are, what makes them sweet and how we might best tap into their life enriching elixir is a process that begins only when we reach the observation posts of our own shores of life and pause to look out on all that is there before us.

Have you, through the journey of these pages:

- Understood more fully the sweet side of nature, and made your own connection with living things?

- Considered the healing powers of water, picked out your own stream or pond or rock by the sea and let yourself be calmed simply by being there?

- Looked up at night and seen the brilliance of more than the stars?

- Discovered the energy of color and light and opened your eyes to its insight?

- Heard the sounds of silence and life and moved to their rhythm and the spirits they express?

- Touched the floor of the earth and found calmness, tasted its fruits and detected flavors of pure delight?

- Put on the hat of the cat and opened your mind to wonder, turned expectations and memories into creative expressions?

- Realized all that you might give of yourself while finding ways to lighten the lives of others?

- Found awe in the majesty of a tiny flower and fed your soul with the wisdom and meaning of the universe?

The word *finistère* succeeds through both its literal and figurative meanings. Someday, perhaps, we may visit the Finistère of Brittany, or any other head/ end point of land closer to home. Frankly, it doesn't really matter if we set foot and eyes upon their literal grounds. Life is absolutely full of destination sweet spots. They are places of all sorts and numbers whose sweetness is in their finding, in the ways in which we make them our own and fix our sights on their vast and unbounded horizons.

So here's to our continuing journey of discovery. May its path lead you around the corner, over virtual mountains and across the seas to a place known more for its horizons than its shores. May it take you to a new recognition and enjoyment of life's essentially countless sweet spots—just waiting to be had by all.

# More to Explore

Enjoy browsing in this compendium of listings and Internet links to resources, destinations and activities that further support each Case in Point narrative. See them as ways to help open the doors of learning, to stretch our minds and spark our imaginations. Knowledge is an important first step in the journey to joy.

## PART I: DRAWING ON NATURE
### Barbara Parsons:
### Reawaken through Flowers

### Chicago Botanic Garden

www.chicagobotanic.org

Situated on nine islands surrounded by lakes in Glencoe, Illinois, this 385-acre garden with 26 display gardens and four native habitats is a preeminent center for learning and scientific research. Its programs are designed to deliver the therapeutic benefits of gardening activities that build on the belief that plants help promote healing, well-being, physical growth and emotional strength.

### Horticultural Society of New York

www.hsny.org

Offering a wide range of programs that use horticulture to provide job training, science and literacy learning, the Horticultural Society of New York is a multidisciplinary cultural and social service resource in mid-town Manhattan. It is particularly known for its horticultural therapy programs offered to families and children in underserved neighborhoods, adults with special needs and at-risk children, as well as its jail-to-street GreenHouse program on Rikers Island, designed to facilitate the mental and emotional healing of incarcerated men and women.

**Sunflower Lovers**

www.sunflowerlovers.com

Filled with sunflower facts and trivia, as well as "how to grow" tips and links to other sunflower sites of interest, this delightful website is enjoyed especially by recreational growers and fans of this ever popular flower. Professionals and those interested in more advanced information might want to visit the National Sunflower Association at www.sunflowernsa.com.

**The Touchstone Center**

www.touchstonecenter.net

The Touchstone Center for Children in New York City creates interdisciplinary arts programs that explore the role of imagination and poetic thought in learning. Founded on the belief that all persons have natural creative, imaginative and artistic capacities, its workshops and seminars for adults explore ways in which themes based on natural phenomena can strengthen and awaken our human relationship to the natural world.

### Linda Brazill and Mark Golbach: Japanese Gardens

**The Japanese Garden**

http://learn.bowdoin.edu/japanesegardens

Visit the Bowdoin College website for a virtual visit to the gardens of Japan, primarily to the historic gardens of Kyoto and its environs. Experience each garden through the medium of high-quality color images, and learn something of its history. Also included are a general bibliography, glossary, and overview of the history of early garden design, as well as a section on the basic elements of Japanese gardens and links to other reputable websites.

**Japanese Tea Garden**

www.japaneseteagardensf.com

Set on five acres in the heart of San Francisco's Golden Gate Park, this delightful Japanese Tea Garden is the oldest public Japanese-style garden in the United States. Visitors from throughout the world enjoy such classic elements as an arched drum bridge, pagodas, stone lanterns, stepping stone paths, native Japanese plants, serene koi ponds and a zen garden. Cherry blossom trees bloom throughout the garden in March and April.

## Morikami Museum and Japanese Gardens

www.morikami.org

The Morikami Museum and Japanese Gardens in Delray Beach, Florida, is a popular center for Japanese arts and culture; rotating gallery exhibitions, monthly tea ceremonies performed in its Seishin-an tea house and Japanese traditional festivals celebrated for the public several times a year top its list of offerings. The 200-acres surrounding the Morikami's two museum buildings include expansive Japanese gardens with strolling paths, tropical bonsai collection, small lakes and nature trails.

## Portland Japanese Garden

www.japanesegarden.com

Blessed with a climate much like that of central Japan, the Portland (Oregon) Japanese Garden celebrates the similar changes in weather that accompany each passing cycle of the moon with a series of five traditional festivals (*Go-Sekku*). Observed in Japan since at least the 6th century, they are celebrated at the Portland Japanese Garden as important family days, held on Sundays nearest to the traditional dates: New Year's celebration, the Doll Festival, Children's Day, the Star Festival and the Chrysanthemum Viewing Festival.

## George Schoellkopf:
## English and Conservancy Gardens

## Chase Garden

www.chasegarden.org/index.htm

Situated high on a plateau with majestic Mount Rainier rising in the distance, the Chase Garden in Orting, Washington, is a place of almost incomparable serenity and beauty. A Garden Conservancy's preservation project, it is an outstanding example of Pacific Northwest modernist garden style.

## The Garden Conservancy

www.gardenconservancy.org

A national institution established to save and preserve America's exceptional gardens for the education and enjoyment of the public, The Garden Conservancy works in partnership with individual garden owners as well as public and private organizations, providing horticultural, technical and financial expertise needed to ensure long term stewardship of natural assets so essential to the aesthetic and cultural life of our communities.

## Greenwood Gardens

www.greenwoodgardens.org

Take a tour back to an era of country estates, gentleman farmers, and elegant tea parties on wide swaths of lawn. Exquisite plantings at this Short Hills, New Jersey, garden are set against crumbling stucco walls, along set-stone pathways, and under garden statues of mystical creatures and colorful Rookwood tile. Be sure to enjoy this Garden Conservancy property's less formal ponds surrounded by a meadow of grass and wildflowers.

## Hollister House Garden

www.hollisterhousegarden.org

A classic garden in the English manner, with a loosely formal structure, informally planted in lush abundance, Hollister House Garden is set in the hills of northwestern Connecticut's Litchfield County. Open in season for the enjoyment of the public, it offers such special events as its popular Garden Study Weekend.

## Springs Romano:
## Butterfly Gardens

## Butterfly Hawaii

www.Butterflyhawaii.com

Springs Romano and her associates made a promise to help the delicate Monarch butterfly survive in Hawaii and so organized the Pulelehua Project. Butterflyhawaii. com was launched as the project's website to inform, support and connect butterfly caretakers to supportive resources and each other.

## The Butterfly Website

www.butterflywebsite.com

Said to be the oldest and largest website dedicated to butterflies and moths, this popular site features an extensive clipart collection, many photographs, videos, butterfly gardening tips, and stories about ways in which people's lives have been magically touched by butterflies.

## North American Butterfly Association

www.naba.org

The North American Butterfly Association (NABA) was formed in 1992 as a nonprofit organization for the purpose of increasing public enjoyment and conservation of butterflies. NABA focuses on the joys of non-consumptive, recreational butterflying, including gardening, observation, photography, rearing and conservation. Its flagship project, the National Butterfly Center, located in Mission, Texas, showcases live animals, plants and the winged wonders that pollinate and propagate all that grows around us.

### Wings of Hope, Inc. Butterflies
www.wingsofhopebutterflies.org

A not-for-profit environmental and community preservation organization, Wings of Hope, Inc. works with the International Butterfly Breeders Association to donate butterflies for ceremonial release in tandem with the establishment, and/or restoration of permanent butterfly habitats. Its On the Wings of Hope project provides seriously ill or at-risk individuals with exposure to butterflies as a way to begin the healing process, as well as to bring communities together after tragedy.

**Phil Douglass:**
**Touch Something Wild**

### Association of Fish and Wildlife Agencies
www.fishwildlife.org

With more than 87 million Americans who hunt, fish and enjoy other wildlife-related recreation annually, the Association of Fish and Wildlife Agencies recognizes America's fish and wildlife as belonging to all of us as a public trust. In addition to representing state agencies in Washington, D.C., it supports fish and wildlife leaders with species-based programs ranging from birds, fish habitat and energy development to climate change, wildlife action plans, conservation education, leadership training and international relations.

### Children & Nature Network
www.childrenandnature.org

The Children & Nature Network offers parents, youth, civic leaders, educators and health-care providers access to latest news and research as well as practical advice and works to reconnect our children with nature's joys and lessons, its physical and mental bounty.

### Hardware Ranch Wildlife Management Area
www.wildlife.utah.gov/hardwareranch/about.php

Run by the State of Utah, Division of Wildlife Resources, Hardware Ranch is a working ranch with the mission of enhancing big game winter range and other critical habitats while promoting year-round public access for watchable wildlife, hunting, fishing, and other outdoor recreation. Its visitor's center, outside of Hyrum in Blacksmith Fork Canyon, offers a variety of interactive programs and exhibits. Hardware Ranch also contains some 15 miles of streams and rivers with several types of trout.

### National Wildlife Federation
www.nwf.org

As the nation's largest conservation organization, the National Wildlife Federation works to inspire Americans to protect wildlife for our children's future. Programs to educate and inspire as well as to restore and maintain healthy ecosystems are designed to sustain the nature of America for the benefit of both people and wildlife.

### The Nature Connection
www.nature-connection.org

The Nature Connection brings animal and nature programs to people with limited access to the natural world. Working with at-risk youth, people with disabilities and elders, The Nature Connection, based in Concord, Massachusetts, brings together seasonal natural materials, live animals, storytelling, music and other expressive arts to heal and to teach through nature.

**Karrie McAllister:**
**Dig in the Backyard**

### Dirt Don't Hurt
www.karriemcallister.com

Karrie McAllister writes and mothers from "Small Town, Ohio," where she also doubles as the local preschool music teacher. Her blog, *Dirt Don't Hurt*, with its underlying theme of nature, of living inside and out in a world of children, tackles such subjects as hearing like an earthworm and ways to enjoy the winter solstice.

### Children's Nature Institute
www.childrensnatureinstitute.org

The Children's Nature Institute (CNI) in Los Angeles, California, fosters children's natural sense of wonderment through the use of hands-on exploration to discover the natural world, and by encouraging children to ask, "Why?" Whether through looking for worms in the dirt, examining the bark of a tree to discover a line of ants, or spraying a spider web with water to see it glisten in the sunlight, CNI helps its littlest visitor to experience nature through observation and exploration.

**National Environmental Education Foundation**
www.neefusa.org

Chartered by Congress to advance environmental knowledge and action, the National Environmental Education Foundation in Washington, DC, works with a network of health professionals, weathercasters, land managers and teachers to promote daily actions to help people live well while protecting and enjoying nature. Programs include The Children and Nature Initiative, which educates pediatric health care providers about prescribing outdoor activities to children, and Classroom Earth, to increase the environmental literacy of high school students.

### Victoria Impallomeni-Spencer: Learn from the Dolphin Spirit

**Dancing Spirits Dolphin Charters**
www.captainvictoria.com

Visit Captain Victoria's website to learn more about the many adventures she offers, including charter boat exploration of the national wildlife refuges in her Key West, Florida, backyard, communing with dolphins in their own warm water playground, and uplifting your spirits while on a Dancing Water Spirit Retreat.

**Dolphin Research Center**
www.dolphins.org

A not-for-profit education and research facility, the Dolphin Research Center in the Florida Keys rescues and rehabilitates whales and dolphins and provides a variety of educational programs that allow the public a chance to learn firsthand about the world of the dolphin. Visitors are invited to participate in such popular programs as Trainer or Researcher for a Day, Dolphin Encounter and Dolphin Dip.

**Kahua Institute**
www.kahuainstitute.com

The Kahua Institute is committed to the exploration and teaching of new ways of empowering the body through both scientific and spiritual means. Building on the word, *Kahua,* meaning "The Wisdom and Power from Within" in the ancient Hawaiian language, it offers retreats, workshops and recordings, including Kutira de Costard's "The Calling," often played by Captain Victoria while out on the water with the dolphins.

**Reef Relief**

www.reefrelief.org

Based in Key West, Florida, Reef Relief is a nonprofit membership organization dedicated to improving and protecting our coral reef ecosystem. In addition to increasing public awareness of the importance and value of living coral reef ecosystems, it seeks to increase scientific understanding and knowledge of such ecosystems. Its online blog is a rich resource of reef facts, photos, videos, news items, scientific studies and event listings.

## Ed Nicholson:
## Project Healing Waters Fly Fishing

**Federation of Fly Fishers**

www.fedflyfishers.org

Headquartered in Livingston, Montana, the Federation of Fly Fishers (FFF) is an international not-for-profit organization dedicated to the betterment of the sport of fly fishing through conservation, restoration and education. Among other goals, FFF seeks to protect threatened waters and native habitats for future generations, provide resources for fly fishing educators and professionals and build the fly fishing community by sharing knowledge and experiences.

**National Consortium for Academics and Sports**

www.ncasports.org

Located at the University of Central Florida, the National Consortium for Academics and Sports (NCAS) is an organization of some 240 colleges and universities across the 50 states and Canada that celebrates the power and appeal of sport to positively affect social change. Ed Nicholson was honored in 2010 with an NCAS civic award; his story is told in the NCAS 25th anniversary edition of "150 Heroes: People in Sport Who Make This a Better World."

**Project Healing Waters Fly Fishing, Inc.**

www.projecthealingwaters.org

Project Healing Waters Fly Fishing, Inc. is a nonprofit program dedicated to the physical and emotional rehabilitation of disabled active military service personnel and veterans through fly fishing and fly tying education and outings. Its programs are conducted at Department of Defense and Department of Veteran's Affairs hospitals across the nation with the volunteer support of the Federation of Fly Fishers, Trout Unlimited and independent fly fishing clubs.

**Trout Unlimited**

www.TU.org

Based in Arlington, Virginia, Trout Unlimited (TU) is a national organization with more than 140,000 volunteers organized into about 400 chapters from Maine to Montana to Alaska. Along with conservation professionals and scientists, TU works to conserve and assess the health of coldwater fish species throughout their native range.

### Steve Grant:
### Make the Streams Yours

**American Hiking Society**

www.americanhiking.org

Based in Silver Springs, Maryland, American Hiking Society is a national organization that works toward ensuring that hiking trails and natural places are cherished and preserved through outdoor activities, clinics and exhibits. Its signature trail awareness program, National Trails Day, inspires the public and trail enthusiasts to come together on the first Saturday of each June to celebrate trails, recognize volunteers and maintain local trails.

**American Kayaking Association**

www.americankayakingassociation.com

The American Kayaking Association helps people get into the sport of kayaking by helping them select their gear and enjoy their time on the water. Its website offers member opportunities for forums, photo galleries and postings of tips and ideas.

**Rivers, Trails, and Conservation Assistance Program**

www.nps.gov/ncrc/programs/rtca

The community assistance arm of the National Park Service, this Rivers, Trails, and Conservation Assistance Program supports community-led natural resource conservation and outdoor recreation projects. Its initiatives range from urban promenades, to trails along abandoned railroad rights-of-way, to wildlife corridors. Assistance in river conservation spans downtown riverfronts to regional water trails to stream restoration.

**Steve Grant**

thestevegrantwebsite.com

A visit to the site of this environmental journalist will take you to his own journal with photographs that recount his outdoor experiences, including observations of what is happening in the natural world.

**United States Canoe Association**

www.uscanoe.com

The USCA was founded in 1870 for the purpose of uniting all persons interested in the use of canoes and kayaks for pleasure, health or exploration. Today, it still remains essentially the same, with national canoe and kayak championships, adaptive paddling, instructor training, safety and conservation programs being among its many popular membership offerings

### Josh Simpson:
### Fuel Creative Spark with Aura of the Sky

**Art Alliance for Contemporary Glass**

www.contempglass.org

An international membership organization of contemporary glass collectors, the Art Alliance for Contemporary Glass furthers the development and appreciation of art made from glass by encouraging and supporting museum exhibitions, university glass departments as well as specialized teaching programs, regional collector groups, visits to private collections, and public seminars.

**Corning Museum of Glass**

www.cmog.org

Located in the Finger Lakes region of New York State, the Corning Museum of Glass is the world's largest glass museum, featuring 35 centuries of glass artistry, live glassblowing demonstrations, Make Your Own Glass experiences for all ages and an international Glass Market. It is also home to the Rakow Research Library, the library of record on glass and glassmaking, and The Studio, a noted glassmaking school.

**Jamestown Glasshouse**

www.jamestownglasshouse.com

Located on the site of long abandoned glass furnaces built in 1608 when the Virginia Company of London set up glassworks, this site today is an interpretive glassblowing facility. Modern-day artisans dressed in colonial glassblowing garb produce masterful pieces of glass, much as the colonists did almost 400 years ago. Glassblowing was one of the Jamestown, Virginia, colonists' first attempts at industrialization and manufacturing in America.

### Josh Simpson Website

www.joshsimpson.com

Shelburne, Massachussets, artist Josh Simpson's website not only introduces the visitor to the wide range of his contemporary glass creations, but provides insights into the intellectual curiosity and imagination that inspire his work. See Josh in action in his studio, enjoy a behind-the-scenes look at the making of a megaplanet, and find the location of his next exhibit.

### National American Glass Club

www.glassclub.org

Founded in 1933, the National American Glass Club (NAGC) supports the interests of glass collectors, scholars, dealers, artists, educators, students, all those concerned with the study and appreciation of glass. Members receive *The Glass Club Bulletin* as well as the quarterly NAGC newsletter, *Glass Shards*, with news of upcoming glass exhibits, shows and club activities.

## Judy Young:
## Bringing the Sky Down to Earth

### Adler Planetarium

www.adlerplanetarium.org

Located on Chicago's museum campus, Adler Planetarium is home to three full-size theaters, extensive space science exhibitions, and one of the world's most important antique astronomical instrument collections on display. Founded in 1930 as America's first planetarium, it is a recognized leader today in science education, with a focus on inspiring young people, particularly women and minorities, to pursue careers in science.

### Astronomy and Spirituality in Our Daily Lives

www.astronomyandspirituality.com

Learn more about astrophysicist Judy Young, Ph.D., and the Foundation for Astronomy and Spirituality, Inc. and its goals and programs. Workshops, gatherings, and retreats that blend astronomy and spirituality are posted, including weekend retreats in Amherst, Massachusetts, near the University of Massachusetts Sunwheel.

### Living Joyfully with What Is

www.livingjoyfullywithwhatis.blogspot.com

This personal blog of astrophysicist Judy Young, Ph.D., offers private thoughts on embracing life with a diagnosis of cancer, connecting with the universe, both astronomically and spiritually, as well as experiencing the sky and the seasons through stone circle calendars.

### Museum Astronomical Resource Society

www.marsastro.org

Also known as the M.A.R.S. astronomy club, the Museum Astronomical Resource Society provides club news and astronomical information to its membership and to the public. Sponsored by the Museum of Science and Industry in Tampa, Florida, the club's site offers a selection of educational activities to help explain some of the principles and phenomena in astronomy, sky charts, image archives from NASA and the Hubble Heritage Project.

### University of Massachusetts Sunwheel Home Page

www.umass.edu/sunwheel

This University of Massachusetts site explains the Sunwheel project when it was being built on campus, its design, location, latest news and projects.

PART II: TAPPING INTO OUR BODIES
## Brigitte Brüggemann:
## Making Color and Light a Medium for Joy

### Brigitte Brüggemann
www.brigittebruggemann.com

New Mexico artist Brigitte Brüggemann highlights recent watercolors, oils, pastels and giclees created "to lift your spirit and feed your soul" on this colorful website. Meet the artist, visit her studio, learn of upcoming workshops and read some of her journal writings.

### Color Basics
www.ColorBasics.com

This comprehensive educational website presents the science of color in non-technical terms, including definitions of color terms as well as an introduction to the Munsell Color System. Featuring a standardized set of colors that makes it easy for people to communicate in the language of color, the Munsell Color System is popularly used by artists, designers, photographers, printers and more.

### Society of Dyers and Colourists
www.sdc.org.uk

Located in Bradford, West Yorkshire, United Kingdom, the Society of Dyers and Colourists is an independent, educational charity devoted to advancing the science and technology of colour worldwide. Central to its work is the Colour Experience, an educational initiative that introduces people of all ages to the joy and science of colour. Enjoy workshops, talks and online resources covering such topics as colour in history, colour therapy and scientific and technologic aspects of colour, as well as a section for children covering colour in nature.

### National Gallery of Art
www.nga.gov

In addition to its many changing exhibits of paintings and sculpture, this Washington, D.C., gallery offers such installations as that of Henri Matisse's rare and fragile *papiers coupes*. By cutting colored papers into beautiful shapes, which he then arranged on white studio walls, Matisse created an environment of color that transcended the boundaries of conventional painting, drawing, and sculpture.

**Joan Tunstall:**
**See Life Twice**

### Scenic World

www.scenicworld.com.au

Scenic World offers visitors a fun, educational introduction to the World Heritage-listed Blue Mountains of Australia. Scenic walkways, railway, cableway and skyway provide easy access to the natural environment of Jamison Valley, including Three Sisters, Orphan Rock and Katoomba Falls, as well as observation of the rainforest's flora and fauna. For those too far away to make the trip firsthand, a whole beautiful land may be explored through this website's interactive adventures.

### Burnbrae Journal

www.burnbraejournal.blogspot.com

As a photographer who is quite happy to capture the beauty of a thing simply for the enrichment it gives her, Joan Tunstall loves to take a stroll with her camera in the garden and yard and post the results on this blog along with a relevant verse or reflection.

### my.nature.org

http://my.nature.org/photography

A program of The Nature Conservancy, my.nature.org/photography works to help photographers and videographers experience the vibrancy of nature through the camera lens. Through its daily nature photo feature, annual nature photography contest, photo stories and tips and techniques by Conservancy photographers, my.nature.org/photography website serves as "the intersection between you and nature."

### North American Nature Photography Association

www.nanpa.org

Based in Alma, Illinois, the North American Nature Photography Association promotes the art and science of nature photography through education, opportunity and inspiration for all interested in nature photography. Nature Photography Day, showcase competitions, annual photography summits, regional field events and road seminars are just some of its offerings.

### Weekend People

weekendpeople.blogspot.com

Another of Joan Tunstall's photography blogs, Weekend People is a gallery of many whom she caught in her camera's eye as they transformed themselves each Friday night from workers into something different. The project started when Joan was invited to join a 100 Strangers Project, but found herself too busy being a worker and too shy to ask permission and so settled for this form of street photography.

### Erin Wallace:
### Showing the Beauty of Each Moment

#### Bluebirdbaby
www.bluebirdbaby.typepad.com

This delightful blog of photographer Erin Wallace reflects the many and varied moments that she both experiences and photographs in her journey through life. Those who tune in to her regular postings may enjoy topics as diverse as "a little bit of nothing" to invitations to join in her "Eyes Open Creative Photography" six week e-course full of "everything you need to know to take your photography to the next level."

#### Photography.com
www.photography.com

Photography.com, a partner site of Photo.net, is an online source for photography articles, browsing photography articles, equipment and digital camera reviews, finding stock photography, locating a photographer or starting your own online gallery. Eight article categories range from "Five Elements of a Great Photograph" to "Restoring, Preserving and Digitizing Old Photos."

#### Photographic Society of America
www.psa-photo.org

The Photographic Society of America (PSA) is a worldwide organization for anyone interested in photography, including casual shutterbugs, serious amateurs and professional photographers. Founded in 1934, PSA has members in over 70 countries. Individual, Club and Council memberships offer such services and activities as a monthly magazine, online photo galleries, image evaluations, study groups, courses and competitions, and an annual conference.

#### Photo.net
www.photo.net

Photo.net is an online community where photographers may connect and discuss photography, explore photo galleries, share photographs, and learn more about the art of photography. Photo.net has more than 600,000 registered users working to help each other improve as photographers.

## Pam Brickell:
## Journaling to Preserve Delight

### ArtPlantae Today
www.artplantaetoday.com

ArtPlantae Today is an educational website established to increase botanical literacy by encouraging an interest in plants and nature through illustration and observation. In addition to serving as a gathering place connecting artists, educators, and naturalists, ArtPlantae offers various botanical and natural science resources of interest to artists, gardeners, naturalists, and educators.

### Nature Journaling & Art
www.creatingnaturejournals.com

As a nature artist, workshop instructor, and someone who is "obsessive about art journaling," Pam Brickell invites visitors to her blog to "stay awhile and enjoy the sights of the South Carolina Low Country." While there, enjoy some of Pam's many paintings, find out what new workshops and programs are scheduled, and check out links to other blogs and sites of interest.

### The John Muir Global Network
www.johnmuir.org

The John Muir Global Network is a portal to celebrating and encouraging environmental protection through the life of John Muir, founder of the worldwide conservation movement. Links are provided to such resources as the John Muir Collections at the Stockton, California, University of the Pacific, as well as the John Muir Mountain Day Camp in Martinez, California, where kids experience a taste of Muir's legacy through such activities as exploring nature trails, discovering local plants and animals, painting and journaling.

### Sierra Club
www.sierraclub.org/education/nature_journal.asp

Founded by John Muir, the Sierra Club is the nation's oldest and largest grassroots environmental organization. With its primary focus on protecting, strengthening and restoring natural systems such as wetlands, forests, and barrier islands, the non-profit organization offers a wealth of educational and outreach programs. Check out the website's suggestions on "Keeping a Nature Journal," inspired by Muir's journals in which he sketched and penned his observations about the beauty he saw in nature.

## Gordon Hempton:
## Listen in a Quiet Place

### Acoustic Ecology Institute
www.acousticecology.org

The Acoustic Ecology Institute is a non-profit organization based in Santa Fe, New Mexico, that provides access to news, academic research, public policy advocates, and articles and essays about sound and listening.

### Macaulay Library, Cornell Lab of Ornithology
www.macaulaylibrary.org

The Macaulay Library at the Cornell Lab of Ornithology in Ithaca, New York, is said to be the world's largest natural sound and video archive of animal behavior. Its mission is to collect and preserve recordings of each species' behavior and natural history and to make them available for research, education, conservation, zoos and aquaria, wildlife managers, publishers, the arts, and both public and commercial media.

### One Square Inch—A Sanctuary for Silence at Olympic National Park
www.onesquareinch.org

One Square Inch of Silence is an independent research project to protect and manage the natural soundscape in Olympic Park's backcountry wilderness. Located in the Hoh Rain Forest at Washington's Olympic National Park, its exact location is marked by a small red-colored stone placed on top of a moss-covered log at the end of a hike approximately two hours from the Visitor's Center above Mt. Tom Creek Meadows. Directions to the site, along with related links and news postings, may be found on this website.

### The Sound Tracker
www.soundtracker.com

The official site of Gordon Hempton, acoustic ecologist and Emmy Award-winning sound recordist, soundtracker.com serves as source for his personally signed CDs of nature and environmental sound portraits. Visitors to the site are introduced to Hempton through his biographical page and numerous posted reviews.

## Judy Dworin:
## Making Music Speak

### Avodah Dance Ensemble
www.avodahdance.org

Avodah Dance Ensemble is a modern dance company based in New York City that is dedicated to making the world a better place through dance, music and storytelling. Touring nationally, it seeks to build bridges with audiences of diverse traditions and cultures as it performs in such venues as women's prisons, concerts, spiritual services, and educational programs.

### Dance to Live
www.dancetolive.org

Dance to Live is dedicated to helping young lives find peace and joy by helping them express their feelings through dance when there are no words available. Begun as a vehicle to pass on the love of dance held by the late Michelle Parma, Dance to Live offers grants to nonprofit organizations which provide children in their care with dance therapy programs as a means of achieving connection, expression and emotional and physical wellbeing.

### Judy Dworin Performance Project
www.judydworin.org

The Judy Dworin Performance Project, Inc. is a Hartford, Connecticut-based company of performing artists who, on stage and in the community, engage in collaborative dance/theater pieces designed to speak to critical issues of social concern. Its three main program areas are its performance dance ensemble, which performs locally, regionally and internationally, its Moving Matters Residency Program, which brings movement-based multi-arts residencies into schools, correctional institutions and community centers, and its Reaching Out artist's mentoring program.

### National Coalition of Creative Arts Therapies Associations
www.nccata.org

For over 50 years, art, dance/movement, drama, music, poetry therapists, and psychodramatists have provided meaningful therapeutic opportunities for people of all ages in a wide variety of treatment settings and schools. The National Coalition of Creative Arts Therapies Associations is an alliance of professional associations representing over 15,000 individual members of six creative arts therapies associations nationwide.

## Adjei Abankwa:
## Speaking through Music and the BaoBao Festival

### BaoBao Festival

http://baobaofest.org

The BaoBao Festival, held annually in Boulder and Denver, Colorado, brings together local, national and international performers for a celebration of Africa's age-old community theater experience of gathering under the baobao or baobab tree. An icon of unity among many African communities, the baobao tree symbolizes the Festival's mission of entertaining, educating and building community through artistic performances inspired by West African tradition and culture.

### International Storytelling Center

www.storytellingcenter.net

Located in Jonesborough, Tennessee, where the storytelling revival began and each year thousands of visitors return to share the time-honored tradition, the International Storytelling Center is dedicated to inspiring and empowering people across the world to tell their stories and renew their storytelling traditions to build a better life and a better world. It does so by providing knowledge, experiences and tools to help individuals, organizations and communities tap into the power of storytelling.

### Playing for Change

www.playingforchange.com

Playing for Change is a multimedia movement created to inspire, connect, and bring peace to the world through music. It was born out of a common belief that music has the power to break down boundaries and overcome differences in backgrounds, uniting people as one human race.

### Traditional Music Society

www.traditionalmusicsociety.org

The Traditional Music Society is dedicated to the promotion of educational excellence and community cohesiveness through the study of indigenous music and dance from around the world (West Africa, South America, Central America and the Caribbean). Through music and dance, students gain a sense of group dynamics, thereby developing critical thinking, concentration and interpersonal skills.

## Tammy Hendricks:
## Making Treasures that Touch

### My Furever Friend
www.myfureverfriend.com

Tammy Hendricks creates Furever Friends to help people who have lost their best furry friend. As a canine soft sculptress, Tammy designs, sews and sculpts pet memorials using fabric, fibers and/or plush fur in the creation of fabric remembrances of four-legged family members.

### Sewing and Craft Alliance
www.gotsewing.com

The Sewing and Craft Alliance promotes the fun, relaxing and creative benefits of sewing and crafting by providing educational information and creative resources to the sewing and crafting enthusiast. It also offers opportunities for retailers and businesses in the sewing, quilting, crafting or textile industries to showcase their products and services to the creative community through advertising, sponsorships and promotions.

### The Society of Arts and Crafts
www.societyofcrafts.org

Based in Boston, Massachusetts, the Society of Arts and Crafts (SAC) encourages the creation, collection and conservation of the world of craft artists. In addition to promoting the work of over 400 craft artists in its galleries on an ongoing basis, SAC sponsors exhibitions, Artist Awards Programs and educational programming.

### Tammy Bears
www.tammybears.com

Soft sculpture artist Tammy Hendricks shows her handmade teddy bears and dogs on this site. Memory bears are made from articles of clothing, blankets, fur coats or other items that hold a place in someone's heart.

## Jim Sudal:
## Being in Touch with the Earth

### Boyce Thompson Arboretum
www.ag.arizona.edu/bta

The Boyce Thompson Arboretum is virtually a 320-acre living classroom that brings together plants from Earth's many and varied deserts and dry lands and displays them alongside unspoiled examples of the native Sonoran Desert environment. Visitors to the Arboretum, part of the University of Arizona campus near the historic copper mining town of Superior, are invited to explore its many gardens, vistas and trails, see enthralling, otherworldly shapes and forms in the Cactus Garden, and find intellectual stimulation in the Smith Interpretive Center.

## Desert Botanical Garden
www.dbg.org

Located in Phoenix, Arizona, amid the red buttes of Papago Park, the Desert Botanical Garden hosts one of the world's finest collections of desert plants, with emphasis on the Southwestern United States. Its 50 acres are home to 139 rare, threatened and endangered plant species from around the world.

## Jim Sudal Ceramic Design
www.jimsudalpottery.net

Enjoy a virtual visit to Jim Sudal's working artist studio and gallery in Scottsdale, Arizona. The gallery's desert botanical designs range from terracotta or stoneware relief tiles to pots, benches, and wall murals, each reflecting the beauty of the desert landscape through vibrant, garden-inspired colors and well-known imagery such as prickly pears, blooming aloes, and Jim's signature design—the agave.

## The Living Desert
www.livingdesert.org

This interpretive nature trail and preserve in Palm Desert, California, offers visitors an opportunity to observe some of the world's endangered desert plants and animals in a natural setting. Established by the Palm Springs Desert Museum as a means of furthering desert conservation through interpretive exhibits, research and educational programs, The Living Desert is home to some 450 species of desert animals and acres of lush botanical gardens.

## National Council on Education for the Ceramic Arts
www.nceca.net

The National Council on Education for the Ceramic Arts (NCECA), headquartered in Erie, Colorado, fosters global education and appreciation for the ceramic arts. NCECA's programs, exhibitions, publications, opportunities and resources inspire and support its national membership of artists, educators, students, individual and corporate art patrons, gallery owners, museum curators and providers of ceramic arts-related products and services.

## Michelle Krell Kydd:
## Following Your Nose

### The Fragrance Foundation
www.fragrance.org

The Fragrance Foundation was established in 1949 to develop educational programs about the importance and pleasures of fragrance for the American public. Reflecting America's position as the largest fragrance market in the world, The Fragrance Foundation today is an international membership organization based in New York City. In addition to offering one of the industry's most extensive print and video fragrance libraries, the Foundation is known for its annual "FiFi" Awards given to acknowledge and honor the creativity of the fragrance industry. In 2009, Michelle Krell Kydd's *GlassPetalSmoke* blog won second and third place in the FiFi Awards competition for "Editorial Excellence in Fragrance Coverage."

### Glass Petal Smoke
www.glasspetalsmoke.blogspot.com

Glass Petal Smoke is a blog created by Michelle Krell Kydd "out of a personal passion for all things olfactive and gustatory." Filled with photos, reflections, even recipes, it appeals to people who love food and fragrance and want to learn more about the stories of their history, myth and folklore. Its take-aways are nuggets of inspiration, joy and wonder.

### The Herb Society of America
www.herbsociety.org

Following its motto, "For Use and For Delight," The Herb Society of America focuses on educating its members and the public on the cultivation and uses of herbs. Headquartered in Kirtland, Ohio, the Society is organized into seven regional membership districts. Projects include fostering plant collections, investigating promising herb plants, and supporting an intern at the National Herb Garden, located at the National Arboretum in Washington, D.C.

### Schwab Rehabilitation Hospital Rooftop Healing Garden
www.sinai.org/rehabilitation/inpatient/rooftop_therapy.asp

A model design for meeting the unique needs of rehabilitation patients, Schwab Rehabilitation Hospital's rooftop healing garden in Chicago, Illinois, includes a vegetable garden, a stream filled with Koi, a waterfall and a children's playground. Key aspects of the garden include plants that stimulate the olfactory senses and that have tactile qualities. The waterfall and stream also serve as soothing auditory elements.

**The Sense of Smell Institute**

www.senseofsmell.org

The research and education division of The Fragrance Foundation, The Sense of Smell Institute is a one-stop resource for scientific researchers, teachers, students, journalists and the general public to obtain timely information on the sense of smell and its importance to human psychology, behavior and quality of life. Among its popular resources are its Virtual Library of Olfaction, its Science of Smell Links, Smell 101, and a section on Smell Loss Resources.

**Eric Webster:**
**Flavor and Aroma Vie with Visual Appeal**

**ECW Private Chef**

www.ecwprivatechef.blogspot.com

As both a chef and a photographer with a driving passion for both, Eric Webster keeps his *ECW Private Chef* blog as an outlet to share, experiment with and explore his ideas. Eric's thoughts on food, complemented by gorgeous full color photos, leave you with your mouth watering.

**International Association of Culinary Professionals**

www.iacp.com

The International Association of Culinary Professionals exists as a culinary crossroads for chefs, restaurateurs, foodservice operators, food writers, photographers, stylists, marketers, nutritionists and academia to share experiences and expertise in ways that lead to growth and learning. An annual conference, local and regional events, awards program and monthly speaker series are among its favorite offerings.

**Taste Society**

www.tastesociety.com

Taste Society was created by a group of food loving individuals who needed a place to chronicle their food journeys and build up a knowledge base of all known foods and related information. They invite you to share the latest foods you've eaten or recipes you've created, to try out foods others recommend, read reviews of food dishes or showcase your photos of delicious food.

PART III: STRETCHING OUR MINDS AND SOULS

## Miriam Epstein:
## Books Become Paths to Dreams

### Books to Dreams, Inc.

www.bookstodreams.org

Designed to encourage children to read by giving them books of their own to keep, Books to Dreams, Inc. is based in Manchester, Connecticut. Made possible through the support of a network of contributors and volunteers, services provided since its launch in 1996 have included distribution of books and literacy materials to low income housing areas and inner city summer school programs, to Head Start programs and other children's organizations, as well as development of permanent children's libraries in shelters and inner city schools.

### The Eric Carle Museum of Picture Book Art

www.carlemuseum.org

Founded by Eric Carle, author and illustrator of such classic children's books as *The Very Hungry Caterpillar*, the Eric Carle Museum of Picture Book Art in Amherst, Massachusetts, offers children and their families an opportunity to explore images that are both familiar and beloved. Activities and events include story time programs, films and professional development workshops, as well as an extensive collection of scholarly books on children's literature.

### Pajama Program

www.pajamaprogram.org

Fulfilling its campaign motto of "Better Bedtimes, Brighter Tomorrows," the Pajama Program delivers warm sleepwear and nurturing books to children in need. A not-for-profit organization founded in 2001, the Pajama Program interacts with thousands of children every year in its Westchester County, New York, reading centers where children participate in reading sessions and are given snacks, new pajamas and a book.

### ProLiteracy

www.proliteracy.org

Formed through the merger of Laubach Literacy International and Literacy Volunteers of America, Inc., ProLiteracy works with its members and partners, along with local, national, and international organizations and the adult learners they serve, to build the capacity and quality of programs that are teaching adults to read, write, compute, use technology, and learn English as a new language.

**Reading Is Fundamental**

www.rif.org

Reading Is Fundamental (RIF) is considered to be the largest children's literacy nonprofit in the United States. It prepares and motivates children to read by delivering free books and literacy resources to children and families who need them most, working to make reading a fun and beneficial part of everyday life. RIF's highest priority is reaching underserved children from birth to age eight.

## Tracy Kane:
### Joy Has a Tendency to Hide, Just Like the Fairies Do

**Association of Children's Museums**

www.childrensmuseums.org

In an increasingly complex world, children's museums provide a place where all kids can learn through play with the caring adults in their lives. The Association of Children's Museums seeks to strengthen and promote children's museums in the United States and throughout the globe through professional development, advocacy and such partnership initiatives as Born Learning, Playing for Keeps, Worldwide Day of Play, and Week of the Young Child.

**Center for Education, Imagination and the Natural World**

www.beholdnature.org

The Center for Education, Imagination and the Natural World at the Timberlake Earth Sanctuary in the foothills of Greensboro, North Carolina, offers programs for children and young adults to support its vision of a universe in which both the child and the earth find fulfillment—the child through discovering the wonder, beauty and intimacy of the earth, and the earth through the love and care of the growing child.

**Columbus Museum of Art's Center for Creativity**

www.columbusmuseum.org/center-for-creativity

The Columbus (Ohio) Museum of Art's Center for Creativity is a hub for experiences that foster imagination, critical thinking and innovation. People of all ages may explore, think, imagine, collaborate, play, learn, problem-solve, wonder, design and create. Programs range from working together with your family to build a giant sculpture or fort, to using one of the Center's Mac laptops and green-screen capabilities to inspire ideas.

**Fairy Houses**

www.fairyhouses.com

The Fairy Houses site features books connecting kids and nature—with a pinch of fairy magic. Hosted by artist and author, Tracy Kane, the site introduces parents and educators to the world of fairy houses, explaining why they are important, and invites membership in its Fairy Houses Club.

## Robert (Sidewalk Sam) Guillemin:
## Spreading Creativity on the Sidewalks

**Americans for the Arts**

www.artsusa.org

Americans for the Arts is the nation's leading nonprofit organization for advancing the arts in America. Working in partnership with local, state, and national arts organizations as well as government agencies, business leaders and educators, this Washington, DC-based organization seeks to create opportunities and policies for every American to participate in and appreciate all forms of the arts.

**Community Art Center**

www.communityartcenter.org

Founded in 1938 by a group of Cambridge, Massachusetts, community residents, the Community Art Center is committed to nurturing children and young adults with limited financial resources so they may achieve personal and cultural growth and have a positive impact on their world through joyful experiences in the arts.

**Creative Arts Network 4 Community Action**

www.CANCA.org

Creative Arts Network 4 Community Action (CANCA) is a Wake Forest, North Carolina-based resource for creative individuals who want to make a difference in their community. CANCA develops projects and events based on belief in the ability of individuals to take small ideas and move forward together as a powerful means of empowering and inspiring others and their communities to reach full creative potential.

**The Heidelberg Project**

www.heidelberg.org

The Heidelberg Project was started in 1986 in response to the tragic effect of the Detroit riots. Then twelve year old Tyree Guyton cleaned up vacant lots on Detroit's Heidelberg and Elba Streets and began to transform the street into a massive art environment. Vacant lots literally became "lots of art" and abandoned houses became "gigantic art sculptures." Today the Heidelberg Project is known as one of the most influential art environments in the world.

## Elizabeth St. Hilaire Nelson:
### Paper Paintings Extend Beyond Surface Image

### American Craft Council
www.craftcouncil.org

The American Craft Council, headquartered in Minneapolis, Minnesota, is dedicated to promoting understanding and appreciation of contemporary American craft. Members include artists as well as institutions and individuals with an interest in the crafts, such as teachers, collectors, gallery owners and professionals in many fields. Popular benefits include annual juried marketplaces in Baltimore, Atlanta, St. Paul and San Francisco featuring original work by more than 1,500 of the country's top contemporary craft artists.

### Art Imitates Life—Paper Paintings Collage
www.elizabethsthilairenelson.blogspot.com

This delightful blog by "paper paintings" collage artist Elizabeth St. Hilaire Nelson not only offers the viewer a glimpse of her latest creations made from torn bits of hand-made, hand-painted, and found papers, but features a new collage process video, news of collage workshops, and fun postings covering various tricks and techniques to bring your own creations to life.

### Collageart.org
www.collageart.org

The Collageart.org website provides a list of links to collage and collage-related sites, including collage artists on the internet, collage exhibition opportunities and reviews, presenters of collage workshops, books, tools, supplies and technical information.

### National Collage Society
www.nationalcollage.com

The National Collage Society, Inc. is an art foundation with individual and collage artist membership that works to foster appreciation and interest in the art medium of collage. It promotes the advancement of collage as a major art medium and assists in the education of the public through exhibits, workshops, lectures and publications.

## Marilyn Douglas:
## Tap Talents and Instincts to Volunteer

### Hospice Foundation of America

www.hospicefoundation.org

Hospice Foundation of America (HFA), based in Washington, DC, serves as an information center offering end of life care resources for patients, families and professionals. Visitors to its website are provided guidance regarding care for those with life limiting illness, kept informed about what's happening at HFA, and advised of upcoming conferences and events.

### Pet Partners

www.petpartners.org/

Dedicated to improving human health through positive interactions with animals, Pet Partners is a nonprofit organization that provides educational programs and services for volunteers and health-care professionals, as well as for individuals with disabilities. Its goal is to help people live healthier and happier lives by incorporating therapy, service and companion animals into their lives. Its Pet Partners® program is recognized as the first comprehensive, standardized training for volunteers and their pets for visiting in hospitals, nursing homes, rehabilitation centers, schools and other facilities.

### Points of Light

www.pointsoflight.org

Points of Light works to put people at the center of transforming their communities. Main initiatives of its HandsOn Network of 250 local volunteer centers across the country and around the world include generationOn, a youth service movement, as well as AmeriCorps Alums, a national service alumni network that activates the next generation of service leaders. Its Points of Light Corporate Institute enables companies to engage their employees and customers in volunteer service.

### Threshold Choir

www.thresholdchoir.org

Based in Inverness, California, the Threshold Choir is an organization of small-group, all women, choirs, dedicated to singing at bedsides, memorials and services of remembrances. In addition to providing background on the Choir's history and purpose, its website features information on where choirs are located and how to join or start a choir, as well as offering CDs of its music repertoire.

**Volunteers of America**

www.voa.org

Volunteers of America helps underserved and most vulnerable people achieve their full potential through services that promote self-sufficiency for the homeless, care for the elderly and disabled, and foster independence. Based in Alexandria, Virginia, with local offices throughout the continental United States and Puerto Rico, Volunteers of America believes that everyone has a talent to give and that tapping into people's skills and knowledge creates a more meaningful experience for the volunteer and those he or she serves.

## Lynn White:
## Turn Professional Skills into Life Skills

**American Horticultural Therapy Association**

www.ahta.org

American Horticultural Therapy Association is concerned with the promotion and development of horticultural therapy programming. Based in King Prussia, Pennsylvania, with more than 800 individuals and organizations located across the US, Canada, Japan and beyond, the nonprofit professional organization is a recognized source of information to both members and the public about the benefits of horticultural therapy.

**International Mentoring Association**

www.mentoring-association.org

The International Mentoring Association (IMA) provides mentoring support and information to professionals and interested parties to help create global communities for sharing best practices that lead to the development of effective mentoring programs. By building on strengths provided by dialogue across all settings and contexts, IMA sees mentoring as a tool for increased learning and performance.

**Mentor**

www.mentoring.org

The National Mentoring Partnership, MENTOR, works closely with a network of Mentoring Partnerships to develop and deliver resources to more than 5,000 mentoring programs and volunteer centers nationwide. Serving more than three million children in all 50 states, MENTOR promotes mentoring quality through standards, research and state-of-the-art tools.

**Sustainable Urban Landscape Information Series**

www.sustland.umn.edu/design/healinggardens.html

This highly informative site of the University of Minnesota provides information on such topics as what is a healing garden and how to design one, including pointers on specific uses, spatial layout and plant selection. Links are provided to outstanding examples of hospice gardens, including sensory gardens, meditation gardens, and gardens for the visually impaired.

**Bonnie Waldron:**
**Add a Smiley Face to Hope**

**Make-A-Wish Foundation**

www.wish.org

Since 1980, the Make-A-Wish Foundation has given hope, strength and joy to children with life-threatening medical conditions by granting wishes that typically fall into one of four categories: I wish to be…, to go…, to have…, to meet…. A network of nearly 25,000 volunteers serves as wish granters, special events assistants and in numerous other capacities.

**Mary Kaye Waldron Quality of Life Project**

www.marykayewaldron.org

Established at Boston College to assist children in Massachusetts with disabilities, the Mary Kaye Waldron Quality of Life Project was inspired by the caring presence of Mary Kaye Waldron, a student at Boston College who passed away shortly before her graduation. Sustained through contributions from the Mary Kaye Fund, the Project perpetuates Mary Kaye's vision of helping others with disabilities improve their quality of life.

**The National Children's Cancer Society**

www.nationalchildrenscancersociety.com

Headquartered in St. Louis, Missouri, The National Children's Cancer Society works at home and abroad to improve the quality of life for children with cancer and their families by serving as a financial, emotional and educational resource for those in need at every stage of illness and recovery. Its "Beyond the Cure" survivorship program assists survivors and their parents in preparing for life after cancer.

**Twilight Wish Foundation**

www.twilightwish.org

Twilight Wish Foundation, the first national senior wish-granting organization, was formed in 2003 when Cass Forkin noticed several elderly women struggling to piece together change to pay their bill at a Doylestown, Pennsylvania diner and Cass anonymously paid it for them. Dedicated to the needs of the elderly, Twilight Wish Foundation has a vision of making the world a nicer place to age, one wish at a time.

### Herb Ouida:
### Preserve Legacy with Gifts of Help and Hope

**Association of Small Foundations**

www.smallfoundations.org

The Association of Small Foundations (ASF) is a national membership organization of nearly 2,200 small foundations with few or no staff. ASF works to enhance the power of philanthropy by providing donors, trustees and professionals with information and peer learning opportunities, inspiration and connections to some of the most passionate members of the philanthropic community in the country.

**Philanthropedia**

www.myphilanthropedia.org

A division of GuideStar, USA, Philanthropedia provides research and reviews on over 400 top nonprofits across 32 causes. Its philosophy is built on the belief that it is important to follow your heart when deciding where to give and to pick a cause or issue that you care deeply about, whether it is to help change the life of a child, improve the environment, or help someone less fortunate have a second chance.

**Todd Ouida Children's Foundation**

www.mybuddytodd.org

The Todd Ouida Children's Foundation was created following September 11, 2001, in order to celebrate Todd's life and preserve a meaningful legacy. Born out of Todd's own struggle with childhood anxiety, the Foundation exists to financially support psychological services and other mental health initiatives for children of families in need.

**The Survivor's Club**

www.thesurvivorsclub.org

Popularly known as the Place for Surviving and Thriving, The Survivor's Club is dedicated to helping people in crisis survive and thrive. It does so by offering information to guide one through adversity and to provide practical tools to encourage the support of family and friends.

### Carol Kortsch:
### Be Awed in the Wonder of the Flower

**The Bloedel Reserve**

www.bloedelreserve.org

Created simply to provide people with a chance to enjoy nature through quiet walks in the gardens and woodlands, the Bloedel Reserve on Bainbridge Island, Washington, offers approximately 150 acres of either second growth forest or altered landscapes, including various gardens, ponds and meadows. Henry Domke, M.D., physician and artist specializing in healthcare fine art, considers it to be "the perfect healing garden."

**Cheyenne Botanic Gardens**

www.botanic.org

Located in Lion's Park, Wyoming's largest municipal park, Cheyenne Botanic Gardens is the largest public botanic garden in Wyoming. Begun in 1977 as the Olympic Community Solar Greenhouse, it was one of the nation's first large scale solar greenhouses built by volunteers. The property is rich with many individual gardens and attractions, including a children's garden and a labyrinth for quiet contemplation.

**The Joy Garden**

www.thejoygarden.com

This charming New Freedom, Pennsylvania, Victorian garden and conservancy was created as a special place where people could visit and find joy in just being. Nancy and Tim Swingler developed the private property with the hope of bringing joy to others as they celebrate life and its special moments. Visitors to the grounds and the tea house, which are generally open to the public two to three days a week, are invited to enjoy tea in the Conservatory overlooking the garden and fountain or to come for personal retreat and to meditate in the prayer garden.

**Peace Awareness Labyrinth & Gardens**

www.peacelabyrinth.org

Built on the grounds of a classic turn-of-the-century Italian Renaissance mansion, Peace Awareness Labyrinth & Gardens is a mid-city oasis where people can relax in nature without leaving the city of Los Angeles. Visitors may walk the hand-carved stone outdoor labyrinth. Peace and quiet are certain to be found in the meditation garden, a sanctuary to reflect and recharge in natural beauty with the sounds of water all around.

## Anne Rowthorn:
## Feel the Rhythm of the Universe

**Anne Rowthorn**

www.annerowthorn.com

As a writer specializing in ecology and eco-spirituality, Anne Rowthorn posts word of her latest books on this website as well as of workshops, retreats and other eco-events built around nature as "the world's best tranquilizer."

**Spirituality & Practice**

www.SpiritualityandPractice.com

A website of resources for spiritual journeys, *SpiritualityandPractice.com* offers ideas on how to find and get the most from books, films, prayers, imagery, art, music, and more. In its annual ranking of the 50 best spiritual books of the year, *SpiritualityandPractice.com* selected Anne Rowthorn's *Your Daily Life Is Your Temple* as a best book of 2006.

**The Trust for Public Land**

www.tpl.org

The Trust for Public Land (TPL) is a national, nonprofit, land conservation organization that conserves land for people to enjoy for generations to come. Its website is rich with inspiring stories of preservation initiatives in parks, community gardens, historic sites, rural lands, and other natural places. Refer to it regularly for ideas on special places to visit, places perfect for hiking, reflection and getting in touch with yourself.

**Abdul Muhammad:**
**Tough Love Speaks Volumes**

### National Center for Fathering

www.fathers.com

The National Center for Fathering provides research-based training and resources to reverse the cultural trend toward fatherlessness by helping dads learn how to be fathers. The Center reaches more than one million dads annually through seminars, training, the WATCH D.O.G.S. (Dads of Great Students) program and a daily radio program.

### National Fatherhood Initiative

www.fatherhood.org

National Fatherhood Initiative has a goal of improving the well-being of children by increasing the proportion of children growing up with involved, responsible and committed fathers. To accomplish this, it works with local, state and national organizations throughout the country to reach fathers at their point of need with skill-building resources to help them be the best dads that they can be.

### National Responsible Fatherhood Clearinghouse

www.fatherhood.gov

Funded by the Office of Family Assistance, The National Responsible Fatherhood Clearinghouse is a national resource for fathers, practitioners, programs, states and the public-at-large who are serving or interested in supporting strong fathers and families through curriculum-based or other programs. Its Fatherhood Buzz is a Clearinghouse initiative designed to support neighborhood barbershops in connecting dads with local resources to help build strong families.

### National Association of Mothers' Centers

www.motherscenter.org

The National Association of Mothers' Centers recognizes the challenges, realities and value of mothering by offering programs that give a sense of camaraderie, peer support, empathy, information and resources for moms and other caregivers. These include referrals to professionals and organizations that serve the needs of mothers and families, as well as educational materials about parenting, advocacy and work/life programs.

## William Renzulli, M.D.:
### Discover Who You Are and Nurture Relationships

### Healthcare Fine Art

www.healthcarefineart.com

Henry Domke, M.D., creates nature art for healthcare. His photographic work, which is known for its fresh views of nature, can be found in hospitals and healthcare facilities across the country. After working as a family physician in Jefferson City, Missouri, for 25 years, Domke gave up his medical practice to turn the beauty he sees in nature into artistic images that inspire and heal.

### National Art Education Association

www.arteducators.org

A leading membership organization for more than 20,000 visual arts teachers, art museum educators, professors, students and artists, the National Art Education Association advances visual arts education to fulfill human potential and promote global understanding. Mentoring, networking and art education conferences are just a few of its professional initiatives.

### Reflections on a Life in Medicine, Art, and Pasta

www.williamfrenzullimd.blogspot.com

After 31 years of pursuing two careers, medicine and art, Dr. William Renzulli retired from medicine to spend full time working at his art. In addition to posting his latest paintings on this blog, he shares his thoughts and reflections on topics as diverse as linguini with eggplant, mushrooms and sundried tomatoes, and love.

### Thomas Merton Center

www.merton.org

The Thomas Merton Center at Bellarmine College, Louisville, Kentucky, is the official repository of the artistic estate of the Trappist monk and author, Thomas Merton. The Center serves as a regional, national, and international resource for scholarship and inquiry on Merton and his works, including the classic *Seven Storey Mountain, No Man Is an Island* and *New Seeds of Contemplation,* as well as on the ideas he promoted: contemplative life, spirituality, ecumenism, East-West relations, personal and corporate inner work, peace, and social justice.

# In Their Words

**Chapter One—The Earth**

Barbara Parsons, Kent, Connecticut
Linda Brazill and Mark Golbach, Madison, Wisconsin
George Schoellkopf, Washington, Connecticut
Springs (Christine) Romano, Kahaluu, Hawaii
Phil Douglass, Hooper, Utah
Karrie McAllister, Orville, Ohio

**Chapter Two—The Sea**

Victoria Impallomeni-Spencer, Key West, Florida
Ed Nicholson, Port Tobacco, Maryland
Steve Grant, Farmington, Connecticut

**Chapter Three—The Sky**

Josh Simpson, Shelburne, Massachusetts
Judy Young, Amherst, Massachusetts

**Chapter Four—The Vista of Sight**

Brigitte Brüggemann, Rowe, New Mexico
Joan Tunstall, Lawson, Australia
Erin Wallace, Damariscotta, Maine
Pam Johnson Brickell, Bluffton, South Carolina

**Chapter Five—The Pulse of Sound**

Gordon Hempton, Port Angeles, Washington
Judy Dworin, Bloomfield, Connecticut

Adjei Abankwa, Boulder, Colorado

## Chapter Six—The Essence of Touch

Tammy Hendricks, Blanchard, Oklahoma
Jim Sudal, Scottsdale, Arizona
Michelle Krell Kydd, Ann Arbor, Michigan
Eric Webster, Saint Helena, California

## Chapter Seven—Wonder and Imagination

Miriam Epstein, Manchester, Connecticut
Tracy Kane, Lee, New Hampshire
Robert Guillemin, Boston, Massachusetts
Elizabeth St. Hilaire Nelson, Longwood, Florida

## Chapter Eight—The Heart of Giving

Marilyn Douglas, Simsbury, Connecticut
Lynn White, Willimantic, Connecticut
Bonnie Waldron, Boston, Massachusetts
Herb Ouida, River Edge, New Jersey

## Chapter Nine—The Spirituality of Life

Carol Kortsch, Radnor, Pennsylvania
Anne Rowthorn, Salem, Connecticut
Abdul Muhammad, Newark, New Jersey
William Renzulli, Paducah, Kentucky

# About the Images

Images on the pages of *Life Is Full of Sweet Spots* are grayscale reproductions of original photographs, screened to provide just a whisper of their original full color imagery. To view more of an artist's work, visit his or her website as noted (when available) in the following summaries.

## Chapter 1: The Earth

**"Sunkissed"**—Known for her work in oils and watercolors, artist Diane Morgan of the Los Angeles area of California, uses powerful lighting effects, reflected surfaces, exaggerated contrasts and unusual compositions to transform simple everyday life into un-ordinary, not-so-still life. In "Sunkissed," she captures the light on the sunflower's open and happy face, inviting the viewer to take a closer look. More of Diane's work may be seen at www.DianeMorganPaints.com.

**"Buddha"**—Mark Golbach of Madison, Wisconsin, makes art with both his garden and camera. His love of photography actually began back when he was a struggling art student, but took off years later when, along with his wife, Linda Brazill, he began to create and document the evolution of their Japanese-style garden. Today, he has shifted his photographer's focus to the fine art and lines of the garden's content, be it the delicate beauty of a lotus blossom or the wise face of the stone Buddha that oversees the place that Mark defines as his artist's studio. More of Mark's photos may be seen on the couple's blog, www.eachlittleworld.typepad.com.

**"Pond Frog"**—Norlyn Wade is an artist of whimsy and delight, which she demonstrates in her "Pond Frog" portrayal of this favorite and enchanted creature with its long legs, and smiley face. The brilliant and varied greens of frogs in her pond, along with the colors and scenic beauty that surrounds her California home in the Santa Cruz mountains, inspire her to celebrate the joy of life. Her paintings of pond frogs are enchanting and full of mischief. They also, as Norlyn sees and paints them, bring smiles to the faces of her young son, Mark, and grandson, Ryan, both of whom left this earth far too soon and whom she knew would want their own personal frogs to keep in their pockets. More of Norlyn's work may be seen at www.norlynstudio.com.

## Chapter 2: The Sea

**"Between the Waves"**—Environmental artist Apollo first started painting dolphins when he moved to Maui in 1980. Since that time he has continued to portray the popular and beloved dolphin, along with other marine life, to boost appreciation and understanding of the ocean and its creatures. Drawing on his love of snorkeling and diving, he combines the style of realism with a touch of animation, as seen in his acrylics painting, "Between the Waves." More of Apollo's work may be seen at www.apolloworldgalleries.com.

**"Wood Duck"**—Hebron, Connecticut, photographer Julie Carlson loves to photograph most anything in nature, but her obsession is birds. It is a passion that has driven her and her husband, Bob, to spend weekends and vacations shooting— sometimes from a duck blind on the Sound, other times from her backyard deck, often as far away as the hummingbird havens of Buenaventura, Ecuador. While she has entered the award winning results in competitions and made them available on annual calendars, she mostly just enjoys the challenge of catching their finery and antics in unforgettable photographic images. More of Julie's work may be seen on www.mary-oconnor.com/photos.html.

## Chapter 3: The Sky

**"The Trees Only Dance at Night"**—Inspiration for the work of New Jersey artist Lance Blum comes from his experiences in life, which he sees as a magical journey. Typically celebrating nature and spiritual yearnings, his paintings use symbolic images that the viewer can internally recognize and hopefully share. Seeing each sunrise and sunset as unique with colors that sparkle and change daily, he creates images that reflect his feelings about these scenes. More of Lance's work may be seen at www.lanceblum.com.

**"Blue Moon"**—Pam Johnson Brickell of Bluffton, South Carolina, is obsessive about plein air art journaling. Wanting to do more than simply create images of birds or other subjects in their environment, she chooses to format her paintings similar to the pages of her nature journal, combining imagery with specific calligraphic information. Dedicated to Apollo II astronaut and moon walker, Neil Armstrong, "Blue Moon" reflects her sentiment of happiness that the universe lined up with Armstrong's passing so that he could be laid to rest during a blue moon. Enjoy more of Pam's work on www.creatingnaturejournals.com.

## Chapter 4: The Vista of Sight

**"Tree of Life"**—Brigitte Brüggemann's work is inspired by nature and her connection to a spiritual reality. Her work, such as "Tree of Life," usually has a source in her conscious or unconscious life. Painting in oils, pastels and watercolors, she uses symbolic abstraction as her own personal visual language, trying to make the invisible visible through color and lyrical abstractions. Visit www.brigittebruggemann.com to see her work in the vivid colors for which they are known.

**"Maple Leaves"**—Joan Tunstall lives in the town of Lawson, in the Blue Mountains of Australia, an area so incredibly beautiful that when in 2007 she had a year off work, she decided to explore the mountains by walking each day, taking photographs and learning to name the flowers and birds. Naming the trees continues to elude her, she says, but that doesn't stop her from continuing to capture their images and reflecting on God's word. Follow her posts over time and enjoy the sight of nature's living things as they turn from the pale delicate colors of spring into bold autumn farewells: www.burnbraejournal.blogspot.com and www.bluemountainsjournal.blogspot.com.

## Chapter 5: The Pulse of Sound

**"Becoming as One"**—There is a moment at which it all comes together—the bow, the strings, the concentration of the mind, the beautiful sound. Damariscotta, Maine, photographer, Erin Wallace, has a way of seeing and capturing those pieces and life moments. More of her photos may be seen on her blog, www.bluebirdbaby.typepad.com or her Flickr photostream, www.flickr.com/photos/biggoofydog.

**"Performance"**—Photographer Erin Wallace of Damariscotta, Maine, believes that when life is simple, you are able to see the joy and beauty in everything. Connections of the movement of dance, music and play are simply one small part of her larger creative vision. For more of Erin's thoughts and photos, visit her blog, www.bluebirdbaby.typepad.com.

## Chapter 6: The Essence of Touch

**"Bentley"**—Soft sculpture artist Tammy Hendricks of Blanchard, Oklahoma created this little teddy baby in memory of her great nephew, Bentley, who lived only seven hours after birth due to a rare heart condition. She hand painted Bentley's footprints on the pad and weighted the bear to be Bentley's weight. Made in part from fur and a blanket Bentley was held in, he is dressed in Bentley's jammies. More of Tammy's creations may be seen at www.tammybears.com.

**"Butterflies and Bees"**—Scottsdale, Arizona, artist Jim Sudal is widely recognized for his Southwest desert inspired ceramics, notably for such handmade sculpted stoneware murals as this one of a kind piece that graces the walls of Muhammad Ali's home. Drawn by the beauty of the desert landscape, Jim reflects its beauty in his work through the use of such vibrant desert imagery as his signature agave and the prickly pear, as chosen for the Ali piece. Layered in its cactus blossoms are hundreds of tiny clay butterflies and bees, a tribute to the fighter's iconic saying, "Float like a butterfly, sting like a bee." More of Jim's work may be viewed at www. jimsudalpottery.net.

## Chapter 7: Wonder and Imagination

**"Butterfly Dance"**—Mary O'Connor of Old Lyme, Connecticut, puts a camera in her pocket whenever she walks where she might see a simple wonder—which is most everywhere. Nature and wildlife are a particular fascination, leading her to snap the shutter on everything from leopards hiding in the grasses of Africa's Serengeti plains to butterflies marking the end of summer as they dance on purple thistle tops. More of her photos may be seen at www.mary-oconnor.com/africaphotos.html.

**"Trevor"**—Longwood, Florida, collage artist Elizabeth St. Hilaire Nelson delivers a world of wonder through the imaginative assembly of tiny bits of paper, colorful scraps of found and cherished items, and splotches of paint and glitter, all arranged to form treasured fine art paintings of paper. To visit her online gallery at www. elizabethsthilairenelson.blogspot.com is to open the doors to a place where such whimsical creatures as Trevor, the Florida box turtle, Jersey Cow Girl, Chi Hua Hua, and a pair of parrots names Hoo Hoo 1 and Hoo Hoo 2 never fail to prompt a smile and delight.

## Chapter 8: The Heart of Giving

**"Riley"**—Terry Logozzo of Lyman, New Hampshire, knows firsthand how much the presence of a dog can soothe and cheer those whom they accompany or visit. As one who has never strayed far from having a four legged friend such as Riley close by her side, Terry knows just how to see and record their soulful expression and personality through her camera's lens. Her photos are portraits of love.

**"Meditation among the Daisies"**—Abby Schultz of Madison, Wisconsin, describes herself as "by no means a professional photographer—just someone who enjoys letting her creativity loose." An event planner by profession, Abby subscribes to the saying that it's all in the details, whether for an event, a photo, or life in general. Capturing life's little moments is most important to her, something she manages perfectly in this photo for a yoga instructor's meditation class, beautifully depicting the asana practice of bringing breath and focus to long held postures.

## Chapter 9: The Spirituality of Life

**"Path through the Forest"**—Green Valley, Arizona, artist and author Lois Griffel uses color and light to capture the legacy of Earth's world. Her impressionist paintings are invitations to the viewer to travel with her into the setting, down the forest path, as she has done here in this oil. Art, she says, "lifts the spirit and reminds me of the beauty of the world. Painting gives me the opportunity to share that feeling." More of Lois's work is shared at www.loisgriffel.com.

**"Cathedral Woods"**—Created by award-winning textile and mixed media artist Hilary Rice of Stirling, Ontario, Canada, "Cathedral Woods " is from Hilary's "Rare Reflections" series of quiet and contemplative works. In keeping with her aim of creating art as an oasis with the potential to transform, this hand painted and embroidered linen textile piece draws its inspiration from Hilary's feelings of new wonder and closeness with the Creator felt while walking in the woods. Text by Rumi, stitched in gold thread onto the background, along with the use of the Chartres Labyrinth imagery, refers to the many paths we take, but with a goal that is one. Hilary's skills as an artist are self taught, fed by her love of the feel of fibres, the shine of silks, and in her more recent work, the texture created from melting synthetic materials. Photo provided courtesy of Hilary Rice © 2010, www.mestudios.ca.

# Notes

## Introduction

1. The world as a circle: Margaret Fortunato Galt, "Nature as Teacher and Guide: Two Interlocking Poetry Writing Exercises," *The Alphabet of the Trees* (New York: Teachers & Writers Collaborative, 2000), pp. 249-260.

2. "On Language: Sweet Spot": William Safire, *New York Times*, April 1, 2007

## Chapter 1: The Earth

1. Permission from Ralph Waldo Emerson to use piece of land: Richard J. Schneider, "Thoreau's Life," The Thoreau Society, 2006, www.thoreausociety.org/_news_abouthdt.htm.

2. "life-everlasting, johnswort and goldenrod": Henry David Thoreau, *Walden* (Boston: Houghton Mifflin, 1906), p. 126.

3. Nature as a force that will steer us right: Henry David Thoreau, *Walking* (Boston: Beacon Press, 1991), p. 85.

4. Spend four hours a day: Ibid., p. 74.

5. Soft fascination, study by Rachel Kaplan, Stephen Kaplan, University of Michigan: *Michigan Today News-e*, John Lofy (Ann Arbor, MI: University of Michigan, 2005). University of Michigan, accessed August 23, 2012, http://michigantoday.umich.edu/06/Fal06/story.html?awalk.

6. Natural connection with living things: Richard Ryan, University of Rochester (2010, June 4). "Spending time in nature makes people feel more alive, study shows." *ScienceDaily*, accessed August 23, 2012, www.sciencedaily.com/releases/2020/06/100603172219.htm.

7. "Nature calmed me...excited my senses.": From LAST CHILD IN THE WOODS by Richard Louv. © 2005, 2008 by Richard Louv. Reprinted by permission of Algonquin Books of Chapel Hill. All rights reserved.

8. Only write poems and be in the garden: Genine Lentine in Stanley Kunitz with Genine Lentine, *The Wild Braid* (New York: W.W. Norton & Company, 2005), p. 9. Reprinted by permission of the publisher.

9. Tendency to brush against the flowers: Ibid., p. 53.

10. A kind of relationship that could be transacted wholly without language: Ibid., p. 53.

11. Even the snakes brought satisfaction: Ibid., p.53.

12. "not only sharing the planet, but also sharing my life…": Ibid.,p. 54.

13. Barbara Parsons: Interview by the author, May 2008.

14. Traits favored by Japanese theme garden judges: *Sukiya Living, Journal of Japanese Gardening* (JOJG), "North America Top 25 rankings," http://rothteien.com/topics/na-survey.htm.

15. Linda Brazill and Mark Golbach: Interview by the author, September 2009; see also Each Little Word blog at eachlittleworld.typepad.com.

16. Seeds, plants, obey the laws of nature: Russell Page, "In Search of Style," *The Writer in the Garden*, edited by Jane Garmey (Chapel Hill, NC: Algonquin Books of Chapel Hill, 1999), p. 99.

17. "Green fingers extensions of verdant heart": Ibid., p. 99.

18. "The fugitive pleasure which gardening affords…never allows the garden to appear static or disorganized": Ibid., p. 100.

19. George Schoellkopf: Interview by the author, August 2009; see also http://hollisterhousegarden.org.

20. 12,000 known species in North America: Lorus Milne and Margery Milne, University of New Hampshire, *National Audubon Society Field Guide to North American Insects & Spiders* (New York, Albert A. Knopf, 1980, 1996) p. 697.

21. Springs Romano, butterfly gardens: Interview by the author, September 2009; see also www.ButterflyHawaii.com.

22. Shinrin-yoku—forest bathing: Tsinetsugu Y, Park BJ, Miyazaki Y, Forestry and Forest Products Research Institute, "Trends in research related to 'Shinrin-yoku' (taking in the forest atmosphere or forest bathing) in Japan," National Center for Biotechnology Information, U.S. National Library of Medicine, Abstract, www.ncbi.nlm.nih.gov/pubmed/19585091.

23. Phil Douglass: Interview by the author, December 2010; see also http://wildlife.utah.gov/blog/author/phil-douglass.

24. Mary Oliver, *The Truro Bear and Other Adventures* (Boston, MA: Beacon Press, 2008).

25. Karrie McAllister: Interview by the author, September 2009; see also *Dirt Don't Hurt* at www.karriemcallister.com.

26. Sharon Lovejoy, *Sunflower Houses: Inspiration from the Garden—A Book for Children and Their Grown-Ups* (New York, NY: Interweave Press, Inc., Workman Publishing Company, Inc., 1991).

27. "I love that quiet time when nobody's up": Olivia Newton-John quoted in "Showing Her Mettle," Jill Smolowe, *People Magazine*, September 25, 2000, www.people.com/people/archive/article/0,,20132405,00.html

## Chapter 2: The Sea

1. M.G. Harasewych and Fabio Moretzsohn, *The Book of Shells, A Life-Size Guide to Identifying and Classifying Six Hundred Seashells* (Chicago, IL: The University of Chicago Press, Ivy Press Limited, 2010), p. 9.

2.  Represents less than only one percent: *Boston Globe* review of *The Book of Shells, A Life-Size Guide to Identifying and Classifying Six Hundred Seashells* at University of Chicago Press Books, www.press.uchicago.edu/ucp/books/book/chicago/B/bo8748568.html.

3.  Number of bivalves exceeded only by vast armies of insects: Solomon H. Katz, editor-in-chief, *Encyclopedia of Food & Culture* (New York: Charles Scribner's Sons, 2003), www.enotes.com/food-encyclopedia/mollusks.

4.  "stands out from the common disorder of perceptible things": Paul Valéry, *The Collected Works of Paul Valery, Vol. 13, Aesthetics,* translated by Ralph Manheim (© 1964 by Bollingen Foundation). Reprinted by permission of the publisher.

5.  "It delights my eyes and fingers": Ibid.

6.  "A strange union of ideas...law and exception": Ibid.

7.  "Living nature": Ibid.

8.  "Break the sun's rays into their wave lengths": Ibid.

9.  "Fragment of the foundations of a continent": Ibid.

10. Shells she greedily collected: Anne Morrow Lindbergh, *Gift from the Sea* (New York: Random House, Inc, Vintage Books Edition, 1965), p. 113. Reprinted by permission of the publisher.

11. "One can collect only a few...": Ibid, p. 114.

12. Ghost crab, estimated to travel at as much as 4.4m/sec.: Malcolm Burrows, Graham Hoyle, *The Mechanism of Rapid Running in the Ghost Crab, Ocypode Ceratophthalma.* (Department of Biology, University of Oregon, Eugene, Oregon, and Hawaiian Institute of Marine Biology, Coconut Island, Hawaii, 1972), *The Journal of Experimental Biology* Website, http://jeb.biologists.org/content/58/2/327.abstract?sid=96885229-1d1b-49ca-86bf-b5686edbe2f7.

13. Giant clam, *Tridacna Gigas*: the website for the *National Geographic,* accessed September 25, 2012, http://animals.nationalgeographic.com/animals/invertebrates/giant-clam.

14. Popular shelling beaches compiled from multiple sources: Steve Millburg, "Top 10 Shelling Beaches," *Coastal Living,* March 2007, www.coastalliving.com/travel/top-10/top-10-shelling-beaches-00400000000216; also *Beach Bum Paradise*, "Ten Best Beaches for Finding Shells," www.beachbumparadise.com/10-best-beaches-for-finding-shells.

15. Captain Victoria Impallomeni-Spencer: Interview by the author, November 2010; see also www.captainvictoria.com.

16. *The Hidden Messages in Water*, Masaru Emoto, English translation by David Thayne (Hillsboro, OR: Beyond Words Publishing, Inc., 2004).

17. *The Secret Life of Water*, Masaru Emoto, English translation by David A. Thayne (Hillsboro, OR: Beyond Words Publishing, Inc., 2005).

18. "The cure for anything is salt water: sweat, tears or the sea": Isak Dinesen [Karen Blixen], accessed on Karen Blixen – Isak Dinesen Information Site, www.karenblixen.com/question43.html.

19. Therapy that soothes the pain in the side, chest and back: Jethro Kloss, "Hippocrates and the Water Cure, History of Water Cure," from *Back to Eden*, www.watercure2.org/hippocrates.htm.

20. Patients who inhaled a specially mixed saltwater solution significantly improved: Peggy Peck, "Studies look to sea for cystic fibrosis treatment," *CNN Health, MedPage Today*, January 19, 2006, http://articles.cnn.com/2006-01-18/health/cf.saltwater_1_cystic-fibrosis-mucus-lung-function?_s=PM:HEALTH.

21. Ed Nicholson: Interview by author, November 2010; see also Project Healing Waters Fly Fishing, Inc., www.projecthealingwaters.org.

22. Herbert Hoover, *Fishing for Fun— and to Wash Your Soul*, edited by William Nichols (NY: Random House, 1963).

23. To go fishing is the chance to wash one's soul with pure air: Herbert Hoover, "Men Are Equal Before Fish," (speech, Florida Speaks, September 1951), Herbert Hoover Presidential Library Association, www.hooverassociation.org/hoover/speeches/men_are_equal_before_fish.php.

24. Some quarter of a million rivers, running roughly 3,500,000 miles. "River Facts, Rivers of the United States," American Rivers Website, www.americanrivers.org/library/river-facts

25. Running Waters to Love: Multiple sources consulted: Best of America: www.americasbestonline.com/flyfishing.htm; Great Outdoor Recreation Pages (GORP): www.gorp.com/parks-guide/united-states-wild-and-scenic-rivers-outdoor-pp1-guide-cid62-ctid566.html; National Park Service Nationwide Rivers Inventory (NRI): www.nps.gov/ncrc/programs/rtca/nri/index.html; National Park Service – National Wild & Scenic Rivers System: www.rivers.gov; US Fish & Wildlife Service, National Wildlife Refuge System: *www.fws.gov/refuges*.

26. "Rivers know this: there is no hurry.": A.A. Milne, *Pooh's Little Instruction Book* (New York, NY: Dutton Children's Books, E. P. Dutton & Co., Inc., 1954), p. 8.

27. "Spring rain fills": Haiku by the author, unpublished.

28. "The fish filled brook": Haiku by the author, unpublished.

29. "With a single splash": Haiku by the author, unpublished.

30. Steve Grant: Interview by author, August 2010; also see thestevegrantwebsite.com.

31. "the meadow's love of the willows…always interested spectators of the angler.": John Burroughs, essay, "Speckled Trout, In the Catskills" (New York, NY: Houghton Mifflin Company, 1910), pp., 187–219; Catskill Archive: www.catskillarchive.com/jb/speckledtrout.htm.

## Chapter 3: The Sky

1. Marshall Island legend of beginning of the sky: *New Larousse Encyclopedia of Mythology*, Introduction by Graves, Robert. (New York, NY: Crescent Books, 1987), p. 460.

2. Eygptian mythology of sky creation: http://en.wikipedia.org/wiki/Nut_(goddess).

3. Circa 1102-952 B.C. papyrus of Tameniu: Karl W. Luckert, "Ancient Eygptian Religion—Mother of Neoplatonism and Christian Orthodoxy," *The History of Religions*, The Third Hypostasis (Level 3), 1991, 1999, www.historyofreligions.com/helio.htm.

4. Nut, goddess of the sky: *Routledge dictionary of Egyptian gods and goddesses*, George Hart (Routledge, 2 edition, 2005), p. 111, http://en.wikipedia.org/wiki/Nut_(goddess).

5. Michael Jones McKean, Virginia Commonwealth University, creates own rainbows: Bemis Center for Contemporary Arts, Omaha, NE, Exhibitions, June 22 – September 15, 2012, www.bemiscenter.org/art/exhibitions/rainbow-project.html.

6. John Simpson: Interview by author, November 2009; see also http://joshsimpson. com.

7. Seeing stars: Multiple sources consulted: International Dark Skies Association: www.darksky.org/DSDestinations; National Park Service: www.nps.gov; Gadling, a *Huffington Post* blog: www.gadling.com/2006/06/06/best-stargazing-destinations-in-america.

8. "I have long thought that anyone who does not regularly—or ever—gaze up...": Brian Greene, *Dark Skies,* NASA Science Website, http://science.nasa.gov/science-news/science-at-nasa/2001/ast01nov_1quotes.

9. Professor Judith Young: Interview by author, July 2010; see also www.umass.edu/sunwheel; www.astronomyandspirituality.com/foundation.html.

## Chapter 4: The Vista of Sight

1. The eye is the window of the soul: Leonardo da Vinci, Universal Leonardo, University of the Arts, London, 2012, www.universalleonardo.org/essays.php?id=550.

2. "Cannot visualize such beauty as is seen by the eye": Leonardo da Vinci, Universal Leonardo, University of the Arts, London, 2012, www.universalleonardo.org/trail.php?trail=543.

3. "nothing less than a thorough knowledge of the function of the eye...": The Notebooks of Leonardo da Vinci, http://en.wikiquote.org/wiki/Leonardo_da_Vinci.

4. The brain allows us to interpret the visual image: "What Is Visual Perception?" Conjecture Corporation, *wiseGEEK*, 2003-2012, www.wisegeek.com/what-is-visual-perception.htm.

5. "paint a board with various colours...": Recipe book for light effects, Leonardo da Vinci; Universal Leonardo, University of the Arts, London, 2011, www. universalleonardo.org/media/101/leonardos_recipe_book.pdf.

6. Brigitte Brüggemann: Interview by the author, June 2010; see also www. brigittebruggemann.com.

7. What colors mean: Multiple sources consulted: Color Wheel Pro, http://color-wheel-pro.com/color-meaning.html; Sensationalcolor.com; www.sensationalcolor.com/color-meaning-symbolism-and-psychology; *Color Psychology: How Colors Impact Moods, Feelings, and Behaviors,* Kendra Cherry, about.com Guide; http://psychology.about.com/od/sensationandperception/a/colorpsych.htm.

8. "talking, singing, sniffing the air, watching for tracks": Richard Louv, *The Nature Principle* (New York: Algonquin Books of Chapel Hill, 2011, 2012), pp. 9-10.

9. Joan Tunstall: Interview by the author, July 2009; see also www.burnbraejournal.blogspot.com.

10. Erin Wallace: Interview by the author, September 2009; see also www.bluebirdbaby.typepad.com.

11. Pam Brickell: Interview by the author, October 2009; see also www. creatingnaturejournals.com, www.pamjohnsonbrickellart.com.

12.   "Three Days to See": Helen Keller, *The Atlantic Monthly*, Volume 151, No. 1, January 1933, pp. 35-42, www.theatlantic.com/past/docs/issues/33jan/keller.htm.

13.   "Use your eyes as if tomorrow you would be stricken blind....": Ibid.

## Chapter 5: The Pulse of Sound

1.    At 23 days, the human fetus is able to feel sound: Maryann Harman, M.A., "Music and Movement – Instrumental in Language Development," Earlychildhoodnews.com, www.earlychildhoodnews.com/earlychildhood/article_view.aspx?ArticleID=601.

2.    Role of the ear in hearing: "How does the ear hear," www.ehow.com/how-does_4574056_the-ear-hear.html#ixzz1cU1DDfI2.

3.    John Cage, 4'33: "The Sounds of Silence, John Cage and 4'33"," copyright © 1998, rev 2002 by Larry J Solomon, http://solomonsmusic.net/4min33se.htm.

4.    "no such thing as an empty space..." John Cage, *Silence*, (Hanover, NH: Wesleyan University Press, 1973), p. 8.

5.    Silence touches us in many ways, offers sanctuary and tranquility: John Lane, *The Spirit of Silence: Making Space of Creativity* (Devon, UK: Chelsea Green Publishers, 2006); www.chelseagreen.com/bookstore/item/the_spirit_of_silence:paperback/press_release.

6.    'The three great elemental sounds in nature are the sound of rain...": Henry Beston, *The Outermost House* (New York, NY: Henry Holt and Company, 1928, renewed 1977), p. 43.

7.    Gordon Hempton: Interview by the author, August 2010; see also www.onesquareinch.org and www.soundtracker.com

8.    Gordon Hempton, John Grossman, *One Square Inch of Silence: One Man's Search for Natural Silence in a Noisy World* (New York, NY: Free Press, 2009).

9.    Songbirds need to learn their language: Melissa B. Dolinsky, Department of Biology, University of Miami, "Missing a Crucial Step?" 1999-2011 Jackie Collins, www.starlingtalk.com/BirdSong.htm.

10.   Baby birds babble softly: "How birds learn songs likened to way humans learn speech," Larry Weist, *Deseret News*, Dec. 9, 2004, www.deseretnews.com/article/595111048/How-birds-learn-songs-likened-to-way-humans-learn-speech.html.

11.   Many variations in both technique and sound of bird's music: ornithology.com, www.ornithology.com/Lectures/SongsandCalls.html.

12.   Fascinated by bird's songs, describing through use of mnemonics: Cornell Lab of Ornithology, www.birds.cornell.edu/AllAboutBirds/studying/birdsongs/whysing.

13.   Echolocation, otherwise known as ultrasonic sonar: National Marine Fisheries Services – NOAA Fisheries, National Marine Mammal Laboratory, Marine Mammal Education Web, www.afsc.noaa.gov/nmml/education/cetaceans/cetaceaechol.php.

14.   Horseshoe bats and Old World leaf-nosed bats emit their echolocation call: Alain Van Ryckegham, School of Natural Resources, Sir Sandford Fleming College, Lindsay, Ontario, Canada, *Scientific American*, December 21, 1998, www.scientificamerican.com/article.cfm?id=how-do-bats-echolocate-an.

15. If we want to hear the nuances of sound: The Anstendig Institute, San Francisco, CA, "Our Bodies Are Affected by the Vibrational Quality of our Surroundings" 1983, www.Anstendig.org/EnvVibes.html.

16. Sound and music intimately connected to movement: Caroline Frizell, "Dance Movement Psychotherapy and Music," *e-motion* vol. XVIII No. 3 ISSN 1460-1281.

17. "Music has been my magic carpet to the world." Paul Winter quoted in "Paul Winter on the 32nd Annual Winter Solstice Concert," Joseph Vella, *Jazz Online – The Voice of Jazz*, December 13, 2011, http://jazzonline.com/blogs/paul-winters-on-the-32nd-annual-winter-solstice-concert.html.

18. Judy Dworin: Interview by the author, May 2009; see also www.judydworin.org.

19. Michelle Parma: Interview with her mother, Susan Parma, by the author, May 2009; see also http://www.dancetolive.org.

20. Adjei Abankwa: Interview by the author, November 2010; see also http://baobaofest.org.

## Chapter 6: The Essence of Touch, Taste and Smell

1. National Hugging Day, created in 1986 by Rev. Kevin Zaborney: "A Concerned Cupidian Named Kevin Zaborney Squeezes National Hugging Day into the Calendar," *People*, January 23, 1989, Vol. 31, No. 3., Archive, www.people.com/people/archive/article/0,,20119408,00.html.

2. Emperor Claudius II, outlawed marriage for young men: "This Day in History: Feb. 14, 278, St. Valentine Beheaded," history.com, www.history.com/this-day-in-history/st-valentine-beheaded.

3. Studies at the University of Carolina-Chapel Hill, School of Medicine, one 20-second hug: "The Power of Love – Hugs and Cuddles Have Long-term Effect," *NIH News in Health*, February 2007, http://newsinhealth.nih.gov/2007/February/docs/01features_01.htm.

4. U.S. couples aren't very "touchy-feely" in public: Marilyn Elias, "Study: Hugs warm the heart, and may protect it," *USA TODAY*, March 10, 2003, http://usatoday30.usatoday.com/news/health/2003-03-09-hug-usat_x.htm

5. Tammy Hendricks: Interview by the author, December 2010; see also www.tammybears.com.

6. "Laura Bridgman, a delicate plant of a girl": Sally Hobard Alexander, Robert Alexander, *She Touched the World, Laura Bridgman, Deaf-Blind Pioneer* (New York, NY: Houghton, Mifflin Harcourt, 2008), p. 1.

7. "She felt the soft muzzle of a calf ... As her hands worked, her mind stirred." Ibid., pp. 6-7.

8. Our backs far less sensitive to tactile activity: "Touch," faqs.org, 2011 Advameg, Inc., www.faqs.org/health/topics/3/Touch.html.

9. Roman Caracella Baths, 1,500 bathers at a time: Rome File – Rome tourist information and city guide; www.romefile.com/sights/baths-of-caracalla.php.

10. Dead Sea Mud: MedIndia Network for Health, Medindia.com, www.medindia.net/alternativemedicine/mudbaths/mud_bath2.htm#e.

11. Karlovy Vary Mud: Melinda Minton, "Mud: Dig It!" *Massage Magazine*; www.massagemag.com/spa/treatment/mud.php.

12. Moors of Austria Mud: MedIndia Network for Health, Medindia.com; www. medindia.net/alternativemedicine/mudbaths/mud_bath3.htm#f.

13. "The pressure of the hands causes the springs of life to flow": Tokujiro Namikoshi, quote accessed from CenterPoint Massage &Shiatsu Therapy School & Clinic Website, www.centerpointmn.com/shiatsu.shtml.

14. Hippocrates prescribed rubbing as means of loosening too rigid joint: David K. Osborn, L.Ac., "Massage and Bodywork – Hippocrates and massage": Greek Medicine.net, 2007 – 2010, www.greekmedicine.net/therapies/Massage_and_ Bodywork.html.

15. Shiatsu massage therapy: "Shiatsu Massage Guide," www.topshiatsumassage.com.

16. Touch plays leading role in development of human sensory response: "Therapeutic Qualities of Clay-work in Psychotherapy: A Review," Michael Sholt and Tami Gavron, Haifa, Israel, *Art Therapy: Journal of the American Art Therapy Association*, AAIA, 2006, pp. 66-72, www.hebpsy.net/files/mrXujBChRsV8maksZzwl.pdf.

17. Soft, earthy material formed as a result of the weathering or erosion of mineral containing rocks: "What is Clay?" *The Science Learning Hub*, Ministry of Science + Innovation, The University of Waikato, New Zealand.govt.nz, 2007-2012, www. sciencelearn.org.nz/Contexts/Ceramics/Science-Ideas-and-Concepts/What-is-clay.

18. Jim Sudal: Interview by the author, October 2009; see also www.jimsudalpottery. net.

19. "Butterflies and Bees," Jim Sudal, 2011, http://jimsudalpottery.net/images-2011/ arcadia.pdf.

20. Average human nose can discriminate between 4,000 and 10,000 different odors: *Smell,* Advameg, Inc., 2012, see www.faqs.org/health/topics/99/Smell.html.

21. Michelle Krell Kydd: Interview by the author, December 2010; see also Glass Petal Smoke, © 2007-2012, http://glasspetalsmoke.blogspot.com.

22. Eric's Citrus Vinaigrette: Eric Webster, interview by the author, October 2011; see also http://ericcwebster.com and www.ecwprivatechef.blogspot.com.

## Chapter 7: Frontiers of Wonder

1. Jules Verne, father of science fiction genre: *Jules Verne Biography*, Classic Literature Library, www.jules-verne.co.uk.

2. Nonsense a necessary ingredient in life; it wakes up the brain cells: Dr. Seuss, as quoted in *Wisdom for the Soul: Five Millennia of Prescriptions for Spiritual Healing* (2006) by Larry Chang, p. 376, accessed at http://en.wikiquote.org/wiki/Dr._Seuss.

3. Miriam Epstein: Interview by the author, January 2010; see also www. bookstodreams.org.

4. C. S. Lewis spoke "to the adult, the child, and the child within the adult": Dr. Don W. King, Montreat College, "The Childlike in George MacDonald and C. S. Lewis," 1986, *Into the Wardrobe*, a C. S. Lewis website, http://cslewis.drzeus.net/papers/ childlike.html.

5. Tracy Kane: Interview by the author, September 2009; see also www.FairyHouses. com.

6. "How to build a fairy house": Tracy Kane, *The Fairies Rules*, www.fairyhouses.com/pictures/how-to-build.

7. *The Cat in the Hat,* Dr. Seuss (New York: Random House, Inc., 1957, renewed 1985, Dr. Seuss Enterprises, L.P.).

8. *Charlotte's Web*, E.B. White, illustrated by Garth Williams (New York: HarperCollins Publishers Bros., 1952).

9. *Eloise*, Kay Thompson (New York: Simon & Schuster, Inc., 1955).

10. *Madeline,* Ludwig Bemelmans (New York: The Penguin Group, Penguin Putnam, Inc., 1939, Ludwig Bemelmans, renewed 1967, Madeline Bemelmans and Barbara Bemelmans Marciano).

11. *The Tale of Peter Rabbit*, Beatrix Potter (London, England: Frederick Warne & Co., 1902; Special Green Edition, Penguin Group, USA, 2009).

12. *Winnie the Pooh*, by A.A. Milne (New York: E.P. Dutton & Co., Inc., Dutton Children's Books, Division of Penguin Books USA Inc., 1926, 1954).

13. Robert (Sidewalk Sam) Guillemin: Interview by the author, July 2009; see also www.sidewalksam.com.

14. Elizabeth St. Hilaire Nelson: Interview by the author, November 2009; see also *Paper Painting*, http://elizabethsthilairenelson.blogspot.com.

15. "Sometimes—when I watch the flight…": Mary O'Connor, "Wonder," *Dreams of a Wingless Child* (Tuscon, AZ: Wheatmark, 2007), p. 12.

## Chapter 8: The Heart of Giving

1. "a terrific happiness habit…": Christine Carter, Ph.D., UC Berkeley's Greater Good Science Center, "What we get when we give," Feb. 18, 2010, *Raising Happiness, Science for Joyful Kids and Happier Parents*, http://greatergood.berkeley.edu/raising_happiness/post/what_we_get_when_we_give/.

2. "the warm glow of internal satisfaction": James Andreoni, "Impure Altruism and Donations to Public Goods: A Theory of Warm-Glow Giving," *The Economic Journal*, Volume III, Issue 401 (June 1990), pp. 464-77, http://econ.ucsd.edu/jandreon/Publications/ej90.pdf.

3. "We give of ourselves when we give gifts of the heart": Wilferd A. Peterson, *The Art of Giving*, (New York: Simon & Schuster, 1901), accessed at www.appleseeds.org/art_giving.htm.

4. Marilyn Douglas: Interview by the author, July 2010.

5. Connection between brain anatomy, brain activity and altruistic behavior: Researchers from the University of Zurich, "Science News - The More Gray Matter You Have, The More Altruistic You Are," *Science Daily*, July 11, 2012, www.sciencedaily.com/releases/2012/07/120711123005.htm.

6. University of Oregon researchers observe significant activation of pleasure areas: "It's Official: The Act of Giving Effects the Brain," Carol Kirschner, *Dollar Philanthropy*, http://dollarphilanthropy.typepad.com/weblog/2007/06/its_official_th.html.

7. University of British Columbia research shows toddlers happier when they give goldfish crackers to monkey puppet friends: Lara B. Aknin, J. Kiley Hamlin,

Elizabeth W. Dunn, Psychology Department, University of British Columbia, Vancouver, British Columbia, Canada, "Giving Leads to Happiness in Young Children,", PLoS—One, June 14, 2012, www.plosone.org/article/info:doi/10.1371/journal.pone.0039211.

8. "Mr. Mandela taught us to love ourselves…": Archbishop Emeritus Desmond Tutu, statement, Mandela Day 2002; www.mandeladay.com/news/entry/statement-by-archbishop-emeritus-desmond-tutu-on-mandela-day-2012.

9. Lynn White: Interview by the author, July 2009; see also Growing Stronger, Inc., http://iamgrowingstronger.org.

10. Heart chakra bridges the gap between the physical and spiritual worlds; color of the heart chakra is green: Kate Smith, CMG, CfYH, *Sensational Color - All About the Color Green*, www.sensationalcolor.com/color-messages-meanings/color-meaning-symbolism-psychology/all-about-the-color-green.html.

11. Bonnie Waldron, Smiley Green Balloon Project: Interview by the author, February 2011; see also Mary Kaye Waldron Quality of Life Project, www.marykayewaldron.org/qualityoflife.html.

12. Angel Network: Greta Hendricks Johnson, graduate student, Ferris State University, Grand Rapids Campus, "Winfrey, Oprah (Paper I)," *Learning to Give*, see Learningtogive.org, http://learningtogive.org/papers/paper135.html.

13. Herb Ouida: Interview by the author, October 2008; see also The Todd Joseph Ouida Memorial Children's Fund, www.mybuddytodd.org.

14. Instead of answers, peace: "Answers: Here," Jennifer Payne, *Random Acts of Writing + Art*, July 22, 2012, http://randomactsofwriting.wordpress.com/2012/07/22/answers-here.

## Chapter 9: The Spirituality of Life

1. Places "that speak of the divine and the unknown, and which allow us to rejoice in the great mystery of our connection to the world and our place in it.": Rebecca Hind, *Sacred Places, Sites of Spirituality & Faith* (New York: MJF Books, Fine Communications, Carlton Books Limited, 2007), back cover.

2. Bungle Bungle, Purnululu National Park, Western Australia: Ibid., pp. 241-43.

3. Castlerigg Stone Circle, Cumbria, England: Ibid., pp. 55-57.

4. Delphi, Fokís, Greece: Ibid., pp. 106-07.

5. Kii Mountains, Honshu, Japan: Ibid., pp. 214-17.

6. Petra, Jordan: Ibid., pp. 112-15.

7. Rapu Nui (Easter Island), Southern Pacific Ocean: Ibid., pp. 248-51.

8. To be spiritual is to be amazed: Abraham Joshua Heschel, see Richard Louv, *Last Child In the Woods*, (Chapel Hill, NC: Algonquin Books of Chapel Hill, 2008), "The Spiritual Necessity of Nature for the Young," pp. 291-92.

9. "A way of connecting with the worl": Hilary Rice, Textile & Mixed Media Artist, www.mestudios.ca/index.htm.

10. Carol Kortsch: Interview by the author, September 2009.

11. Peace Awareness Labyrinth and Gardens: www.peacelabyrinth.org.

12. Labyrinths followed since days of King Nestor: Glastonbury Pilgrim Reception Centre, www.glastonbury-pilgrim.co.uk/labyrinths.php.

13. Basilica of Reoperates, Orleansville, Algeria: www.bcuc.org/PDFs/WALKING_THE_LABYRINTH.pdf.

14. Chartres Cathedral, Paris, France: www.lessons4living.com/chartres_labyrinth.htm.

15. Glastonbury Tor, Somerset, England: www.glastonburytor.org.uk.

16. Grace Cathedral, San Francisco, California: www.gracecathedral.org/visit/labyrinth.

17. Ohio State University Chadwick Arboretum, Columbus, Ohio: http://chadwickarboretum.osu.edu/walking-the-labyrinth.

18. Sacred Garden of Maliko, Maui: www.sacredgardensmaui.com/SG/index.htm.

19. World Wide Labyrinth Locator: www.labyrinthlocator.com

20. Anne Rowthorn: Interview by the author, July 2010; see also www.annerowthorn.com

21. *Earth and All the Stars*, edited by Anne Rowthorn (Eugene, OR: Resource Publications, 2000).

22. *Feast of the Universe*, edited and compiled by Anne Rowthorn (Leeds, MA: Leader Resources, 2009).

23. "Namaste—I honor the place within you where the entire universe resides": Mahatma Gandhi, accessed at http://hinduism.about.com/od/artculture/p/namaste.htm.

24. "To love is recognize yourself in another": Eckhart Tolle, *A New Earth: Awakening to Your Life's Purpose,* (New York: PLUME (SA) Inc., The Penguin Group, Eckhart Tolle, 2005), p. 105; quote accessed at Eckhart Tolle, Quotes from a New Earth, www.quedox.com/be/tolle.html.

25. "love is our true destiny": Thomas Merton, *Love and Living,* edited by Naomi Burton Stone and Brother Patrick Hart, (San Diego, CA: Harcourt Brace Jovanovich, 1985, © 1979) p. 27.

26. "I like to laugh and be with my family and friends...": Anjelica Huston. Zoë Sallis, *Ten Eternal Questions* (San Francisco, CA: Chronicle Books LLC, 2005), p. 194.

27. Abdul Muhammad: Interview by the author, November 2010.

28. Fathers Now, a program of Newark Now, http://newarknow.org.

29. William Renzulli: Interview by the author, October 2009; see also *Reflections on Life in Medicine, Art, and Pasta*, www.williamfrenzullimd.blogspot.com.

30. *Have I Told You Today that I Love You*, William F. Renzulli, M.D., (Bloomington, IN: AuthorHouse, 2007).

CPSIA information can be obtained at www.ICGtesting.com
Printed in the USA
BVOW021908280313

316743BV00002B/2/P